Cultural Memory

in

the

Present

Mieke Bal and Hent de Vries, Editors

STRUCTURES OF MEMORY

Understanding Urban Change in Berlin and Beyond

Jennifer A. Jordan

STANFORD UNIVERSITY PRESS

STANFORD, CALIFORNIA

2006

Stanford University Press
Stanford, California
Printed in the United States of America on acid-free, archival-quality paper

Library of Congress Cataloging-in-Publication Data

Jordan, Jennifer A., date-
  Structures of memory : understanding urban change in Berlin and beyond /
Jennifer A. Jordan.
      p. cm.--(Cultural memory in the present)
  Includes bibliographical references and index.
  ISBN 0-8047-5276-1 (cloth : alk. paper)--ISBN 0-8047-5277-X (pbk. : alk. paper)
  1. City planning--Germany--Berlin. 2. Land use--Germany--Berlin.
3. Memorials--Germany--Berlin. 4. Berlin (Germany)--Buildings, structures, etc.
5. Berlin (Germany)--History--20th century. I. Title. II. Series.

HT169.G32B3876 2006
307.1'2160943'155--dc22   2006003647

Original Printing 2006
Last figure below indicates year of this printing:
15   14   13   12   11   10   09   08   07   06
Typeset by Bruce Lundquist in 11/13.5 Adobe Garamond

STRUCTURES OF MEMORY

For Jim, Sandy, and Carl

Contents

Acknowledgments

This research received generous support from many organizations and individuals. The year that I spent as the Cohen Family Fellow at the U.S. Holocaust Memorial Museum's Center for Advanced Holocaust Studies provided the time, resources, and intellectual atmosphere that made it possible to finish the book. The German Academic Exchange Service also funded my work in a variety of ways, from my first summer learning German at a Goethe Institute to all-important short-term research trips to gather additional information. I am also grateful to the Social Science Research Council/Berlin Program for Advanced German and European Studies for generous support of my research in 1998 and 1999. In addition, the Center for 21st Century Studies at the University of Wisconsin-Milwaukee helped me begin the challenging process of transforming a dissertation into a book, and provided an exciting environment in which to grapple with these challenges. Finally, the University of California, San Diego, and the Center for German and European Studies at the University of California, Berkeley, helped fund early stages of the research and writing.

Many people made this project possible on the ground. Berlin district council member (and chair of the memorial plaques commission) Volker Hobrack was my instructor in the complex world of memorial plaques and provided me with everything from hard-to-find files to historical musings to fantastic brunches. He read a rickety manuscript at an early stage, and I am sincerely grateful for his investment in the project that has slowly come to fruition. Kerstin Bötticher at the Landesarchiv patiently dragged cardboard boxes full of files out of storage and forged a path for me through the wilderness of pre-1989 archival material. Indeed, everyone I encountered at the Landesarchiv was extremely helpful. Harmut Häußermann at the Humboldt Universität Berlin provided on-site support, was inquisitively tolerant of my work, and introduced me to an important friend and colleague, Bettina Reimann, to whom I also owe many thanks. The list of people who opened up their homes, offices, and filing cabinets to this Californian with the unusual project is far too long to include here, but includes Brian Ladd, Margit Mayer, and Bruno Flierl, as well as many others at the State Historical Preservation Office, the Aktives Museum Faschismus und Widerstand, the district city hall of Mitte, the Berlin state government archives, and many district museums, from Schöneberg to Marzahn.

I am very grateful to the many people who spoke with me in the midst of busy workdays and packed calendars; their insights and wisdom greatly aided the research process. In addition many thanks are due to Norris Pope, Mariana Raykov, Angie Michaelis, and Peter Dreyer for their work in bringing this book to print, and to Donna Genzmer and the UW–Milwaukee Cartography and GIS Center for the creation of the maps. Thanks are also due to Alexander Käsbohrer and Anje Werner for filling my hasty photographic requests from afar.

At the University of California, San Diego, Rick Biernacki graciously served as my dissertation advisor, helping me to think through and narrow down what began as a mammoth research project. He patiently read everything from very rough notes to more polished chapters, consistently helping me to hone the project. Martha Lampland has also read much of the project at various stages, offering vital suggestions. In addition, Dick Madsen, Amy Bridges, Todd Kontje, and Chandra Mukerji all provided valuable insights and critiques.

Jasmine Alinder and Brian Ladd merit special thanks for having read the entire manuscript in draft form, along with Ed Linenthal. Laura Brahm, Karen Buerkle, Carrie Yang Costello, Claudia Curio, Josh Dunsby, Kristin Espinosa, Laura Fingerson, Susan Funkenstein, Dominik Göbel, Sara Hall, Tom Lekan, Brent Maner, Aims McGuinness, Steve McKay, Stacey Oliker, Ellen Reese, Oren Stier, Rebecca Wittmann, Vera Zolberg, and especially Aron Rodrigue all provided valuable help by reading chapters or discussing key elements of the book. I am very grateful for their insights and suggestions, and grateful too to the many people whose names I have surely (and inadvertently) forgotten to list.

A fleet of lovely friends in many cities kept me company everywhere I went in the long process of researching and writing this book—Pacific Grove, Burbank, San Diego, San Francisco, Milwaukee, Washington, D.C., Evanston, Chicago, Berlin, Falkensee, and, finally, Vienna. Thank you most of all.

STRUCTURES OF MEMORY

1

Landscapes of Remembering
and Forgetting

How are some places of great cruelty or great heroism forgotten by all but eyewitnesses, while others become the sites of public ceremonies, well-tended outdoor museums, or at least enduring markers of some kind? To answer this question, this book turns to the landscape of contemporary Berlin and to places marking persecution by or resistance to the Nazi regime. Because of its past as the capital of the Third Reich, as a central symbol of the Cold War, and as the new capital of a united Germany, Berlin is a particularly powerful context in which to examine the social origins of memorial landscapes. Whether sites of torture by the Gestapo or mass deportations to concentration camps, the places examined in this book have marked the city's Nazi past, and have often been rendered off limits to use as apartments, shops, or offices. At the same time, however, not all proposed memorial projects are actually built, and only a small portion of all "authentic" sites—places with direct connections to acts of resistance or persecution during the Nazi era—actually become infused with official collective memory. Why, then, are some sites ensconced in official collective memory, while others fade into the landscape? And how can we account for these patterns of concentrated collective memory amid volatile real estate markets, mammoth construction projects, and rapid political change?

Remembering can, and does, leave its marks on the skin of the city. But in order to observe precisely *how* it does so, I examine both successful and failed memorial projects, and compare those places that have emerged into the official memorial landscape with those that remain only in the memories of eyewitnesses or diligent researchers. I find that collective memory shapes the urban landscape in part at the observable intersection of four specific factors: land use, landownership, the resonance of the site's meaning with a broader (often international) public, and the presence or absence of what I call a "memorial entrepreneur," which is to say, someone willing to lobby on behalf of memorialization.[1] Memory thus shapes the landscape through the day-to-day practices of memorial construction, which range from international debates about art and history to the bureaucracies of local parks departments, historic preservation offices, or property registries.

Few places bear the traces of their past unaided, in Berlin or elsewhere. The theoretical framework presented here illuminates the concrete processes of place making and memorial construction in Berlin, but also promises to speak to the production of memorial spaces in other settings as well. The question of how to treat real estate with a difficult past has recently become an issue of widespread concern in the United States, for example, in the wake of the Oklahoma City bombing, and then the attacks at the World Trade Center, where some of New York's (and the world's) most expensive real estate became, in the words of many, "hallowed ground."[2] This book offers a guiding set of questions with which to examine the dynamic interactions of memory, markets, and politics in cities around the world, whether in Lower Manhattan, Phnom Penh, or Buenos Aires.[3] How are we to understand the presence of "hallowed ground" in the middle of a bustling metropolis? Put more broadly, how do groups of people anchor collective memories to the landscape? How does a given patch of land or a particular building go from being meaningful only to a handful of eyewitnesses or historians to being a significant element of local, national, and even international collective memory?[4]

Collective memory operates within economic, physical, and political limits, including the four elements mentioned above, as well as broader political, cultural, and economic climates.[5] These limits become visible in the analysis of the stories of places like a small workshop in the heart of Berlin, at Rosenthaler Straße 39, where a man named Otto Weidt attempted to save the lives of his employees, most of whom were both Jewish and blind, between 1941 and 1943. Each of these four factors is clearly evident in the transition of this workshop from a set of vacant rooms in postwar East Berlin to an internationally recognized exhibition and a place infused with the memory of Weidt and the people he hoped to save.[6] On a sunny morning in late winter 1999, Berlin district city council member Volker Hobrack held a brunch for a small group of people engaged in various memorial projects throughout the city. At the end of the meal, the breakfast guests and their host all decided to drive together the short distance into the city center of eastern Berlin to see a newly opened exhibition entitled "Blindes Vertrauen: Versteckt am Hackeschen Markt, 1941–1943" ("Blind Trust: Hidden at Hackescher Markt, 1941–1943"), which told of Otto Weidt's struggle to save the blind Jewish factory workers he employed making various kinds of brushes.[7] Curated by a group of students from a museum studies program at the University of Applied Sciences (Fachhochschule für Technik und Wirtschaft, or FHTW), the exhibition occupied three rooms in a labyrinthine building next door to the Hackesche Höfe, a sprawling art nouveau complex of apartments, shops, and restaurants that currently attracts tens of thousands of visitors to this corner of the former East Berlin every year. Unlike the Hackesche Höfe, the building that housed the exhibition was decrepit and run-down, untouched by renovators or even a paintbrush since well before World War II. The rooms of the exhibition itself had stood essentially vacant for decades.

After finding their way through a long, crumbling courtyard and up a set of creaking stairs, the group of breakfast guests arrived at the exhibition, where they viewed glass cases full of letters, photographs, and other objects, ranging from a cloth Star of David worn by one of the workers to a postcard sent to the factory owner from his lover on her way to Auschwitz. The walls were rough and unpainted, the floors bare. At one end of the exhibition was a tiny room where Weidt had hidden a Jewish family until their betrayal by a trusted friend. In another room, interviews with eyewitnesses, including the writer Inge Deutschkron, one of the breakfast guests who had joined in this late morning excursion, played continuously on a TV installed in an old coal stove. Deutschkron, who is Jewish, had survived by means of an elaborate combination of forged papers and hiding places, spending part of the war as a secretary in the small factory rooms that served as the exhibition's stage.[8] Originally, the exhibition was scheduled to run for just four weeks, from March 5 through April 4, 1999. More than six years later, it is still open, now as an official annex of Berlin's Jewish Museum.[9] But in 1999 there was no guarantee that this would be the case.

For years, Deutschkron acted alone in her efforts to place a plaque for Otto Weidt at the entrance to the building, writing in vain to the East

Berlin magistracy in the late 1980s. In 1993, however, after the change in the political system, Deutschkron's efforts succeeded, and a plaque was placed on the site. Furthermore, by the late 1990s, the site had a group of increasingly active memorial entrepreneurs. In 1997, the artist Helen Adkins (who ran an arts center in another wing of the building) suggested that an exhibition be developed in the workshop rooms, and a group of six students (including Kai Gruzdz and Ariane Kwasigroch, who were later hired to oversee the exhibition) took up her suggestion. They worked closely with Deutschkron and others, and the exhibition on the site of Weidt's factory opened in 1999. The fact that the rooms were essentially vacant in the late 1990s certainly paved the way for the exhibition, but no marking would have taken place without the concerted effort of these advocates. (See Figures 1.1–1.3.)

FIGURE 1.1. Rosenthaler Str. 39. Photograph by Jennifer Jordan. All photographs by the author were taken between 1998 and 2004.

FIGURE 1.2. Rosenthaler Str. 39, courtyard. Photograph by Jennifer Jordan.

FIGURE 1.3. Rosenthaler Str. 39, courtyard. Photograph by Jennifer Jordan.

As word of the exhibition spread, this project increasingly resonated with a broader public, initially in small groups and book readings and Sunday brunches, but quickly spreading to local and national newspapers. These activities helped to begin the process of rooting these spaces in official collective memory, in part by generating further resonance through newspaper reporting, the work of elected officials, and visits by high-ranking politicians, including the federal president at the time, Johannes Rau, and the speaker of the German Parliament, Wolfgang Thierse, as well as other dignitaries. It may not seem surprising that Germany's president and other dignitaries would visit a place where a German citizen defied the Nazis and saved lives. But for more than fifty years, the rooms had been far from the public eye and their history forgotten by all but the surviving eyewitnesses.

Unlike many of the other sites in this book, the building housing the Blind Trust exhibition was actually private property until 2005, mired in a dispute among the more than two dozen heirs about what do to with the property. (See Chapter 4 for a more in-depth discussion of this dispute.) There were so many owners because the property had been restituted to the heirs of the Jewish property owner who fled Berlin in the 1930s. His children and grandchildren, scattered on several continents, were unable to come to an agreement about whether to sell or hold onto the property.[10] The years of disagreement created an opportunity to mark the history of these rooms, because there were no competing uses in the late 1990s. After much uncertainty, the property was sold to the district housing authority in 2005, and the fate of the site now seems secure.

One of the elements of the exhibition's longevity is its powerful claim to authenticity, to having a direct connection to compelling historical events. Soon after it opened, Deutschkron gave a reading from one of her books to an audience of three dozen people seated in the exhibition rooms. During the question-and-answer period after the reading, a woman in the audience compared the rooms to the Anne Frank House in Amsterdam in their authenticity and their power to convey their history, saying, "When you are really there, you *feel* it."[11] But neither the Anne Frank House nor the Blind Trust exhibition would have such power for subsequent generations without the actions of a wide array of people writing about these places, advocating on their behalf, and envisioning them as uniquely instructive and deeply authentic. What is now known as the

Anne Frank House, Prinsengracht 263, was slated for demolition by its new owners in 1955. The Anne Frank Foundation's account of the transformation of the land follows a similar trajectory to that of the "Blind Trust" exhibit, albeit on a much larger scale:

In the meantime, however, public opinion had been alerted. Newspapers both within the country and abroad announced the threatened demolition and urged that the Secret Annexe be saved. Under the heading "Anne Frank's Secret Annexe Awaits the Wreckers' Ball", the daily newspaper *Het Vrije Volk* reported on 23 November 1955: "The plan to demolish the Secret Annexe must not continue! If there is one place where the fate of Dutch Jews is most clearly revealed, it is here. The Secret Annexe does not appear on the list of protected monuments, but it nevertheless has become a monument to a time of oppression and man-hunts, terror and darkness. The Netherlands will be subject to a national scandal if this house is indeed pulled down."[12]

A foundation was established to organize preservation efforts, and fund-raising began. In honor of their company's own anniversary, the building's owners donated the structure to the Anne Frank Foundation in 1957, and the museum officially opened in 1960.[13] In order for the status of the Anne Frank House to change so dramatically—from being officially condemned to being visited by literally millions of people in the subsequent decades—clearly much work had to be done. The diverse activities of lobbying, fund-raising, letter-writing, long evening meetings after work, writing books, writing letters to the editor, talking, thinking, reading, mourning, and celebrating all contribute to the landscape of material memory, in Amsterdam, in Berlin, and elsewhere.

It is precisely this kind of work that is the subject of this book. As James Young and others have asserted, no site speaks for itself.[14] There is nothing inevitable about either the Blind Trust exhibition or the preservation of the Anne Frank House. As the historian Rudy Koshar observes, "objectively considered, such historical sites are mere constructions of stone, wood, brick, concrete, and steel. Their meanings derive from public action."[15] In this book, I provide an analysis of such public action, but I also offer two approaches that are difficult to find in other studies of memorialization. First, I focus, not only on the places that emerge as official markers in the landscape, but also on those that go unmarked. Second, I place these sites not only in their cultural, artistic, and historical contexts, but also in the economic, bureaucratic, and legal contexts utterly essential in shaping the production of memorial space, paying attention to property registries, land use guidelines, and other elements that rarely find their way into discussions of memorial construction.

This book reveals the hidden struggles behind the terrain of memorials in Berlin, and also delves into the many struggles that never actually result in markers at all. Previous studies of memorialization in Berlin and elsewhere in Germany have resulted in thorough accounts of the existing landscape and nuanced discussions of German memorial culture, including, most prominently, Brian Ladd's *The Ghosts of Berlin* (1997), as well as Michael Wise's *Capital Dilemma* (1999), Gavriel Rosenfeld's *Munich and Memory*, James Young's writings, including *At Memory's Edge* (2000), and Rudy Koshar's studies of historic preservation and memory in Germany, *Germany's Transient Pasts* (1998) and *From Monuments to Traces* (2000). By and large, they address the markers ensconced (sometimes briefly, sometimes permanently) in Berlin's landscape, elaborating on the story of successful projects and official memory. This means they offer in-depth discussions of the imprint of history (and its interpretations) on the landscape, and even an understanding of the kinds of debates and back-and-forth that lead to their construction. Yet in order to understand the social origins of memorial space, it is necessary to compare that which is forgotten (at least officially) with that which is remembered.[16]

The framework presented here emerges out of my work on Berlin, but it can also serve as a foundation for the investigation and analysis of memorial construction in other settings as well. Forgetting and remembering alike shape any given urban landscape, but recent scholarship on memorial construction has tended to focus more on remembering rather than forgetting, and on those memorial projects that are actually erected rather than those that never see the light of day. Many compelling studies of memory sites (in history, geography, art history, sociology, architecture, and neighboring disciplines), then, focus primarily on completed projects, including Edward Linenthal's books on Oklahoma City and the U.S. Holocaust Memorial Museum, Marita Sturken's book on the AIDS quilt and the Vietnam Veterans Memorial, and even Pierre Nora's multi-volume study of the construction of the French past.[17] Taking a comparative approach and examining "forgotten" places, however, yields additional information about the social, political, and material forces behind memorial construction, and places memory projects into their material, political, and economic contexts.[18]

In addition to its specific analysis of Berlin and the broader literature on memory and memorials, this book also builds on a growing body of work in urban sociology, where political and economic analyses are joined with a focus on culture and symbols. I take up the concerns of urban scholars like Sharon Zukin, Christopher Mele, and Harvey Molotch, who have developed intriguing approaches to the study of real estate markets and the range of symbolic meanings of urban spaces in an array of settings, from southern California to New York's Lower East Side. I combine these concerns with the theoretical sensibilities of sociologists like Chandra Mukerji or Rick Biernacki, who have studied eighteenth-century French gardens and nineteenth-century labor practices, among other things, to analyze cultural behavior in the context of political and economic transformation.[19]

I ask, then, how these kinds of transformations of urban space occur—how a dusty row of poorly lit rooms could sit empty for decades, and yet now resonate so widely with schoolchildren, journalists, and politicians alike, as has happened in the case of the "Blind Trust" exhibition. But I also ask why, given the power of "authentic" sites, most sites with similar authentic connections to the past fail to become memorials. The memorial landscape is not determined solely by the traces left in the built environment or in memory, official or otherwise, even as memorials come to seem self-evident and unmarked places seem to become ordinary. The "Blind Trust" exhibition and others like it did not come about solely because of intrinsically powerful meanings or direct (or authentic) connections to past events. The success of this and other memorial projects resulted from a convergence of factors, especially the four I identify above. Central patches of urban land become infused with widely salient meanings, but they do not do so of their own accord. These buildings and memorial complexes travel a long and uncertain road. Their fates, including those of sites now most engraved in the cityscape and the public consciousness, are anything but given. Social activity thus periodically transforms empty lots and forgotten buildings into places of powerful and wide-ranging collective memory and symbolism.[20] Post-Wall Berlin offers a unique window into these processes, both because of its own history and because of the nearly overnight transition to a market economy and a democratic government.

There are two poles of memory and forgetting in any city: total erasure or forgetting, and total memorialization, or the marking of every site that housed violent or courageous events. To begin to solve the puzzle presented by the patterns of Berlin's memorial landscape, it is helpful to imagine these two impossible extremes between which the city's residents have navigated a path since the end of World War II. On the one hand, envisage a city whose past has been blotted out by the homogenizing forces of wartime bombing, postwar urban planning schemes, real estate markets, globalization, and forgetting (intentional, incidental, and otherwise), and whose vacant spaces have been filled by freeways, shopping malls, corporate headquarters, and other familiar contemporary urban forms. On the other hand, imagine a city made fully a museum, where every patch of land or brick wall with a connection to Berlin's Nazi past is marked and cordoned off from the mundane practices of commerce, dwelling, governance, or recreation.

It is, of course, politically, culturally, and physically impossible to mark every site of resistance to or persecution by the Nazis. A memorial landscape can only partially reflect actual events. At the same time, though, it is politically, and perhaps psychologically, impossible to forget entirely and to eradicate all traces of that past, and to refuse to construct new reminders of it. Where precisely on the continuum between these absolutes does Berlin lie, and how did the city arrive at that point and not closer to one extreme or the other? In other words, how do places come to tell their stories-or particular versions of particular elements of their pasts?

Despite wildly fluctuating property values and unprecedented amounts of renovation and construction in commercial, residential, and governmental sectors, the majority of the memorials that existed before 1989 in Berlin have remained in place. Even with a burgeoning and potentially highly profitable real estate market, existing memorial spaces rarely disappear beneath skyscrapers or shopping malls, or even beneath new government buildings. Furthermore, at the same time that property values were skyrocketing and the city was being primed to be the capital of a unified Germany, new memorial spaces appeared. The years since the Wall fell have seen the construction of new memorial sites, some internationally recognized and centrally located, others tucked away on quiet residential streets or even in building foyers. At the same time, a difficult, heroic, or brutal past is not sufficient condition for a plot of land or a building to be devoted exclusively to memorial use. A given site must also meet other preconditions.

Four Forces

First, stories of individual courage or systematic annihilation during the Nazi era do not become memorials on their own. They must have advocates—memorial entrepreneurs—and the advocates' calls must be heard. In most cases, an identifiable individual begins a campaign to transform a site into a memorial. A catalyst either spurs him or her to action or suddenly brings greater attention to his or her efforts. A growing circle of supporters develops, often in response to the active efforts of memorial entrepreneurs. These supporters, as well as the original memorial entrepreneur(s), in turn contact the press and political officials. Memorial entrepreneurs may be city council members, citizens' groups, Holocaust survivors, tour guides, university professors, or historically inclined residents. For some, their professional lives are intricately connected to these activities. For others, their day jobs have little to do with the evening and weekend hours spent campaigning for memorial plaques or sitting on the boards of directors of memorial sites.[21] These bureaucrats, officials, professors, students, artists, and other activists have an existing (if also ever-transforming) repertoire of techniques that help to produce officially recognized sites of memory. These actors are also frequently connected to a well-entrenched institutional framework for memorializing in Berlin. Clubs, local history workshops, district museums, universities, three levels of government, historical preservation offices, offices of political education at different levels, publishing houses, pedagogy, tourism, existing *Gedenkstätten,* or memorial complexes, conferences, guidebooks, and newspapers all contribute to this memorial landscape. The physical imprints on the landscape include plaques, monuments, and street names. The motivations of memorial entrepreneurs vary widely, from marking the site of their own resistance to the Nazis to seeking their own notoriety and political capital. At the same time, their actions are a necessary but not sufficient element of memorialization.

Second, the calls of memorial entrepreneurs must resonate with a broader public. After initially being meaningful only to a handful of people (generally intellectuals or those with firsthand experience of the events), memorial projects follow a trajectory of increasing visibility through use of the press, university courses, and/or voluntary organizations by memorial entrepreneurs to publicize the meaning of a site. As pressure on political representatives grows, and press coverage increases, the campaign seems to reach a point of no return, a moment at which any alternative use of the land becomes unthinkable, and it becomes politically difficult *not* to support a given memorial project. Resonance is also a part of a circular cultural process. In the U.S. context, for example, David Chidester and Edward T. Linenthal find that "although spearheaded by specific cultural entrepreneurs, cultural brokers, or cultural workers, struggles over the ownership of sacred space inevitably draw upon the commitment of larger constituencies."[22] Memorials happen only if they are approved, but they then can and do affect public opinion and deeper-seated ideas about history and ethics.

Resonance may also happen at the local, national, and international level.[23] A small group of local history enthusiasts or a group of students may publicize a site to the point where the district council or even state administration takes notice, and supports the endeavor. A project such as Blind Trust may also break out beyond the bounds of the local and begin to receive coverage in national newspapers and attention from national-level officials. Furthermore, some of these sites break out even farther, begin to resonate internationally, become the subject of articles in the *New York Times*, and are visited by international dignitaries. With unification and the subsequent transfer of the German capital from Bonn to Berlin, some local debates about memorialization became national or even international.[24] Since 1989, the landscape of Berlin has had an increasingly international audience, not only when it comes to the architectural debates and new capital buildings, but also in terms of Germany's confrontation with its Nazi past in the "Berlin Republic." Throughout the 1990s, the U.S. press, for example, also consistently covered issues of memorialization and confrontation with the past in Berlin and in Germany more generally.[25] Economic, political, and military legitimacy in the international community also often appear intertwined with questions of Germany's relationship to its Nazi past.[26]

But memorial entrepreneurs and resonance alone are not enough to determine whether a site will become a memorial. Land use and ownership are the third and fourth of the forces in question here, and significantly shape whether memorial entrepreneurs will be successful in their efforts, and whether resonance will actually result in memorialization. I consider land use and ownership as distinct categories, because they function in different ways. Specifically, there are many cases where the ownership status is ideal for memorialization (namely, a site is publicly owned) but existing uses such as apartments or shops prevent exclusive memorialization. Alternately, a given land use may be compatible with memorialization, but if the site is privately owned, there is no way for the state to intervene, and it will go unmarked unless (as has occurred in a few cases) the property owner is also in favor of some kind of marking. Most memorials erected in Berlin since the 1990s are on state-owned property, and in places where there was no preexisting use. Property in public hands but already in use as offices or apartments remains difficult to convert to exclusively memorial use. Private but vacant space (and with unclear property relations, such as the rooms at Rosenthaler Straße 39) may offer a window of opportunity for memorialization, but since the change of governments and economic orders in 1989, no memorializing can take place without the consent of the property owner. Official memory of the Nazi past thus settles far more frequently on state property than on private property. Because private property is the order of the day, collective material memory has to fit into that grid. In a democratic system based on the conventions of private property, not even the most skilful of memorial entrepreneurs or the most resonant of meanings can force the hand of a property owner without providing compensation. In some cases, activists will push the district or state authorities to place a plaque on the sidewalk in front of a building (that is, on public property) when the property owner refuses to have a plaque placed on the building itself. Collective memory, then, tends to occupy spaces that have few other demands made on them, and thus on land already designated as open space (such as a traffic island or park), and already owned by the state.

Within a larger web of contingencies, structures, and cultural, political, and economic trends, these factors play central roles in rooting specific narratives of the German past in the landscape of Berlin. Clearly, the first two elements differ significantly from the second two. Ownership and land use are not agents in the way that memorial entrepreneurs are, nor are they as fluid or conditional as resonance can be. Private property, buildings already in use, places whose meanings do not resonate with a broader public, and sites without a committed advocate generally do not become memorials. As the following chapters will demonstrate, in most cases a site can fulfill three out of four of these criteria and still fade into the cityscape unmarked.

Authenticity

The memorial projects constructed in recent years have generally been on "authentic" sites. Many people involved in discussions about memorials and historic preservation distinguish readily between authentic and inauthentic sites, the former being those on which (or in which) recorded and/or remembered events actually occurred.[27] There is a widespread focus on the specificity of place, emphasizing the pedagogical power of the authentic floorboards, wallpaper, or cellar walls that were witness to atrocity or heroism. James Young confirms the prevalence of this focus, finding that "some people claim intuitively to sense the invisible aura of past events in historical sites, as if the molecules of such sites still vibrated with the memory of their past," and this certainly seems to be happening in the Blind Trust exhibit.[28] No other lasting uses of the space had intervened since the rooms at Rosenthaler Straße 39 were used as Otto Weidt's factory, and their poor condition contributed to their perceived "authenticity" (a term used frequently by activists and journalists to describe the site), which was a fundamental reason for preserving them as a museum, its advocates argued in the 1990s. "The fact that the workshop room and the hiding place of the Jewish family Horn [the family whom Weidt hid in a small back room until their betrayal by a family friend in 1943] are preserved almost in their original condition in their entire oppressive expressiveness [*Aussagekraft*], inspired the students [who curated the exhibit] to make this place publicly accessible."[29] One of the students who played a central role in the creation of the exhibit, Kai Gruzdz, explained the motivation behind the project thus: "Change is perceptible in the city every day, and we have noticed that places worthy of preservation disappear in the process. It was important for us to seek out such a hidden and forgotten monument and make it into the substance of an exhibit."[30] Urban change in the new Berlin threatened to erase this and other authentic sites.

The argument of authenticity is prevalent and powerful, yet most authentic locations slip into mundane usage. The authenticity of a site does not always guarantee memorial status. Throughout Berlin, and indeed far beyond its borders, places with so-called authentic ties to past acts of great cruelty or great courage disappear from view, their pasts recalled only by eyewitnesses or, perhaps, historians. Historical events alone are not sufficient to create a memorial space. Particularly if we follow Émile Durkheim's understanding of the construction of the sacred, no place evokes its own untouchability.[31] Of all of the potentially memorializable sites, ultimately only a very few are even proposed as memorials, and even fewer actually achieve memorial status. Most slip into the fabric of daily life. There are apartments built on the site of Hitler's chancellery, for example, constructed in the 1980s by the East German government, and Sony's European headquarters were built in the 1990s on the site of one of Berlin's most infamous Nazi courts. Nazi bunkers, forced labor camps, damaged synagogues, and anonymous buildings used as deportation centers have slipped out of public memory. Most "authentic" locations never actually become memorial sites, and not all proposed memorial projects are actually constructed.

What of the projects that never come to fruition? And what of the countless places of heroism or cruelty—technically "authentic" in the sense used by so many memorial entrepreneurs—that remain in the personal memories of eyewitnesses and even on the pages of meticulous chronicles of resistance and persecution, but that are invisible in the urban landscape? I expand on the concern for the origin stories of memorials shared by many scholars by adding a crucial comparative dimension, investigating failed proposals and forgotten places alongside the landscape of existing memorials. I investigate the origins of sites of concentrated collective memory, and the ways in which people transform mundane patches of urban land into sites of wide-ranging meaning. I then compare that which is remembered with that which is forgotten—or, those events that are marked officially in the urban landscape with those that are left unmarked, either because memorial proposals fail or because no such proposal was ever made. I address the aesthetic debates and the existing markers in the landscape, but I also place these debates over history and aesthetics in the necessary context of land use, ownership patterns, and the framework of institutions and regulations that shapes this terrain. This approach, in turn, yields a basis from which to understand and analyze the social patterns of memorialization.

The collective memory involved in memorialization in Berlin is not solely the product of an underlying consensus, but also a result of public controversy and debate. Memory is made collective over time and thus has a dynamic quality, in part because of its collective properties.[32] As extensive analyses of memory have made clear, either the past has to be experienced firsthand or it has to be narrated in images, texts, oral stories, stone markers, or other communicative forms that link not only past generations to the present (or vice versa) but also those who were not there to the original events.[33] Drawing on Henri Bergson, Jeffrey Olick and Daniel Levy assert that "collective memory . . . should be seen as an active process of sense-making through time," a premise confirmed by the "active processes" whose description is at the heart of this book.[34] Olick and Joyce Robbins see the influence of the past on the present as "conscious and unconscious, public and private, material and communicative, consensual and challenged."[35] Today's conflict is, in many instances, tomorrow's consensus, as public memorials are concretized both in the urban landscape and in the collective memory.[36]

Urban memory sites offer an intersection of forces that do not often meet up in sociological studies—collective memory, urban planning, culture, real estate, and multiple levels of politics. This case brings into bold relief the dynamics more difficult to trace where history is not as close to the surface as it is in Berlin. To understand how memory gets made, and why some places become repositories of official collective memory, while others do not, I combined archival research, interviews, and German-language secondary sources.[37] I conducted extensive archival work in the federal, state, and district archives of Berlin between 1998 and 2004. The archival sources range from photographs to property registries to the records of citizens' groups, and also include an in-depth analysis of legislative and administrative records. I augmented these sources by interviewing architects, urban planners, artists, politicians, activists, public officials, and others directly involved in these processes. I also relied on German-language secondary sources, including catalogs of memorial sites, local histories, and periodicals, seeking out sequences of events and pivotal moments in each project's history, as well as the actors involved, and the terms in which these actors spoke of potential memorial sites.[38] I searched newspaper databases for any mention of these sites and was able to pinpoint the chronology of those memorial sites that received press coverage, matching these chronologies up with the legislative decisions about the sites at the levels of district government (Berlin at the time was divided into twenty-three districts, each with its own city council) and state government (Berlin is both a city and a federal state, so its governing body is a state assembly).[39]

These qualitative and historical approaches offer a view of the ways in which the meanings and uses of land change over time, and specifically how the patterns of remembering and forgetting emerge in the landscape of Berlin. The combination of these materials has allowed me to better understand how government officials, artists, architects, and others actively shape the construction of memorial sites and the terrain of the city. Together, these sources yielded complex histories of each site, but also revealed patterns in memorial sites' transformations from anonymous patches of urban land to places of wide-ranging significance. Two limitations bear mentioning, however. First, in any investigation of urban change, not only contingency but also activities difficult (and sometimes impossible) to access through conventional methodological channels play important roles. There is always a terra incognita involved in studying urban change in the broadest sense, because people sometimes forget, or lie, or break the law, or, above all, negotiate behind the scenes in ways that do not necessarily show up in newspapers, archives, or interviews. This is an enduring problem of urban research. Second, these landscapes are intrinsically in flux, and it is entirely possible (indeed likely) that the understanding and even physical form of some of the sites I have examined will have changed by the time these words are printed. Even as I write, once-forgotten places are being pulled into the limelight, and other sites once foremost in many people's minds are receding from view.

My research serves as the basis for a new theory of the production of urban memorial space, attuned to the complexity of collective memory and place construction. This book thus both details the concrete ways in which these forms of remembering and forgetting occur in Berlin and offers a framework with which to explore the intersection of markets and culture, not only in Berlin, but in a range of other contemporary cities as well. This framework illuminates the concrete production of memorial spaces in Berlin, and speaks to such production in other cities as well. By examining multiple sites in the same city and comparing officially remembered and publicly forgotten sites, this book develops an approach rarely taken in other studies of memory, most of which tend to focus only on those places that actually appear in the landscape.

As in other cities, the memorial landscape in Berlin is not a straight-forward result of political history, but the product of a matrix of forces operating in varying strengths and across time. Place construction happens at the intersection of ownership patterns, land-use regulations, individual investment in places, and broader political and cultural sets of meanings. The memorial landscape of Berlin—and arguably of many other cities as well—arises out of the intersection of a multitude of forces, ranging from the original event itself to fleeting artistic trends to decades of entrenched land-use policy and ownership patterns. The places discussed here high-light both the observable patterns in memorial construction and the role of contingency: nothing here is predetermined, or inevitable. Granted, no scholar (and no savvy passerby) would assert that these sites are inevitable. But once constructed, memorials, like buildings in general, tend to mask the often conflictual conditions of their creation and to take on an appar-ent permanence that belies their social origins. Many proposed projects teeter on the brink of failure for years, yet become profoundly uncon-troversial (if also often ignored) once construction is complete. This past materializes into memorial spaces through a mixture of quiet consensus and passionate dispute.

In cities throughout the world, for purposes of remembering, peo-ple demarcate places where great cruelty has occurred or great heroism has been manifested. As Chidester and Linenthal (1995), Young (2000), and others have asserted, the unique qualities of a memorial space that set it apart from nonmemorial spaces are not intrinsic—they must be produced. The particular constellation of remembering and forgetting is by no means inevitable. Sometimes debates over sites of memory may be tempests in the proverbial teapot, bitter battles over tiny patches of political turf. But debates over memorials may also be of dire urgency, not only for survivors, but also for broader formations of local or national identity, international political relations, urban development, and collective moral frameworks. Ultimately, these interpretations of the past of a given place (and of a given collectivity) are also intertwined with visions of the future. Not only in Berlin, but also at the Tuol Sleng Museum of Genocidal Crimes in Phnom Penh, or the Parque de la Memoria in Buenos Aires, or the Robben Island Museum off the coast of South Africa, marking a site of past cruelty or courage serves, in part, as a way to envision both the past and the future, the latter ideally free of the kinds of troubles being recalled.[40]

These landscapes of remembering and forgetting are, after all, tied up with the memories of bodies, and of the intense materiality of physical harm. For many people, spirits lurk in cemeteries and burial grounds, and so must also linger on in former detention centers, concentration camps, and killing grounds, the meanings of which are marked and conveyed by survivors, artists, and historians, among others. This process can be both a key component of place making and a vital element of the study of place, helping to answer the sociologist Tom Gieryn's question, "How do places come to be the way they are, and how do places matter for social practices and historical change?"[41] Public book readings, impromptu question-and-answer sessions, chance meetings, and lifelong visions all combine to create such places of concentrated meaning in the cityscape. These are the deeply social ways that places *do* begin to speak. The question of why some places are collectively recalled with markers in the landscape, while others are not, can also be phrased in the following way: How do groups of people live with collective memories? There are many answers. We write about them, tell grandchildren about them, read about them, ignore them, dispute them, and forget them. And we also transform them into concrete places in the landscapes around us. In this book, then, I focus on the ways in which a particular set of "ghosts"—those generated by personal stories and collective memories of persecution by and resistance to the Nazi regime—take on the tangible form of bronze plaques, glass-encased exhibits, and public sculpture.

Chapter Overview

Chapter 2 addresses the shifts in memorial culture from 1945 to the current era, examining the changing perception and treatment of the urban memory of Berlin's Nazi past. After 1945, the residents of both East and West Germany navigated between a strong impulse to forget the Nazi past and—at times—a powerful impulse to remember it, resulting in a range of memorial projects in both halves of the city. But what happened to these "uncomfortable monuments" in the wake of the falling of the Wall?[42]

In the final weeks of 1989, construction and demolition in East Berlin ground to a halt, with one well-known exception. The only sound of hammers and bulldozers came from the thin strip along the Wall, as demonstrators, tourists, and hawkers chiseled away at the concrete panels, followed by bulldozers and cranes. Everywhere else in the city, construction sites fell still, the dynamite holes bored in condemned buildings remained empty, and everyone waited to see what would happen next. The dramatic shifts in political and economic structures, as well as new paradigms of urban planning and land use, set the stage for subsequent memorial practice. In particular, the commodification of land and buildings in post-1989 eastern Berlin, coupled with new political forms, has had significant effects on the city's social and material landscape.

Given this political and economic upheaval, the post-1989 memorial landscape of Berlin presents a set of what might seem, at first glance, to be paradoxes, addressed in Chapter 3. As property values skyrocketed and construction boomed, at least some existing memorial sites might have been expected to give way to the pressure of this escalating demand for urban land. Yet even with the total collapse of the East German political and economic spheres, the majority of the memorials the East German government had built dealing with the Nazi past in Berlin remained in place.

Chapter 4 turns to new memorials put up after 1989, revealing the step-by-step production of memorial space. How, for example, can a given plot of land in the center of Berlin be a parking lot one year and a solemn memorial site where thousands of tourists stop to snap photos and dignitaries gather for official ceremonies a year later? No city is ever a blank slate, even with the fall of one political and economic regime and the rise of another, as the example of Berlin so clearly shows. Moreover, most cities have at least a few patches of land devoted to memorials, even amid shopping malls, corporate headquarters, and government ministries. Here I begin to focus in greater depth on the role of land use, landownership, memorial entrepreneurs, and resonance in memorial production.

Although most preexisting memorials persisted in Berlin after 1989, and new memorials were constructed in the 1990s, many proposed memorial projects have failed, and still more "authentic" sites have gone unmarked in the landscape. Chapter 5 sets out to explain why this has occurred. Over the past six decades in Berlin, synagogues have been demolished to make way for parking lots, playgrounds, or apartment blocks. Cellars and bars used by the SS and the SA as places to incarcerate, torture, or murder people they considered to be enemies of the Nazi regime have been reused as storage rooms, laundries, or restaurants. Barracks built to house forced laborers have been pulled down, abandoned, or used for other purposes. In a few cases, a plaque was attached to a building façade to remind passersby of what once happened in one of these locations, and in even fewer cases, a larger memorial was erected.

Chapter 5 compares places that are officially marked with those that vanish into the landscape. The messages emanating from an existing memorial site may give the impression that the stones or bronze are themselves speaking, that there is something intrinsically communicative about such a site. But stones do not speak for themselves, and many places that should—following the prevalent logic of authenticity in German memorial culture—emit a sense of sorrow and warning, for example, actually do not do so for anyone but eyewitnesses without years of work. Contrasting marked sites with unmarked sites offers a way of thinking more broadly, and theoretically, about the infusion of place with meaning and memory, and of investigating what kinds of circumstances lead to the exposure in the landscape of a particular moment in a given site's history. Chapter 5 brings into greater relief the forces that contribute to the memorial landscape that actually emerges.

Chapter 6 illuminates further tensions between authentic historical sites, market pressures, and the political volatility of the city's remembrance of its Nazi past. By examining a "failed" project, as well as a new set of small-scale memorials, I explore the intersections of the local and the global in Berlin's memorial landscape. One example of the failure of a site to capture both public imagination and governmental approval is the so-called "drivers' bunker," attached to the complex of bunkers underneath Hitler's chancellery. When it was rediscovered in 1990, a long debate ensued about what to do with it, but the state government of Berlin finally voted not to place it under historical preservation. At the other end of the spectrum are the new "stumbling stones" being set into sidewalks across Berlin to mark the lives of single individuals who suffered at the hands of the Nazis. These stones seem to have captured international public attention, despite (or perhaps because of) their modest scale. In both of these cases, and many others, the processes of memorialization are simultaneously very local and very international. However, theories of collective memory in general and memorialization in particular have tended to remain resolutely located within national borders, and they clearly need to expand beyond their traditional bounds. Memorial projects and historic preservation efforts, in Berlin and beyond, operate in an increasingly international context, one in which artists, donors, survivors, historians, political officials, and even the people who visit sites of memory are often aware of the actions of their counterparts in far-off places.

Blank Slates and Authentic Traces: Memorial Culture in Berlin After 1945

No city is ever a blank slate. No amount of bombing or bulldozing can fully eradicate the traces of what came before, either in the landscape itself or in the memories and habits of its residents. Even in the midst of dramatic political, economic, and material change, traces of the past persist in the urban topography, as well as in technocratic practices and individual and collective memory. Cellars, pipes, and subway tunnels still lurk beneath the surface of the most decimated city, encouraging reconstruction in patterns that reflect the remaining infrastructure. Memory also persists in the minds of residents, even when the traces of these memories have disappeared from the visible city. But the precise constellation of sites of memory—the imprint of individual and collective memory on the cityscape, and vice versa—changes over time, in ways that are sometimes subtle and sometimes dramatic. This process has occurred with particular intensity in post–World War II Berlin.

A city's stock of historical buildings and markers may feel permanent to passersby, but this permanence obscures the profound contingencies and extensive efforts behind the cultural landscapes we inhabit. How, then, did Berlin change from the smoldering ruins of 1945, fraught with what would later come to be called "authentic" sites, into a place renowned for its difficult and public confrontations with its Nazi past—a city whose "commemorative apparatus" has "become a rather well-oiled machine," as Jeffrey Olick puts it?[1] In James Young's words: "Holocaust memorial-work in Germany today remains a tortured, self-reflective, even paralyzing preoccupation. Every monument, at every turn, is endlessly scrutinized, explicated, and debated. Artistic, ethical, and historical questions occupy design juries to an extent unknown in other countries."² Young's and Olick's descriptions certainly apply to contemporary Berlin. But such a scenario would have been difficult to imagine in 1945, when there was little hint of the layers of memorial culture to come.

This chapter examines three kinds of changes in Germany's commemorative culture. First, not surprisingly, there have been substantial changes in the aesthetic forms of the memorials designed to mark resistance to or persecution by the Nazi regime, including a growing focus on "authentic" sites and nontraditional memorial forms. Second, the categories of events and individuals that count as worthy of memorialization have changed distinctly from one decade to the next. Third, the relationships between states, their residents, and their territories have changed as well. That is, there have been considerable changes in the ways in which states craft landscapes of memorials, and, in particular, in the political and bureaucratic routes through which they do this, and the degrees to which popular opinion and citizen activism figure in the construction of such landscapes. Taken together, these processes also offer a way to more precisely understand the overlaps and disjunctures between official landscapes of memory and a broader "collective memory."

As later chapters will show, each marker in the landscape comes about only through years of effort. The actions that lead to a marker include not only the initial acts of persecution or resistance but also years of work on the part of artists, politicians, survivors, activists, intellectuals, and local, national, and even international constituencies. A range of motives has driven these actors over the past five decades, among them, mourning, pedagogy, guilt, political calculation, and idealism.³ The landscape today is shaped by decades of decisions that cement official collective memory. These decisions, the way they are made, and the form and content of their imprint on the landscape changed throughout the postwar period. But they did so in uneven ways, mediated through decades of political wrangling, economic fluctuation, and artistic and historiographic processes. This kind of memory is rooted not only in the landscape but also in professional journals, high school and university curricula, museum studies, guidebooks, and an array of governmental and private organizations.

Here, then, I am concerned with how the East and West German states have created particular landscapes of (official) memory treating the city's Nazi past.[4] Investigating these intersections opens a more nuanced way to talk about the relationship between a state, its landscape, and its subjects in terms of representations of official collective memory. No concentrated site of collective memory happens of its own accord. Every plaque, every engraved stone, and certainly every interpretive exhibition is the result of years of activity. Today this landscape of erasure and marking is shaped not by a unified vision of the city's past, but by decades of artistic activity, historical research, and public debate.

Terrains of memory create layers not identical with collective memory or with any official stance on the past at a given moment, for at least four reasons. First, in any political system, there is necessarily some degree of disjuncture between the representations of the past created by the state in the landscape and the broader popular understandings and interpretations of the past. Second, of course, there is also a lack of consensus among the people as well, under any political system, albeit to varying degrees (a fact not always captured in analyses of collective memory). Simply because the narrative is there does not guarantee that it is accepted by the population in uniform ways, or that a collection of monuments and plaques creates a homogeneous collective memory or national identity. Third, the layers of past remembrance often remain in place. It is rare that the traces of previous ways of treating the landscape are fully erased. Statues are pulled down in public displays of revolution or regime change, but, to varying degrees, the terrain of past political eras combines with new efforts to shape landscapes of memory to create a multiple and even conflicting narrative of different elements of the past. Finally, the channels for the creation of these imprints vary as well, ranging from the executive decree of one-party rule to a cacophony of citizens' groups and memorial entrepreneurs with a multiplicity of agendas and intentions.

Approaches to Memory

Not only does the content of memorial culture change over time; so do the political and bureaucratic channels through which memorial landscapes are created. Hence the importance both of a historical perspective in studies of collective memory and of studying the channels through which memory's various forms enter into and shape the material and social world.[5] Influenced in part by Maurice Halbwachs and Pierre Nora, many sociologists, historians, geographers, and others have increasingly turned their attention to collective memory.[6] Some of the recent sociological work on collective memory opens the subject up to notions of conflict, which are especially visible when collective memory is viewed over time. Other approaches operate with a more unified notion of collective memory, and of the relationship between the complicated entity of memory and the tricky notion of the collective. In one recent analysis, Amy Adamczyk examines the collective memory and rituals surrounding Thanksgiving over a period of three centuries, focusing more on the symbols themselves and less on the changes in the factors shaping and transmitting these memories.[7] Adamczyk draws on Halbwachs to assert that "collective memories change according to the needs and concerns of each generation," and that "present interests and needs are the main source of change in collective memory and commemoration."[8] This approach seems to imply a more unified set of "needs and concerns of each generation" than might actually be present, reiterating Nora's, Halbwachs's, and Durkheim's emphasis on the consensual roots of collective memory.[9] Often such approaches may be exactly right, given that sometimes elements of collective memory do in fact become broadly consensual.[10] But in these approaches, there is not as much talk of memory as a struggle over dominant narratives of the past, for example, or as a part of a contentious and layered project of national identity or state formation that may not overlap with the understandings that broad swathes of the population may have of the past.

Olick and Levy turn their attention to the role of conflict in producing elements of collective memory, asserting that, "collective memory . . . should be seen as an active process of sense-making through time."[11] Furthermore, Olick finds that states use aspects of memory for political legitimation, creating what he calls "legitimation profiles," a concept "useful for appreciating the ways in which diverse symbolic elements and issues congeal through time into relatively coherent yet dynamic systems."[12] Rudy Koshar also sets out to examine the contingent and layered elements of landscapes of memory, offering a three-point approach with relation to German memory and finding

that framing strategies may be used by the state and its agencies or by social groups representing a variety of interests and ideologies. It is assumed, furthermore, that framing strategies themselves are "path-dependent" . . . because they get their legitimacy from past uses and articulations. When groups mobilize framing devices, they may establish social consensus, or they may promote or exacerbate conflict, depending on historical circumstances. Framing devices are rarely unilaterally imposed from above [in democracies] . . . but emerge from negotiation and conflict. This book [*From Monuments to Traces*] is about a triad, a three-cornered relationship among highly resonant parts of a memory landscape, individuals, and groups that struggle to invest that environment with meaning through the use of framing strategies, and the themes and symbols that are the raw material of the framing devices and meanings themselves.[13]

Some outcroppings of official collective memory thus result from intense personal connections to past events, while others are stripped-down symbols that fit an official party line, and sometimes official memory (especially in the West after the 1970s and in unified Germany) responds to various grassroots pressures. But even in settings where citizen activism shapes a fair amount of the memorial landscape, there is neither a perfect match-up NOR perfect opposition between official and unofficial memory.

Clearly, the project of officially remembering the resistance to and persecution by the Nazi regime in Germany changed significantly on both sides of the Iron Curtain in the years following World War II. I detail some of the key changes in post-1945 memorial culture here, in order to provide a context for the discussions of post-1989 memorial practice that will occupy the rest of the book. An interdisciplinary array of scholars has been involved in understanding these transformations of memorial culture, resulting in detailed analyses of the ways in which it has changed over time, and a general agreement that these changes fall loosely into four eras, discussed in greater detail below. (Not all analysts share the same conceptions of these periodizations, but many do overlap.)[14] I build on these analyses and draw on newspaper articles, German- and English-language secondary sources, archival sources, and catalogs of monuments, combined with an analysis of the memorial landscape itself, to consider some of the theoretical implications for the study of collective memory and urban change. The intentions of those doing the memorializing are often apparent in the transcripts of public meetings, dedication speeches, op-ed pieces, or in the pamphlets or other interpretive information available on-site. These sources can illuminate the approaches of governments at various times and at various levels, as well as the intentions of citizens' groups, district history museums, and history workshops involved in memorialization—revealing changes in aesthetics and in content, and in the relationships of states to their landscapes and citizens.

Immediate and Provisional Memory, 1945–1949

In the night of May 8, 1945, Germany officially surrendered to the Allies in the eastern Berlin neighborhood of Karlshorst.[15] Berlin and Germany entered what many called the Zero Hour.[16] Despite the language of the Zero Hour, however, and the strong impulses to suppress detailed memory of the Nazi era, leaving no trace of the Nazi past in the landscape was simply never a viable option.[17] Even in the summer of 1945, survivors and politicians were turning their attention to issues of how to remember resistance to and persecution by the Nazi regime. As much as the capitulation signaled the beginning of a new political era in Germany, there was also widespread continuity on many levels, including in the built environment. The physical, psychological, and social traces remained either fully exposed or hidden just beneath the surface. At the time of the capitulation, Hitler's bunker lay partially exposed at the city center, and almost the entire population had firsthand memories of World War II. The city was in ruins, there was no state, and most memorial work appeared to be shaped by survivors. From the perspective of the individual, Berlin was never a blank slate, but rather a landscape layered with personal memory. There was obviously an immediacy of memory in May 1945 differing significantly from the kind of memory of the Nazi era circulating in Germany today.

Many of the places that became important locations of memorialization toward the end of the twentieth century were, in 1945, at least partial ruins and were not singled out for memorialization. Much of Berlin was destroyed or heavily damaged by Allied bombing and the Soviet advance, leaving behind fifty-five million cubic meters of rubble, Jeffry Diefendorf notes, but he argues that this is only part of the story, and that there was much structural continuity even in areas that were bombed most heavily or that experienced firestorms.[18] Not only did many masonry walls remain standing even in heavily bombed areas, but most of the underground infrastructure also remained in place. The intact sewer systems and gas lines necessarily also shaped reconstruction. Bombing or burning do not necessarily level a building. Someone has to make a decision either to leave it a ruin, to tear it down completely, or to reconstruct it based on what is salvageable. Many salvageable buildings were torn down in both East and West to do away with politically fraught structures such as Hitler's chancellery or the imperial palace, to make way for new city planning schemes, or to remove dangerous ruins. In rebuilding the city, sites that are now the subject of intensive archaeological investigation or widely publicized rediscovery were, in the years immediately following the war, simply parts of the topography of the city, steeped in the personal memories of perpetrators and those victims who survived, but not entrenched in a broader landscape of official collective remembrance and pedagogical practice. Such sites include synagogues damaged but not destroyed during the 1938 pogroms and the Gestapo headquarters, whose cellars were rediscovered in the 1980s. I should note that the language of "rediscovery" is somewhat problematic because it implies that the traces of these events vanished through some natural process, which obscures the active forgetting and demolition through which many people, officials and regular citizens alike, attempted to erase the Nazi past. Furthermore, as noted elsewhere, for eyewitnesses to past events (whether victims or perpetrators), the memory of what happened in a given place surely did not fade, so that "rediscovery" may be accurate in describing an arc of collective forgetting and remembering, but in no way conveys the continuity of individual memory, or the considerable lengths people went to (including demolishing salvageable buildings) to erase evidence of the sites that might later be rediscovered.

Some people certainly had a vested interest in suppressing memories, either as perpetrators or victims. Others pushed quite early on for public markers and ceremonies to remember the victims of persecution and the agents of resistance. During the occupation, from 1945 to 1949, there was as yet no clearly established official memorial culture. In these years, there was a memorial vacuum of sorts. Initially, victims' organizations played key roles in memorialization, including the Hauptausschüsse für Opfer des Faschismus (Central Committee for Victims of Fascism), or OdF, and the Vereinigung der Verfolgten des NS-Regimes (Union of the Persecuted of the Nazi Regime), or VVN, as well as ethnic and religious groups, particularly Jewish communities, and the newly allowed German Communist Party (KPD) and Social Democratic Party (SPD).[19] Photographs from September 1945 capture fleeting memorials set up in the city, hand-painted posters hung with garlands, calling on people to honor the victims of the concentration camps, living or dead, and in particular to remember the heroism of anti-fascist resistance fighters.[20] Stefanie Endlich and others have found that at this point, the public remembrance of the Nazi past entailed a comparatively diverse grassroots set of efforts to create sites marking persecution and resistance, often in forms that allowed for public ceremonies. "The first memory signs [*Erinnerungszeichen*], remembrance stones, and gravestones originate in the first weeks and months directly after the end of the war, and from the early postwar years," Ulrike Puvogel notes.[21] Wreathlaying, the erection of pillars or urns, reburials, large public ceremonies, and countless acts of personal remembrance took place. One account also describes memorials made of "plaster, wood, papier-mâché, flag cloth," and other relatively temporary materials.[22]

In his analysis of memory on both sides of the Iron Curtain in Germany, Jeffrey Herf found that "[a]mong the Communists returning to East Berlin, those who had been political prisoners in German concentration camps attempted, with some success, to shape the form and content of political memory. In so doing, they displayed a generosity and compassion which became rare following the codification of East German antifascism."[23] This local and individual nature of memorialization differed significantly from the more centralized and official memory that developed just a few years later, when the two Germanys were founded.[24] In the late 1940s and early 1950s, there were a few markers for Jews who had been killed throughout Germany. These were often on a relatively small scale and erected on local initiative, marking cemeteries, the sites of mass murders, and death marches.[25] Even so, given the magnitude of the Holocaust, there were relatively few markers or ceremonies devoted explicitly to recalling the murder and persecution of Jews, and this would remain the case in both halves of Berlin until the 1970s in the West, and the late 1980s in the East. At this point there was also no hint of the more elaborate kinds of memorialization that would become prevalent in later decades. Some memory work did happen, but most authentic sites vanished into the landscape, some to be rediscovered later.

State Formation and the Cold War, 1949–1968

Once the German Democratic Republic and the Federal Republic of Germany were founded, issues of state formation and political legitimacy came to the fore alongside the pressing problems of economic recovery and physical reconstruction. Both sides began officially to mark certain sites connected to resistance to Nazi power. At the same time, polarization and simplification characterized much official memory of the Nazi era. Herf finds, for example, that "the public language of memory was related to occupation-era policies of denazification and judicial procedure," so that memory was mediated through these broader political and institutional processes.[26] At the time the two German states were founded, in 1949, people were still navigating the especially treacherous waters of personal memory and national politics in the midst of this bombed-out landscape. There was a mixture of centralized and selective remembering, on the one hand, and widespread erasure and forgetting, on the other, in both halves of Berlin. As early as 1948, with the increasing division of the city, official representations of the Nazi past became more ideological and more divided, and linked more to the Cold War. Thus even before 1949, East and West had already embarked on different paths of remembering the Nazi era. "[E]ach nation had perceived and publicly proclaimed that the other was the continuation of a totalitarian, whether fascist or communist, state while each was itself a rebirth of German democratic traditions."[27]

Authorities, artists, survivors, and enthusiastic Communist Party members made this antagonism quite plain in the memorial landscape. Both sides sought a tradition of resistance (whether military or communist) in which to root the origins of their respective states. In the West, the quest for a legitimate, and usable, national past took the form primarily of honoring "conservative, military, Church, and social democratic" resistance.[28] In the East, the focus was on socialist and communist resistance to the Nazi regime, and these public markers centered on what were officially referred to (until 1989) as "anti-fascist resistance fighters." Official memorialization took place in ways that coincided with and bolstered the ideological position and political legitimacy of each side of the Cold War. Memorialization, both in physical monuments and at public ceremonies, quickly became tangled up with Cold War politics.[29]

As in the West, in East Berlin and East Germany in the 1950s and 1960s, memorial culture emphasized public ritual and the marking of sites connected to officially recognized "anti-fascist resistance fighters." In 1948 and 1949, the foundation of the German Democratic Republic and the "Stalinization" of the ruling Sozialistische Einheitspartei Deutschlands

(SED) "led to a growing narrowing, simplification, abstraction, and ritu-alization of official remembrance."[30] This process included the disbanding of victims' organizations and increasing official reliance on the red trian-gle as the sole symbol of anti-fascist/communist (and thus officially rec-ognized) resistance. At this point, the red triangle—the symbol used in concentration camps to indicate political prisoners, particularly socialists and communists, and which had been used spontaneously after 1945 as a symbol of persecution and resistance—also became a more official symbol. The SED also transferred responsibility for the documentation of anti-fascist resistance from the Union of the Persecuted (VVN) to the Marx-Engels-Lenin Institute.[31] There were clear efforts to concentrate control of memorialization in the hands of the SED, and this included the exclu-sion of communist concentration camp internees from discussions about memorials and the dismantling of the VVN, although former members of the VVN continued to be individually active, volunteering their time for smaller projects.

While there was more memorialization in the East early on, including centralized and decentralized memorials, public ceremonies, and memo-rial plaques, these projects quickly became the work of the state and not of independent individuals or groups. Throughout the history of the GDR, memorial construction was largely a top-down process, and this remem-bering generally took the form of heroic portrayals of anti-fascist resistance fighters, an important element of establishing East German national iden-tity. In an account of East German monuments published in 1970, Volker Frank wrote:

The aim of antifascist monuments is to recall the years of the fascist dictatorship, to honour the dead and to express vividly in the eyes of the artist the moral quali-ties which the resistance fighters displayed, their steadfastness and their unflinch-ing valour. But the antifascist monument should at the same time produce in the observer a negative reaction to all forms of neofascism and should help to devel-op an awareness of past events. This includes as prerequisites of our present-day socialist life, the struggle against fascism and the unity of the working class which was prepared during the resistance.[32]

The focus on anti-fascist resistance fighters thus provided the German Democratic Republic with an account of the Nazi era that allowed them to claim a proud anti-fascist heritage.

Most memorialization in this period also followed traditional representational forms in both East and West, including statues, plaques, engraved stones, and courtyards—which is clear in the landscape even today.[33] Peter Reichel finds "crosses, crypts and churches, inscribed walls, gravestones and columns, as well as . . . the figurative representations of victims of violence and war."[34] Many sites had more a ritual than a pedagogical function and emphasized the possibility of public ceremony rather than the preservation of original structures or sites of persecution and resistance. Outside of Berlin, one set of authentic sites that received more attention was the concentration camps. The East German government began to turn concentration camps into memorial sites and educational centers earlier than the West did. In the West, no large-scale memorials were established at the concentration camps until the 1960s. In the late 1950s, the East German government began building *Nationale Mahn- und Gedenkstätten* ("National Sites for Commemoration and Admonition") at the sites of former concentration camps, dedicating memorials at Buchenwald in 1958, at Ravensbrück in 1959, and at Sachsenhausen in 1961.[35] The dedications of these memorials clearly served a larger political and ideological project, according to Herf. "Both Otto Grotewohl at Buchenwald in 1958 and Walter Ulbricht at Sachsenhausen in 1961 delivered speeches that drew political significance from past suffering. Both came to praise fallen soldiers more than to mourn innocent victims. The texts were major statements of official antifascist memory in East Germany."[36]

At the concentration camps in East Germany, through the 1980s, the exhibits and ceremonies gave little or no recognition to the Jewish victims of the Holocaust, or to anyone who was not a communist or socialist. This phenomenon persisted well into the 1990s, either intentionally or due to a lack of funds for new exhibits. At Sachsenhausen, outside of Berlin, the original state socialist exhibits still occupied the bulk of exhibition space at the end of the 1990s, and decades-old concrete memorial structures were crumbling over the crematoria. Similarly, until its complete redesign after the fall of the Wall, the German History Museum in East Berlin, largely a product of the 1950s and 1960s, failed to mention "German national participation in the events of the Third Reich." In these representations, and in official GDR history, fascism was a product of capitalism, and "Jewish victims seem[ed] an embarrassment."[37] In the process of building the Buchenwald memorial, for example, many of the original buildings were also actually torn down, a stark contrast with the attention given to "authentic" sites like the Gestapo Headquarters and the House of the Wannsee Conference in the 1980s and 1990s.[38] With only a few exceptions, detailed below, this style of memorialization continued in the East until 1989.

Despite its close connections to the government and to the commemoration of military resistance, official memorialization in the West was still more democratic and more dependent on some degree of civil society and activism than memorialization in the East. But at this point, it bore little resemblance to the later scale of citizen activism, with none of the kinds of history workshops, school projects, and pedagogical work on the scale seen by the 1980s. The earliest official and large-scale memorial sites in West Berlin were Plötzensee, dedicated in 1952, and Stauffenbergstraße, where the central courtyard was fashioned into a monument in 1953 (part of this building has now been turned into the Gedenkstätte Deutscher Widerstand, a museum dedicated to the history of German resistance to the Nazis). The West Berlin Senate sponsored the Plötzensee project after being pressured by relatives of members of resistance groups, particularly military officers who had attempted a coup against Hitler. Between 1933 and 1945, more than 2,500 people were executed in the Plötzensee prison. Many of them were political opponents of the Nazi regime and were sentenced to death at the Volksgerichtshof in the city center. Parts of the complex were destroyed near the end of the war, but the area was put to use once again as a prison after the war's end. The execution room was left unused, however, and was made into one of West Berlin's first official markers relating to the Nazi past, which honored military and elite resistance to the Nazis and, like other projects of the era, was rooted in part in an effort to found a tradition of German resistance on which the new West German government could construct a legitimate national identity.[39]

Overall, fewer markers of resistance or persecution during Nazi era appeared in the West than in the East during the 1950s and 1960s. Holger Hübner, a local author who wrote one of the more exhaustive accounts of Berlin's memorial plaques, credits the East with having a much more extensive memorial culture treating the Nazi past much earlier than the West. He recalls visiting East Berlin in the 1970s (from his home in the West) and being surprised by the extent to which the East had engaged in the marking of the Nazi past in the landscape, particularly in the form of memorial plaques dedicated to anti-fascist resistance fighters.[40] In the 1950s, plaques adorned with red triangles were mounted throughout East Berlin, with texts like the following: "In this building lived the anti-fascist resistance fighter Werner Seelenbinder, born on August 2, 1904, murdered on October 24, 1944, in Brandenburg. Honor his memory." Even into the 1980s, however, when these communists and socialists were also Jewish, official representations generally ignored that fact.

The two sides shared much in terms of memorial culture, especially an emphasis on palatable foundational narratives. Both sides also continued to omit any significant acknowledgment of the murder of Jews as well as Sinti and Roma (Gypsies), gays, and other "forgotten" groups. In the 1950s, the East differed little in this respect from the West. Neither German state marked the sites of deportations or destroyed synagogues to any significant extent; both commemorated individual social democratic or communist resistance by Jews, but rarely mentioning that they were Jewish. In Reichel's opinion, this "was probably no oversight, but rather a historical-political calculation."[41]

During this period there was also a widespread willingness to tear down or build over sites deeply intertwined with resistance and persecution during the Nazi era. Authenticity had not yet become a predominant category of memorialization.[42] The repair and reconstruction of damaged structures also began to erase places that would later be considered authentic sites of memory. In the West, the "Economic Miracle" and early, widespread construction and reconstruction also resulted in the disappearance of many authentic sites. Extensive urban reconstruction erased authenticity, not only of sites tied to resistance and persecution during the Nazi era, but also in terms of historical preservation and the aesthetics of façades. Thus in the East the lack of resources for renovation meant that crumbling but beautiful building facades remained in place, while such façades were systematically stripped and plastered over in the West. In many cases, synagogues, deportation centers, and other sites that later became the objects of archaeological excavation, careful preservation, extensive research, and public memorialization were torn down as the city was rebuilt.

One of the most striking examples of the erasure taking place throughout Berlin was the removal of most traces of once-robust Jewish communities from the landscape in both East and West.[43] On November 9, 1938, most of the prominent synagogues in Berlin were severely damaged, most of the interiors destroyed and many of the buildings set on fire by the SS and others. Bombing during World War II damaged many of the structures further.[44] Many synagogues survived the war, even if they were damaged in the 1938 pogroms or in the early 1940s, only to be leveled in the 1950s, not just in Berlin but throughout Europe.[45] In the years following the war, Berliners walked past ruins every day. As the economy improved, particularly in the West, resources for rebuilding became increasingly available, which also meant that it became possible to remove existing ruins to make way for new construction.[46] Jackhammers, dynamite, and bulldozers have all contributed to the shape of the memorial landscape.

Demolition orders were followed, in some cases (and much later), by excavations both in the cityscape and in the archives, which led in turn to a new landscape of plaques and sculptures. The synagogue at Behaimstraße in the western district of Charlottenburg, for example, was damaged in 1938 and again in 1941, demolished in 1957, and then marked with a memorial plaque decades later, in 1994. According to Sabine Offe, the demolition of synagogues, or their reuse as fire stations, a building housing an electrical transformer, even a fish smokehouse, were not simply the result of "forgetting . . . rather [they were] consciously and intentionally removed."[47]

These vastly different approaches to the built environment reflect two very distinct political, cultural, economic, and urban planning eras. During the first, the people making decisions about city planning and historic preservation placed far less emphasis on authentic traces of the city's decimated Jewish population. During the second, beginning in the late 1970s, such traces played greater (if not always consistent) roles in planning, preservation, and memorialization. Indeed, the demolitions essentially created work for later archaeologists and historians.

Memorial Trends in the 1970s and 1980s: Change in the West, Continuity in the East

With a new generation assuming power, and World War II increasingly receding into the past, official memorial practices changed throughout both Germanys. Both sides saw a decentralization of the responsibilities for commemorative activities, including memorials, plaques, publications, and events. The categories of memorialization also broadened in this peri-

od, albeit far more in the West than in the East. In the East, the SED funded more decentralized projects by assigning more responsibility to lower
levels of the party, increasingly delegating responsibility for plaques and
publications to local committees and councils. But the overall aesthetic
form and content stayed largely the same, as did the broader techniques
employed by the state to create these landscapes of official memory. In the
West, the overall aesthetic forms changed (including more extensive use of
conceptual memorials and "authentic" places) and categories of memorialization began to be more inclusive, unintentionally laying the foundations
for contemporary memorial culture in Berlin.[48] The memorial landscape
became more heterogeneous, and what was officially remembered also varied, in part because of grassroots involvement and the decentralization of
memorial responsibilities to lower levels of government. The overall number of memorial projects also increased, especially leading up to 1987, the
year of Berlin's 750th anniversary, which was celebrated with great fervor
on both sides of the Wall as the memorial landscape became another site
in which to wage the Cold War.

Memorial Projects in the East

Memorial practice changed far less in the East than in the West during this period, for at least two reasons: East Germany did not experience the same kind of generational upheaval as the West, and international
changes in memorial practices, historical analysis, and artistic approaches
to representations of the past were not taken up to the same extent that
they were in the West. In many respects, the commemorative practices
that had developed in the 1950s and 1960s continued into this era in the
East. The GDR continued to build monuments to the memory of persecution (*Verfolgung*), extermination (*Vernichtung*), and anti-fascist resistance,[49] language exemplified by a large column in the eastern district of
Friedrichshain built in 1975, which lists the names of seven people and
proclaims: "They were murdered / In remembrance of the heroic resistance
fighters / against fascist barbarism / their legacy has been fulfilled / in the
socialist GDR."[50] In the eastern district of Köpenick, a large fist reaches up
toward the sky atop a column covered in socialist realist bas-relief, part of
a larger ensemble built in 1969 to commemorate those killed in 1933 in the
"Köpenick Blood Week."[51]

The plaques put up in the 1950s resemble those put up in the 1970s and even the 1980s—the language of anti-fascist resistance fighters and memorial plaques emblazoned with the red triangle continued to be used throughout the GDR's existence. For the most part, these projects continued to omit Jews and other persecuted groups who were not necessarily socialists or communists. In the 1980s, these representations did show slight indications of turning toward other forms of resistance, but essentially, through 1989, official East German treatment of the Nazi past in the landscape focused on the socialist realist commemoration of anti-fascist resistance. (See Figure 2.1.)

While the East German Culture Ministry continued to link memorial projects to Cold War politics, it also began to delegate increasing amounts of memorial work to the local level. This was a period when monuments of "national significance," including the former concentration camps, were in the charge of the national council of ministers, while city district councils handled more local monuments of "territorial significance."[52] A hierarchy of historical commissions and tradition commissions developed, overseen by various levels of SED leadership.[53] The SED began charging city districts with the task of marking anti-fascist resistance, both in written form and in the imagery and language of plaques and monuments. During this

FIGURE 2.1. Memorial plaque, Linienstr. 154a. Photograph by Jennifer Jordan.

period, there was also a profusion of published sources relating to memorials and to this history in general. Hans Maur, for example, published detailed accounts of sites connected to the "workers' movement" in each district of East Berlin, including sites associated with resistance and persecution during the Nazi era.[54] (Maur has also continued to be active in memorial projects since 1989.) Certainly, memorial culture in East Germany was shaped predominantly by a relatively uniform party line; there were no set conduits for an array of citizens to shape official memorial culture, and the content remained largely limited to anti-fascist, socialist, and communist resistance. But individual East Germans engaged with the Nazi past in a multitude of ways, and many of the people who became actively involved in grassroots or local memorial work after the Wall fell were also eastern Germans.

In part in response to the decentralization efforts in the 1970s and 1980s, guidelines for local officials and researchers were developed. In 1981, the East German Institut für Denkmalpflege (Institute for Historical Preservation) and Culture Ministry published a handbook on political memorials aimed at local governments charged with overseeing a wide range of sites, from small memorial plaques to large ensembles. The introduction made clear the political and pedagogical intentions behind political monuments, including those (the majority of recent memorial projects) marking the sites of anti-fascist resistance. "Monuments of political development are important testimony of the history of our people. They are of great worth for political education, particularly of young people. They deliver authentic impressions of historical events and speak directly to emotions and imagination." Furthermore, "they are well-suited to convey that our society, our state, arose out of the work and the struggle of many generations of the revolutionary proletariat," and "the monuments of political history serve the development of a socialist patriotism and proletarian internationalism."[55] This spirit manifested itself in the copious plaques around the city emblazoned with red triangles, and in a range of memorial stones placed around the city. How well this approach reflected a more broadly shared collective memory is another question, bringing up the complex issue of who such a "collective" would be in the first place.

In 1983, the secretariat of the Central Committee of the SED developed a program for refurbishing the "Museums of the Anti-fascist Resistance in the National Warning- and Memorial Sites Buchenwald and

Ravensbrück." While this project was an acknowledgement that the memorials constructed in the 1950s needed to be updated, the tone of the refurbishing reiterated East Germany's claim to a proud history of anti-fascist resistance and continued the widespread omission of any mention of the treatment of Jews from the official narratives of the concentration camps. The remodeling of the exhibits was clearly linked to a larger national and political project, and not necessarily to a widely shared "collective memory" among East Germans. "That which is represented in the museum should inspire hate and condemnation of the crimes of the fascist German imperialists . . . and, at the same time, should motivate the museum visitor for the struggle against the aggressive misanthropic politics and imperialism today and the struggle for the preservation and securing of peace and societal progress."[56] This was also a statement clearly aimed at the enemy on the other side of the Wall.

Memorial work reached a fever pitch throughout the city in the 1980s, in preparation for Berlin's anniversary in 1987, which provided an occasion, not only to reflect on the city's 750 years of history, but also to engage in a multitude of projects, ranging from small picture books to fully reconstructed neighborhoods. The anniversary created a "pressing deadline" for the construction of memorials and the mounting of plaques.[57] Guidebooks, lecture series, public ceremonies, and other commemorative projects left their mark on the physical and social landscape of the city. These projects continued the battle over who could legitimately claim the history of Berlin, including the history of resistance to the Nazi regime (although by no means limited to that). They became, in part, a kind of competition to see which side of Berlin could more proudly and thoroughly claim the city's past, and interpretations of that past, as important pieces in the larger puzzle of postwar German national identity. In 1987, the Council of Ministers of the GDR issued regulations for the "Production of Sculptural Monuments." Public monument sculpture was to honor some element of socialism, ranging from "warning remembrance of the warriors against fascism and war" to "important events of the international class struggle."[58]

The anniversary involved a clear symbolic waging of the Cold War, an episode in a generally understated battle of housing construction, urban renewal, and historic preservation that continued for almost half a century. But the war of words and historic buildings escalated in the mid 1980s, leading up to the year 1987. In both Berlins, anniversary projects were not only part of a fierce competition with the city's other half, but also an effort to draw in tourists from other parts of both Germanys. These commemorations covered far more than simply the recent past, reaching back to the fishing village that Berlin had been more than seven centuries before.

This flurry of activity in preparation for 1987 illustrates the material effects of anniversaries and commemorations on cultural memory and material landscapes. For the East, the predominant message was the proud origins of the East German state in resistance to fascism, a refrain echoed from the earliest years of the GDR. At least superficially, 1987 solidified the anti-fascist tradition in East Germany and was closely connected to official party doctrine. In June 1987, the SED declared that "on the basis of the resolution of the Eleventh Party Convention of the German Socialist Unity Party [the SED], the connection of the anti-fascist heritage and the revolutionary traditions linked to the development and growth of our worker and farmer state is to be strengthened."[59]

This approach was prevalent essentially until the Wall fell, although in the late 1980s memorial culture in the East did begin to open up very slightly to broader understandings of victims and of appropriate representational forms. Reichel notes:

Only very late did they [the East German government] begin to differentiate their one-dimensional victim definition and to open up to Jewish victims. Since the 1980s, around a dozen places in East Berlin have commemorated the deported and murdered Jews: at several sites in the district of Weißensee, at the Jewish Cemetery in Schönhauser Allee, and at the deportation center in Große Hamburger Straße. But even in this period, the relationship of victims of the Nazis to the workers' movement was still ranked higher than their Jewish background.[60]

Caroline Wiedmer finds that "in East Germany official memory of the war was legislated throughout the Democratic Republic's forty years of existence by the myth of anti-fascism. . . . [although] the late 1980s had ushered in a more avid interest in the war-time persecution of Jewish victims of the Holocaust."[61] Renovation of the New Synagogue in East Berlin also began at this point, and a competition was held to erect a small neighborhood monument in an area that had once been home to many of Berlin's Jewish residents.[62] A handful of residents, activists, artists, and government officials were also beginning to steer away from socialist realism as the predominant aesthetic memorial form and starting to incorporate broader categories of resisters and victims.

Memorial Projects in the West

While memorial culture in the East during the 1970s and 1980s largely continued the trajectory set in the 1950s and 1960s (with small changes toward the end of the 1980s), a different set of conditions was at work in the West.[63] While the East decentralized but essentially stayed the course, in the West, there was a sea change, resulting from a multitude of factors. The generational upheaval of 1968, as well as an international turn toward social history or history from below shifted the focus and form of official memorial culture in the 1970s and 1980s. Officials, artists, activists, and others also began to pay increasing attention to the sites of perpetrators, and to sites with an authentic connection to the Nazi past. Memorial work was increasingly decentralized and democratized and became more pluralistic. The categories of memorialization began to include a broader range of victims and resistance, including not only Jews but also other persecuted groups such as gays, Roma and Sinti, and communists. These changes became the groundwork for the shape of memorial culture after the fall of the Wall. "Beginning in the 1970s, a multiplicity of initiatives arose that—along with survivors, for whom the historical locations had always remained present—committed themselves to the creation of monuments [*Denkmäler*] and concrete memory work [not only] at central locations, but also in many out-of-the-way places," Endlich writes. "Since the mid 1980s a regular 'monument boom' had begun to spread in the western half of the city, rooted in grassroots initiatives of 'trace-searching' [*Spurensuche*], through which the monument topography developed in the 1950s and 1960s was decidedly expanded and locally made more precise."[64] There was a convergence of factors that laid the groundwork for an increase in citizen involvement in memorialization. Various levels of government had to respond to these projects, granting or withholding funding and planning permission, and organizing competitions for new memorial designs. Activities at the federal level at times differed from those at the local level, and the terrain of memorials could look quite different from one district of West Berlin to the next, depending on the interests and actions of local district officials and activists. Thus a somewhat heterogeneous landscape developed, juxtaposed with the markers that had been put in place in previous decades.

The West was particularly affected by the social conflicts of 1968, which contributed to (among other changes) a new type of confrontation with the Nazi past and an expansion of categories, actors, and sites of memory, including previously excluded groups.[65] The student movements themselves, and the broader meaning of this year as a generational changing of the guard, constituted a turning point in many aspects of West German society.[66] Many members of a younger generation, with little or no firsthand memory of World War II, rejected the widespread silence about the Nazi era and contributed to the expansion of categories and forms of memorial culture. In subsequent years, West Germany began a more explicit process of *Vergangenheitsbewältigung*, or confrontation of its Nazi past.[67] In particular, Christhard Hoffmann writes, "the memory of the Holocaust was also politically instrumentalized, above all by a younger generation molded through the student movement. This can be seen particularly clearly in the Federal Republic in the 1980s, when hardly a single major political conflict—from the armament debates to controversies over immigration—was discussed without mention of the Holocaust as both an exemplary lesson and moral legitimation for a particular position."[68] At the same time, in Germany and elsewhere, there was also a growing attention to "history from below." More people became interested in more aspects of Germany's recent history, engaging in research, organizing, and pressing for new and different kinds of memorials, pressure to which various levels of government frequently responded. Local history workshops also emerged, with their members leading walking tours of the city and producing their own publications. University professors and high school teachers also began encouraging their students to investigate the material remains of the Nazi past in the cityscape.

A report on monuments commissioned by the Senatsverwaltung für Bau- und Wohnungswesen (the Senate Administration for Construction and Housing) for example, captures the following key trends in memorial culture throughout West Germany in the 1980s:

1. Political confrontations and debates are conducted with monuments.
2. The circle of monument makers and the groups to whom the monuments are dedicated is broader and more differentiated.

3. The places of the historical events are rediscovered and acquire a great, almost magical meaning.

4. New artistic forms of remembrance are diligently sought simultaneously with the acknowledgment of the impossibility of a total comprehension.

5. Sites of learning and memorials [*Lernorte* and *Gedenkstätten*] appear—increasing pedagogical measures accompany and supplement the monuments.

6. The process of confronting [these issues] is more important than the end result.[69]

Ultimately, a diverse array of projects found their way through the bureaucratic channels of city planning departments and various combinations of state and private funding.

These local, on-the-ground practices also happened in the context of new international trends in both art and historiography. Art schools, history conferences, and, of course, publications all helped to circulate new ideas about ways of representing and interpreting elements of the past and became increasingly important in the 1970s and 1980s. The forms of memorializing the past became not only more pedagogical and more focused on authentic sites, but also increasingly conceptual, rather than directly representational, in part as a rejection of previous aesthetic styles that supposedly closed rather than opened debate and offered viewers an easy answer rather than provoking them to critical reflection. Many memorial projects throughout Germany in the 1980s took the form of what James Young and others call "counter-monuments": "brazen, painfully self-conscious memorial spaces conceived to challenge the very premises of their being."[70] In the words of John Czaplicka, the new conceptual monuments, not only in the 1970s and 1980s, but in the 1990s as well, "effectively conjoin an aesthetic and therefore sensual representation with a mediation of historical facts that may lead to a contemplative and enlightening involvement of the visitor."[71]

A particularly striking component of these memorial activities in the 1970s and especially in the 1980s was the widely shared belief in the importance and pedagogical power of so-called authentic sites. Activists, educators, and officials all turned their attention to authentic sites in the cityscape, rather than to simply ceremonial sites not directly connected to

historical events. Stefanie Endlich, an active participant and prolific analyst of many of these efforts, points to the increasing involvement of many
different citizens' groups who actively insisted on the pedagogical power
of "authentic" sites. The key terms that arose out of this turn toward social
history and the generational upheaval were the "search for traces" (*Spurensuche*) and "the securing of those traces" (*Spurensicherung*).[72] This way of
remembering emerged in the late 1970s, as "little by little concrete crime
sites (*Verbrechensorte*) were 'rediscovered' in all of their variety. . . . The
impulse for the confrontation with Nazi events and crimes in 'forgotten
places' came primarily from groups, clubs, history workshops, and initiatives that concerned themselves with 'history from below.'"[73] Likewise,
Sabine Offe found the 1970s to be a time of the rediscovery of authentic
Jewish sites in the German landscape.[74] The focus on authentic sites was
intended in part to help reduce the abstraction of evil and eliminate some
of the distance caused by the passing of time and the inevitable decline in
the numbers of people with firsthand memory of the Nazi era. This shift
in focus also contributed to an increasing emphasis on "authentic" sites
connected to perpetrators, including the former Gestapo headquarters
and the villa where the Wannsee Conference took place. This shift applied
to a far broader range of historical sites and historic preservation practices than those treated here. As Rudy Koshar points out, "For more than
two decades after World War II, reconstructed buildings and landscapes
were the paradigmatic expressions of political community on both sides
of the German-German border. And finally, in the period from roughly
1970 until the reunification of Germany, historical traces captured either in
archaeological remains or in metaphorical renderings of the memory landscape as a topography of commemorative signs and markers, crystallized
and framed meaning."[75] And this attention to traces continues today.

For the West, public memory in the 1980s increasingly entailed
a close examination of German responsibility and guilt, and there was a
widespread sense that remembering could help to prevent future atrocities.
The people behind these increasingly grassroots projects aimed to transform the cityscape into a place of learning and instruction, and to spread
a moral message by educating school groups, tourists, and pedestrians in
general about the Nazi past. Sometimes they staged impromptu ceremonies or mounted unofficial plaques, but ultimately a diverse array of projects found their way through the bureaucratic channels of city planning

departments and various combinations of state and private funding. Places like the Topographie des Terrors (Topography of Terror) outdoor museum on the site of the former Gestapo headquarters, for example, were supposed to disrupt the urban fabric, and confront people with the reality of the city's Nazi past. Such commemorations were very different from the heroic statuary in large open squares that characterized official memorialization in both halves of Berlin in the 1950s and 1960s, and very different also from the more fleeting memorial activity of the immediate postwar era.

Changes in conceptions of history in general and German history in particular contributed to the expansion of the categories of victims and resistance remembered in the landscape. A variety of citizens' groups and individuals became increasingly involved in memorialization, among them those I call memorial entrepreneurs, whose role in determining whether a given site actually became a memorial expanded as the processes of memorialization were decentralized and democratized. Other groups increasingly involved in memorial work included local district museums (*Heimatmuseen*) (particularly active in the western district of Kreuzberg) and history workshops. This diversity of actors and projects led both to more memorial sites, commemorating a wider range of persecution and resistance, and to networks and memorialization practices that have continued to shape the memorial landscape of Berlin into the twenty-first century.

As in the East, Berlin's 750th anniversary in 1987 spurred new programs in the West to build memorials of all kinds, some more traditional (such as porcelain memorial plaques) and others more conceptual or confrontational. During this period, there was an overall expansion in the number of sites, including memorial plaques, marking the Nazi past in West Berlin.[76] A West Berlin bank sponsored a *Berliner Gedenktafel* (Berlin memorial plaques) program that mounted 211 plaques manufactured by the State Porcelain Manufacturer (originally the KPM, or Royal Porcelain Manufacturer) in West Berlin between 1985 and 1988.[77] The program commemorated a broad range of historical figures and events, including but in no way limited to those persecuted by and/or resisting the Nazi regime. In part in response to this program, which created distinctly uniform and state-sanctioned plaques, which many activists felt to be incomplete and too narrowly focused on elites, the Kreuzberg art administration (*Kunstamt*) began its own plaque program.[78] The programs in Kreuzberg and the neighboring district of Neukölln focused exclusively on persecu-

tion by the Nazis and drew on a variety of artistic styles designed to provoke more interest than the standard memorial plaque form.[79]

The Topography of Terror

The anniversary also offered an incentive to set up a more permanent exhibit on the site of the former Gestapo headquarters, rediscovered
and excavated in the late 1970s and 1980s.[80] Once the Topography of Terror was more clearly marked, this site had tremendous power to evoke the
horror of the Gestapo and the SS for people who had not been eyewitnesses to them, in part because visitors realize they are standing near (if not
in) the cellars used to torture prisoners. Today, the Topography of Terror is
an unusual outdoor exhibition, combined with archaeological excavations
and the site of a planned documentation center, in the heart of Berlin (Figure 2.2). Ulrich Eckhardt and Andreas Nachama suggest that this is

a saving of honor for the city whose name could be read in the return address of
countless death sentences in all of Europe. This "thinking place" [*Denkort*] is better able than any monument to sharpen consciousness and memory; it explains
in a comprehensible way how the unimaginable could arise, who the perpetrators
were, and what the victims suffered. At the very center of the city, in the heart
of the future government quarter, there, where in the [Nazi] imperial capital, the
desks of the perpetrators once stood and a gigantic machinery of surveillance and
extermination encompassing all of Europe was installed, there the questioning
empty urban space works like a wound in the cityscape or a disturbance in the
brave new world.[81]

Although it lies in the West Berlin district of Kreuzberg, the Topography
of Terror site was directly affected by the fall of the Wall because its north-
ern boundary was also the border of East Berlin and the district of Mitte.
Moreover, the exhibition today uses a potentially very valuable piece of
real estate to tell its historical and moral story. Only a block from the Topography of Terror and two blocks from the Holocaust Memorial, for example, the state government of Berlin and the federal government were
fighting each other in 1993 for a site (approximately 20,000 m²) estimated
at the time to be worth more than DM 100 million.[82] But for decades the
site sparked little interest, and had little commercial value. The Gestapo
and SS buildings there were damaged by bombing during the war and

eventually torn down, and the site was put to mundane uses for decades after the war, until a handful of people began to literally scratch beneath the surface of this odd vacant lot. For decades after the war, the land was used as a dumping ground for construction rubble and as an area where student drivers could practice their skills. Other proposed uses for the lot included a helicopter landing pad and a six-lane expressway. In 1962, the state contracted with a construction firm to level the lot.[83]

In the late 1970s and early 1980s, however, the site was called back into public awareness through a series of events. Dieter Hoffman-Axthelm, a Berlin historian, contributed to the initial impetus to mark the site by leading a tour of it and writing an article about it, and others took up the cause as well.[84] "The buildings, fully destroyed near the end of the war, were hauled away in 1949; only in 1986, after massive public pressure, were the bloody traces of history made visible again, and the rest of the Gestapo torture cells uncovered," Peter Neumann writes in a guidebook to Berlin's historical sites.[85] Popular and official recognition of the site followed, in large part because the discovery occurred at a time in which it resonated with broader cultural and academic movements. "That this situation was recognized as inappropriate at the end of the 1970s is connected to the upheaval in historical study," Bernd Matthies notes. "[S]uddenly

FIGURE 2.2. Topography of Terror. Photograph by Jennifer Jordan.

FIGURE 2.3. Niederkirchner Str. (former Gestapo headquarters), 1986. Photograph: Landesarchiv Berlin.

slogans like 'Dig where you stand' arrived from abroad, [and] so-called history workshops competed with academics. . . . In Berlin, [over and] above the victims' leagues, civil rights organizations and the aspiring Alternative List [the Berlin branch of the Green Party at the time] began to move for a rediscovery of the site."[86] The site also had the distinct advantage that, at the time of its designation as a site of memory, it had little commercial value, located as it was with its back (or front) up against the Berlin Wall. Through a series of actions in the 1980s, including the laying of wreathes on the excavated foundations, the clear marking of the Gestapo history of the area began, as did the excluding of other uses. Reinhard Rürup, a historian charged with the task of documenting the site, recalls how quickly it became apparent that researchers had in front of them not only the Gestapo headquarters, but also the headquarters of the SS and the Reichssicherheitshauptamt: "With that it was clear that we were dealing not just with history, but with world history."[87] (See Figure 2.3.)

A temporary exhibition was installed in time for the 1987 city anniversary, which was intended to be taken down at the end of the celebrations.

But, writes a reporter for the *Tagesspiegel*, "the enormous international resonance made that appear fully unthinkable."[88] By June 1989, the West Berlin culture ministry had established a committee to determine the future use of the land, with the plan being to "secure the remaining traces and to interview the remaining eyewitnesses."[89] In its interim report, the Berlin Senate[90] emphasized that the site was "not only a place of Berlin, nor only of German, but rather of European history. Such a place should not be handled simply in the context of the tasks of local politics, but rather must have the rank of an international institution."[91] This vacant lot on the edge of West Berlin began to resonate far beyond its ragged borders.

A first competition to symbolically mark the site was held in 1983, but the results were abandoned, "because the disparate planning concept demanded that the 'historical depth of the place' be brought into agreement with profane uses like a parking lot, playground, and paths."[92] The first competition envisioned a monument built on the land. The winning entry was abandoned after very vocal objections were made to covering over the authentic, original site, and the "open wound" in the cityscape. When discussions about a central memorial for the murdered Jews of Europe emerged in the late 1980s, this site was also suggested as a possible location—a proposal that met with many objections.[93] The Active Museum and a number of victims' organizations immediately objected to this site, in part because it is a place of the perpetrators (*Täter*) and should be remembered as such.[94] As late as 1994, a member of the Free Democrats fraction in the state assembly wanted to know what arguments there were against locating the Holocaust Monument on the former Gestapo land. On August 9, 1994, Minister Wolfgang Nagel replied: "In the land of the perpetrators, the Monument for the Murdered Jews of Europe is necessary in addition to [sites like the Topography of Terror, but]. . . . to plan it on this site would be inappropriate and, particularly, incompatible with the goal of keeping this place as a visible sign as much as possible."[95] Thus the argument about the authenticity of the site, and its effectiveness as an "open wound," appears to have prevailed; the state has determined that, for now, it will not become an inauthentic, monumental monument, but will remain a *Denkort*.

In November 1989, this plot of land suddenly found itself in the very center of the city. "The lot doesn't simply lie 'behind' the Gropius building now, but rather it has a weight of its own. From being on the outskirts of West Berlin, it has once again become a place in the center of Berlin," a Senate commission charged with the task of discussing the future of this area concluded.[96] Over the next few months, the area experienced dramatic changes in both symbolic and financial value.[97] In 1990, the Senate called in the federal government to participate in the planning for this site, in light of its "extraordinary national and international significance," with the intention of shifting some of the cost of the site onto the federal budget.[98] In 1992, the land was handed over to the Topography of Terror Foundation.[99] At this point, the site's future appeared to be secure. It seemed to have become untouchable. All around it, new office buildings, apartments, shops, and government buildings sprang up. But the only construction planned on this lot is some kind of documentation center, the first competition for which was held in 1993.[100] Originally, the Topography of Terror had no permanent exhibition or research space, but there was growing need for such structures. Between 1987 and 1997, 1.5 million people saw the Topography of Terror exhibition.[101] Given the prices of neighboring property, a permanent Topography of Terror building could only be built on the site itself.[102] The design competitions eventually led to the selection of a design by the Swiss architect Peter Zumthor, but the project stalled, and then fell apart in the face of mounting costs and other controversies. By 2005, the project had been abandoned, Zumthor had quit it, and the foundation and the federal government started from scratch to develop plans for a new documentation and exhibition center.[103] There is no question that the site itself will remain some form of marked site for now, even if it is unclear who will fund the documentation center, or if it will ever be built.[104]

This site itself (if not the unbuilt documentation center) is the "result of consensus building among initiatives, organizations and victims' leagues, [and] international memorial/museum experts and specialists, [the] result of an often also painful learning process around the question, what content profile and what physical form this place of the former Nazi terror headquarters should take."[105] This phenomenon may be explained in part by the presence of entrenched and vocal advocates for the site, but also by the fact that its symbolic value had been securely established before the Wall fell and the price of neighboring land began to shoot up.[106] It became a key node in the network of memory sites, and a site of the intersection of citizen activism with state-sanctioned memory. The Topography of Terror provided a central site where authenticity and pedagogy were linked together. The conceptions and networks developed during the process of establishing this as an officially recognized site have also left a lasting impression, not only on the urban landscape, but also on the social landscape of memorial projects and memorial entrepreneurs, in part because "the discussion about the design and future [of the former Gestapo Headquarters, or Topography of Terror] . . . , served to sharpen the public awareness of the meaning of authentic places."[107] This project has been central to contemporary memorial culture in Berlin. The history of the Topography of Terror is well documented, and its status as an active memory site seems to be secure. In part because of the transfer of ownership to the Topography of Terror Foundation, but also because of powerful arguments about the authenticity of the site, the land remains largely what it was supposed to be—an open wound in the cityscape.

By the end of the 1980s, then, an entrenched memorial culture had developed in the West, based to a large extent on grassroots efforts interacting with various levels of government. Increasingly, the anguish of personal memory was giving way to more abstract representations of the Nazi past, fewer and fewer eyewitnesses remained, and the scars of war were disappearing from the urban landscape. During this period, so different from the years immediately after the war, the memorial landscape was also opened up, at least in comparison to the 1950s and 1960s, to more inclusive categories of remembrance, a wider variety of participants in memorialization, and a broader spectrum of forms of memorials, including the preservation of "authentic" sites and the use of conceptual approaches to marking the Nazi past. New avenues for the production of officially recognized symbolic landscapes were created as well, including history workshops, district programs, and *Heimatmuseen*, many of which collected materials and organized exhibits around their district's history of resistance and persecution in the Nazi era. At the same time, even when memorial work seems to become more pluralistic and democratic, it does not necessarily reflect consensually held recollections of the past, but rather the kind of negotiated and partial representations discussed by Olick, Koshar, and others.

Memorials After 1989

By the time the Wall fell, there was a deeply rooted approach to the memorialization of the Nazi past in both East and West Berlin. As a result of memorial practice and, of course, broader political and economic changes, Berlin's memorial landscape has changed dramatically in the intervening years. The landscape is now a patchwork of sweeping new commercial and governmental developments, as well as concentrated pockets of official collective memory of the Nazi past (and a host of other pasts as well). Overall, the democratization and decentralization of memorialization in West Germany in the 1970s and 1980s helped to set the stage for memorial practice in the 1990s.[108] The fall of the Wall revealed, among other things, two different landscapes of memory. Many of the memorial practices prevalent in the East, including socialist realism, an emphasis on the language of anti-fascism, and the use of the red triangle, were abandoned as the Wall fell. Most of the old markers remain in place, however, and are juxtaposed with new markers erected after 1989. There is a tremendous range in the scope of the new sites, from the central Holocaust Memorial to the tiny "stumbling stones" placed in the cobbled sidewalks in front of houses from which people were sent to concentration camps. Some memorial projects have become places where Germany as a whole seems to engage in monumental debates about its relationship to its Nazi past, while others are local projects whose audience is really only people in the local neighborhood.[109]

Many eastern Germans took up the "new" forms of memorialization described in the previous section as well, evident in so many district-level projects and in the work of activists in the eastern districts. After 1989, memorializing was more subject to the vagaries of financing, and districts in East and West alike assumed increasing administrative and financial responsibility for local projects. Anyone hoping to put up a plaque, for example, has had to rely largely on private donors, however, because subsidies for cultural projects in both East and West have dried up considerably. This growing reliance on private funding arguably makes memorial projects more heterogeneous, and perhaps even less representative of some kind of overarching collective memory. The return of private property to eastern Berlin also means that owners now have the final say as to whether their property is to be used for memorial purposes.

While official East German memorial practices ceased immediately after the Wall fell, the landscape of Berlin was not actually purged of all traces of East German collective memory of the Nazi past. The state and district governments of Berlin took a relatively cautious approach to East German monuments in general, and, not surprisingly, few officials were interested in tearing down sites that dealt specifically with the Nazi past. Overall, there was relatively little of the kind of spontaneous destruction of monuments that occurred in other eastern European countries; "the demolition of monuments by the citizens of the GDR never happened. No Lenin, no Thälmann, and no Marx was hauled down from his pedestal."[110] People did surreptitiously remove plaques bearing Honecker's name, but a few days later, they handed them over anonymously to the city museum.[111] Eventually, Lenin did fall, but Marx remained. The predominance of western memorial practices combined with a relatively cautious treatment of the existing memorial landscape, so that unification did not entirely eradicate the physical remnants of the eastern version of history. This caution was due in part to the efforts of groups of students and activists, and later politicians and experts. One group, the "Initiative on Political Monuments of the GDR," took a particularly active role in trying to prevent the wholesale removal of East German markers from the landscape. Consisting primarily of art history students from all of the Berlin universities, eastern and western alike, it began in the spring of 1990 as a working group of the Active Museum of Fascism and Resistance (founded in 1983, with the claim that Berlin "needed an institution that, as an active museum, constructively confronts recent German history between 1933 and 1945, as well as neofascist resurgence in the present").[112] Noting that "the point of departure of our work was the observation that the Berlin Wall was being torn down with great speed, the symbols of power of the GDR were being removed, and as a consequence also the political monuments of the former East Berlin were being taken down,"[113] members of the Initiative organized tours of the city, as well as a public discussion with the cultural administration of the eastern district of Prenzlauer Berg, and even mounted a replacement memorial plaque for one that had been stolen.[114] East German memorial culture was officially abandoned, but not entirely removed. One reason why it was largely accepted by both the public and its elected representatives that relatively few socialist sites be torn down is that the ideology behind these sites ceased, nearly overnight, to be any possible threat to the post-1989 political, economic, and symbolic order.

Furthermore, many of the people who were actively engaged in memorial projects in East Germany continued to play central roles in memorialization after 1989 as well. Many of the politicians and bureaucrats involved were trying, to some extent, to create a memorial landscape that would provoke a kind of confrontation with and rethinking of the past, rather than erasing all remnants of the fallen regime. The question was "how to treat monuments . . . perceived as outmoded [*unzeitgemäß*]. . . . neither letting them remain without comment [*unkommentierte Verbleiben*] nor removing monuments from the urban landscape was envisioned; rather, an active confrontation with monuments and history was called for."[115]

While memorial plaques were the responsibility of each individual district, monuments (*Denkmäler*) were the responsibility of the state government.[116] The Senate established a ten-person commission to review the existing political monuments in the eastern half of the city, following the recommendation of Culture Senator Ulrich Roloff-Momin. They were not responsible for the Soviet monuments, because a treaty with Russia guaranteed that those would remain.[117] All in all, the commission's recommendations tended to "a cautious, carefully considered treatment" of the monuments.[118] At the same time, there was criticism of the fact that the commission only dealt with the eastern half of the city. Critics emphasized that, if there was going to be a reconsideration of the postwar monuments in the East, then a similar reconsideration should take place in the West. Wolfgang Kil and others pointed out that the work of the monument commission was "here, not to evaluate the Berlin monuments of the postwar era, but rather exclusively those monuments in the eastern part of the city," criticizing the commission, and the authorities who had established it, for only focusing on and reconsidering eastern monuments, rather than reevaluating the memorial landscape of both Berlins.[119]

The new political system meant, among other things, a new way of producing memorials.[120] There are also new discussions in this era of the relationship between tourism and the memory of resistance to and persecution by the Nazi regime.[121] In addition, the existing terrain and the approaches generated in the West were now confronted with the singularly new setting of unification. Now that the two Germanys had been united, and Berlin was on its way to becoming the capital again, there was also increased international scrutiny both of Germany's treatment of its Nazi past and of the new "Berlin Republic."[122] As James Young writes, "no other nation has ever attempted to re-unite itself on the bedrock memory of its crimes or to make commemoration of its crimes the topographical center of gravity in its capital."[123] Furthermore, "in suggesting themselves as indigenous, even geological outcroppings in a national landscape, monuments tend to naturalize the values, ideals, and laws of the land itself. . . . What then of Germany, a nation justly forced to remember the suffering and devastation it once caused in the name of its people? . . . Under what memorial aegis, whose rules, does a nation remember its own barbarity?"[124] This relationship takes on a particular intensity in the wake of unification and in the midst of the increasing consolidation of the European Union. Controversy about the Holocaust in the 1990s "has revolved primarily around questions of how to anchor Holocaust commemoration in the national historical consciousness of a unified Germany and how to choose forms of cultural memory that best suit this end in the 'nation of the guilty.'"[125] Olick and Levy find that

the effects of German unification and Germany's central role in the European Community will create (and already have created) new challenges to the way the past is remembered and how it works as collective memory. These challenges, however, have a long and varied history; the accumulation and transformations of this history lie at the center of Germany's ongoing work to define who it is, what it can do, and what it should do. The analysis of political culture, as newly conceived, helps us to appreciate and untangle the complexities of that work, which involves a continuous negotiation between past and present. Collective memory *is* this negotiation, rather than pure constraint by, or contemporary strategic manipulation of, the past.[126]

Within these negotiations that constitute collective memory, a certain skepticism has developed concerning the direct effects of such memorializing. In their 1995 guide to Berlin's memorials, *Gedenken und Lernen an historischen Orten,* Thomas Lutz (a former director of the activist group Aktion Sühnezeichen who has since 1993 been with the foundation set up to run the Topography of Terror) and Stefanie Endlich (who is also involved in the Topography of Terror Foundation) express some of this caution, knowing that memorial sites do not necessarily result in the planned-for transformations in people's awareness of the past.[127] Debates over memorial excesses, as well as the well-established institutions of memorialization, would have been difficult to predict in 1945 and even in subsequent decades. A given memorial's effects are indeterminate and do not necessarily correspond to the intentions of its creators. What do sculptors, politicians, and advocates hope for as they create these memorials—and what do preservationists or teachers or tour guides expect from them later on, months or decades after their original dedication? These efforts are, on many levels, not only representations of the past, but also concentrated visions of the future. That is, memorials—and not only in Berlin—frequently serve to recall versions of what has happened in the past and attempt to shape the future behavior of those who see these memorials. But this effect is not guaranteed. The audience for any of these memorial sites (and indeed for memorial sites in general) is also very heterogeneous. The controversy, the arguments, and the layers of interpretation and debate are difficult to see in the memorial landscape itself, even in countermonuments and conceptual projects that are intended to more actively engage the viewer.

Conclusion

Compare the landscape of 1945 to that of today, when there is an expansive and well-developed memorial culture, and when issues of marking the Nazi past appear frequently not just in local papers but in papers around the world. The Berlin landscape is now punctuated with barely visible memorial plaques, gleaming new educational centers, overgrown memorial stones, and controversial new memorial sites. Acts of remembrance are necessarily coupled with processes of forgetting, and any landscape of memory also exists with a shadow landscape of forgetting.[128] This pairing is not in itself an indictment of the acts of forgetting, but rather a recognition of the necessarily selective and incomplete foundations of memory. Berlin's memorial terrain is clearly both dynamic and the product of a heterogeneous collection of institutions, policies, citizens' groups, academic and artistic sea changes, and local, state, and federal government agencies and elected bodies.

Their creators may have intended these commemorative projects to serve many purposes: to teach history and morality, to help to prevent a recurrence of fascism, to honor a favorite heroic figure, to construct an acceptable past, or even to serve a project of atonement and moral culpability that contributes to contemporary German political identity. These memorials and plaques are moral tales inscribed in the landscape, even if those narratives are not always immediately apparent to the passerby. Memorialization on both sides of the "German-German" border was meant by its supporters not only to promote remembrance but also to instruct and to warn. There is a clear pedagogical content to memorials, in the East as well as the West. Even if the content and message of memorials differed on either side of the Wall, both regimes started with a belief in the moral instructive power of these symbolically and historically charged places and the political necessity (both domestic and international) of such commemoration. This belief only increased in the 1970s and 1980s, particularly in the West, and has lasted to this day. At the same time, as powerful as the arguments about authenticity may be, authentic sites do go unmarked. The shifting approaches to memorialization have tangible consequences for the physical, social, and political landscapes of the city.

In the course of the past few decades, Berlin's landscape has become a potent mix of erasure and concentrated official collective memory, resulting from the interaction of local, state, and international factors, as well as personal and collective memories. These changes help to explain how Berlin has arrived at its particular combination of remembering and forgetting, with its mixture of concentrated pockets of collective memory hinged to messages of warning and remorse, side by side with the legacies of postwar urban planning and the post-1989 real estate market. The meanings attached to these pockets of memory are constructed in a variety of ways, but they are neither flimsy nor inevitable. They emerge as mixtures of happenstance and intention, as the urban landscape holds onto the imprints of past actions, slogans, trends, and convictions, albeit in uneven ways, and through a wide array of bureaucratic, political, artistic, and material channels. What counts as worthy of commemoration changes over time, as do the accepted techniques of commemoration. Furthermore, particularly in democratic settings like the Federal Republic of Germany, representations of the past are not necessarily monolithic or direct reflections of official policy, both because layers of memorials accrue over time and because the processes of memorial production involve a range of groups interacting with the state. The contours of the relationship between the state, its landscape, and its residents are transformed as well, and as the political, economic, and social contexts shift, they leave their imprints in the terrain of the city, and alter the experience and perception of previously constructed memorials. When any of us visit these sites, the often contentious conditions of their creation have generally disappeared behind the smooth surface of educational exhibits or bronze plaques.

Persistent Memory:
Pre-1989 Memorials After the Fall
of the Wall

When the Wall came down, a range of markers treating the city's Nazi past already dotted the eastern half of Berlin, running the spectrum from inconspicuous plaques to large-scale sculptural ensembles. These stones and statues embodied four decades of official East German marking of the Nazi past in the urban landscape. But what happened to these sites in the wake of the introduction of a new political system, new urban planning schemes, and the other major transformations that followed the events of 1989? In October 1990, less than a year after the fall of the Wall, the *Frankfurter Allgemeine Zeitung* reported that Berlin had "become the leading metropolis for real estate investment in all of Europe."[1] After years of division, the city was now experiencing "an unprecedented investment boom." Between 1990 and 1992, average rental prices for office space in the Berlin region doubled, while rents in top locations tripled or even quadrupled.[2]

Despite the collapse of the East German regime and the creation of a real estate market nearly overnight, GDR monuments dealing with the Nazi past remained in place in the early 1990s at more than sixty sites in the eastern half of Berlin, not counting plaques.[3] But the world around them had changed. The fact that these markers still stand does not mean that they are salient in official collective memory or in tourists' or residents' experiences of the city. Many pre-1989 sites, even though they remain physically in the landscape, have slipped out of public awareness and faded from the public view.

Nevertheless, a number of GDR memorials have been extensively incorporated into post-1990s commemorations and are visited by school groups and tourists on walking tours, listed in guidebooks, and featured in newspapers. Some of these have been modified to make them better fit the parameters of post-1989 remembrance, to update information that subsequent research has contradicted, or to counter what some see as overtly socialist language. Others remain more or less as they were before the Wall fell.

The original intentions of the builders of a given memorial cannot guarantee how it will weather the passage of time. This indeterminacy is an integral element of *any* memorial landscape, but it is intensified when the original ideological framework of the sites collapses. When the state apparatus that built a given memorial vanishes, ceremonies that once took place may cease. Funds for landscaping and maintenance may dry up. Governing bodies may suspend the use of these sites for political or educational purposes. Public interest may wane. But even without the kind of sweeping changes that occurred in 1989, the uses and meanings of memorials may change, not only with shifts (both subtle and cataclysmic) in political organization or economic climate, but also with a change in generations. Memorial sites in Berlin and beyond exist in both time and space. Memorials are, of course, a product both of the moment in which they are created *and* the moment in which they are encountered.[4] Their meanings, uses, and significance change over time—something we see with memorials all over the world. Collective memory, historical work, politics, and bureaucracy have all left their mark on Berlin's memorial landscape, sometimes simply in the shape of a small stone nearly overgrown with bushes, sometimes in the form of larger complexes actively used in contemporary memorial practice.[5] As permanent as a memorial site may feel, memorials come and go. And even when they remain in place, they may move in and out of public awareness and use. Physical persistence does not guarantee continued resonance, or that a site will continue to be used in that way that its creators intended.

Markets and Politics

Threats to the physical persistence of these sites could have come from at least two different quarters. First, the market and new urban planning schemes might have squeezed out memorial space in favor of new housing, office space, commercial developments, or government buildings. Second, given the collapse of the East German government, there might have been a systematic removal of the symbolic marks it left in the landscape. Here, it is important to distinguish between memorial sites that take up urban land (stones, columns, courtyards, graves, larger sculptural ensembles, and even museums) and memorial plaques. Certainly, vandals and property owners removed many memorial plaques, and any plaques with reference to the East German government were removed as well. Otherwise, the pre-1989 memorial landscape of East Berlin has remained largely intact, particularly the elements concerned with the city's Nazi past.[6] At any rate, as property values skyrocketed and construction boomed, at least some existing memorial sites might have given way to the pressure of this escalating demand for urban land. The simple increase in demand could have lead to the sale or development of memorial sites to be used for more profitable purposes. That may seem inconceivable—how could anyone consider developing a plot of land saturated with the memory of the Nazi past? But in fact there are plenty of plots of land tied to the Nazi past that are bought and sold and developed, although almost never with existing markers on them. Hitler's bunker and chancellery are the most obvious examples; the site is now covered with blocks of apartments and shops, as well as a parking lot.[7] But given the dire predictions in the early 1990s about shortages of housing, offices, and retail space, and the astronomical rental and sale prices particularly in 1992 and early 1993, it might still seem surprising that no memorial would give way to these pressures.[8] Despite land prices in the city center approaching Tokyo levels at the peak of the real estate boom, however, no existing memorial sites marking persecution by or resistance to the Nazi regime gave way to condominiums or shopping malls. The structural transformations taking place in eastern Berlin in the 1990s have not translated into similarly dramatic changes in the existing memorial landscape treating the Nazi past.

If the market and urban growth did not lead to the disappearance of existing memorials, neither did the loss of the GDR's political legitimacy, with a few exceptions.[9] All of the memorial sites addressed in this chapter were built with the consent, and usually the direct involvement, of the East German government. Certainly, there was still heterogeneity in these memorial processes in the GDR. The landscape of markers changed over time, and while it did not result from democratic processes, it did result from some degree of discussion within the existing political establishment, as well as the work of citizens who were interested in this history. There was variation and disagreement, but what got set in stone did so with the top-down approval of a government that was not democratically elected (see, e.g., Jeffrey Herf's analysis of eastern and western memorial culture).[10] But once that government fell, it might be reasonable to expect that some of the markers it left in the landscape would have been removed, as happened in so many other post-socialist countries.[11] The initial weeks after the falling of the Iron Curtain were less destructive to the memorial landscape in the former GDR than they had been in other eastern European countries. "The soundless collapse of SED [Communist Party] rule and reunification never gave rise to the kind of 'revolutionary people's rage' . . . [in the GDR that it did in] some other eastern European states, so that the remains [*Hinterlassenschaft*] of such 'political monuments' are considerable and diverse."[12] Eberhard Elfert saw public outcry over the official demolition of the Lenin monument in 1991 as having provoked the eventual creation of a high-level government committee to decide the fates of the most visible political monuments, most of which were not connected with the GDR's interpretation of the Nazi past. Elfert rejected the possibility of placing all of the GDR monuments in a monument park, as was done in Moscow and Budapest among other former communist countries, because "the situation in Berlin, where two political systems met, is not comparable with the political relations of eastern European states."[13] Herbert Staroste added that "a threat to the democratic constitution of our society is doubtless no longer going to come from these monuments."[14]

Clearly, in East Germany, the memorial landscape included far more than only monuments connected with the Nazi past. While memorials were in fact removed (particularly those with specifically Communist imagery, including images of Lenin), the landscape of markers dealing with the Nazi past was left largely intact (although memorial plaques were removed with greater frequency than actual memorial sites, a phenomenon discussed in greater detail below). Some of the accompanying texts changed in content or emphasis, but most patches of land officially devoted to marking resistance to or persecution by the Nazi regime remain. The physical imprint of East German treatment of the Nazi past has survived, even without the political scaffolding that created it, and with a widespread land grab.[15] Nearly all sites marking the Nazi past in East Berlin that were built before 1989 carried over into the new political and economic era, albeit not with the same message and implications they had once had. It seems that once a site is built, it is likely to remain a permanent point of official collective memory materialized in the cityscape.

This continuity is not as surprising as it might seem at first glance. First, the East German government marked the Nazi past in ways that have turned out to be at least somewhat consistent, not only with post-1989 memorial culture, but also with post-1989 property relations and urban planning practices. Second, these markers were often built on property that continued to be publicly owned even after 1989, and on land that was already set aside as open space, so they are doubly protected by both ownership and land-use guidelines. In general, after 1989, traffic medians continued to be traffic medians, parks remained parks, and cemeteries remained cemeteries. The physical continuity of the city contributes to the continuity of the symbolic landscape as well. Many of the sites occupy existing green spaces, cemeteries, traffic medians, sidewalks, and other elements of the urban landscape, where there are few—if any—competing uses. They are generally not designated for future construction and are unlikely to be of interest to developers or city planners.

The persistence of these sites can be explained in part by ownership patterns and existing land uses, but also by the resonance of the content in a unified Berlin. The resonance of any site marking the Nazi past—even in the familiar language of "anti-fascist resistance" used so extensively by the Communist Party—also helped to secure these sites' continued presence in the urban landscape. The sites concerned a set of subjects well entrenched in the West as worthy of memorialization. In many respects, then, it was easy to leave these markers in the landscape. They weathered the storm of unification in part because relatively few of them provoked controversy, and there were few conflicting claims on the land.[16] But perhaps they also remain uncontroversial because many have receded into the background. Land is marked, stones are put in place, but these actions do not guarantee specific transformations in public awareness, or that people will notice these places as they walk past them on their way to work or to school.

Memory and Materiality

Drawing on a familiar repertoire of aesthetic approaches and ideological formations, the memorials built in East Germany took on an array of physical forms: memorial plaques attached to building façades; memorial stones placed in cemeteries, parks, traffic islands and other public land; larger ensembles of memorial stones or statuary that take up patches of urban land; and even museums. Few are the type of conceptual monument increasingly favored (at least by many artists and officials) in the West in the 1980s and throughout Berlin after 1989, where the artists and others involved seek to disrupt the urban fabric and to unsettle—and instruct— the passerby. Instead they tend to follow rather traditional forms.[17] Particularly in the 1970s and 1980s, the government encouraged local party leadership to mark sites tied to the broader anti-fascist and socialist struggle, including sites related to resistance to the Nazi regime. This attention to the local level is visible, for example, in the series of books by Hans Maur detailing sites connected to socialist history in each district of East Berlin, published in the 1970s and 1980s. The centrality of the local is also clear in the *Historischer Lehrpfad zu einigen Stätten der Verfolgung und des Widerstands gegen den faschistischen Pogrom November 1938 im Stadtbezirk Berlin-Mitte*, a booklet issued by the Committee of Anti-Fascist Resistance Fighters and the district history museum of Mitte in 1988 (the fiftieth anniversary of the November 1938 pogroms). This is an intriguing document, covering many sites (such as Rosenstraße and Burgstraße 26) where there were, at the time, no plaques or memorials, and clearly addressing the persecution of Jews.[18] In other cases, district-level historians investigated and publicized local sites of resistance, which then frequently led to small monuments or plaques. The GDR very intentionally used the urban landscape as a site of instruction, disseminating a relatively unified message about the GDR's anti-fascist past, and linking this past to concrete sites in the landscape. These small-scale local projects helped to translate elements of the kind of centralized narrative of the Nazi past described in the previous chapter into sites of local meaning and recognition, placing anti-fascism in the midst of the East German citizens. Many of these projects (including the plaques placed on the apartment buildings of "anti-fascist resistance fighters" who were sent to concentration camps, for example) are also premised on a widespread belief in the significance, and instructive power, of "authentic sites."

Some of these sites are barely visible and far from the city center, while others are routinely used for public ceremonies and gatherings, well on the beaten path of tourists and school groups and politicians. Most are quiet, easily overlooked places. One would have to actively seek them out, and would have to know where to look. Even with the aid of maps, a car, and a hefty book cataloging Berlin's markers of the Nazi past in hand, finding many of these presented a challenge. Some are "authentic" sites, some are not. Most are shaped by the ideological and aesthetic approaches widespread in official GDR memorial culture (discussed at greater length in the previous chapter). Some are under official historical preservation; others are zoned as residential green space and thus unavailable for development. Many are in cemeteries, and thus highly unlikely candidates for sale. In fact, only a handful of these sites are even built on land that could possibly be developed after 1989. This collection of plaques, statues, and stones embodies decades of political maneuvering, personal memory, ideology, historiography, and shifting artistic approaches to the problem of the memory and the representation of the Nazi past. These are ideas and intentions translated into urban landscapes through bricks, bronze, and other lasting materials. Taken together, they tell a multifaceted story. Decades of memorial practice in the GDR are left behind, not so much in sedimentary layers, as juxtaposed side by side with post-1989 approaches.

These places result from layers of efforts, over time and at different levels of government and other organizations. But again, simply because they remain in place does not mean that these sites necessarily occupy a central place in public memory of the city's Nazi past, or that all passersby will experience them in similar ways. There is a tremendous range both in their visibility and in their post-1989 use, and in their presence on tourist or dignitary itineraries, in the press, and in other forms of public awareness. These variations, in turn, provide us with some clues as to the afterlife of memorials, and the effects of time (and political, economic, and generational change) on their use and reception. Citizens' groups or local district museums carefully tend some of these memorial sites. Some have become obscured by overgrown bushes or new construction. I would also argue that these sites provide a stock of future spaces of more active memory. An anniversary, a school project, an act of vandalism, or a new historical discovery in the archives may suddenly draw a particular site more directly into public awareness.

Clearly, then, the construction of a given memorial does not guarantee how that site will be experienced and understood by the public. Passersby may be curious, oblivious, ambivalent, or even hostile. Reactions may change over time as well. Many places that are officially remembered are nonetheless unofficially forgotten, or at least rarely noticed. The public that encounters these sites today also possesses a changing set of skills, knowledge, and habits that shape their reaction to and connection with these (and any) memorials. School curricula and curatorial approaches vis-à-vis concentration camps changed in the 1990s, for example, altering their pedagogical and political interpretation. The audience in eastern Germany for sites marking aspects of the Nazi past changed with the change in political leadership, albeit not in lockstep. The variation in the visibility and power of memorial sites also reinforces the caveat that runs through this book and that should run through any analysis of memorials: the intentions of any memorial project are not identical with its consequences. We should also remember that both before and since 1989, these places have been of interest and concern to only a relatively limited part of the population.

This landscape is comprised of the left-behind layers of decades of memorial practice. The state that supported the installation of these markers in the landscape has disappeared from the scene, but the physical remnants of its efforts remain. Since 1989, some of these memorials have witnessed regular public ceremonies, sometimes vandalism, and sometimes both.[19] Some are removed, some are simply neglected. They may become stops on a tour or the subject of widespread media attention and new publications, or known only to people living nearby. In order to show this variation, I highlight four different examples of the post-1989 treatment of pre-1989 memorial sites in the eastern half of the city. I begin with a site that has remained essentially unchanged—and indeed has become a central element of contemporary memorial practice—even as the buildings and vacant lots in its vicinity changed dramatically. I then turn to the question of memorial stones, most of which remain in place, but most of which also seem to blend into the background as the city changes. A third example involves a cemetery in a district on the eastern edge of Berlin, well off the beaten path, but the site of extensive pre-1989 memorialization and home also to new memorial sites that have been added since 1989. Finally, I also discuss memorial plaques, in part to highlight the contrast between these somewhat more fleeting markers and the larger memorial sites more rooted in the landscape and far more difficult to remove.[20]

Große Hamburger Straße

In the middle of a densely built section of Berlin sits a patch of grass and two small monuments marking the former site of a Jewish *Altersheim*, or retirement home. There is no trace of the building, which was badly damaged by bombing during World War II and eventually torn down. But in 1942, before it was bombed, the Nazis turned it into a deportation center, from which thousands of Berlin's Jewish residents were sent to concentration camps. Standing before it today, it is difficult to picture the former structure. The memorial, installed in 1987 by the city government of East Berlin, consists of a plot of grass with a stone path leading up to a vertical monument, resembling a headstone. The plaque on the monument reads, "On this site was once the first rest home of the Jewish Community of Berlin. In 1942 the Gestapo turned it into a deportation site for Jewish citizens. Fifty-five thousand Berlin Jews from infants to the elderly were deported to the concentration camps Auschwitz and Terezin and brutally murdered. NEVER FORGET, PREVENT WAR, PROTECT PEACE." To the right, closer to the neighboring Jewish cemetery, stands a group of bronze figures by Willi Lammert (based on a design by John Heartfield),

FIGURE 3.1. Große Hamburger Str. Photograph by Jennifer Jordan.

placed there in 1985. The ensemble is unusual among pre-1989 memorials in the East in that it directly addresses the persecution of Jews. Unlike more conceptual memorials (some of which are discussed in the next chapter), it is also immediately apparent what is being remembered, because the primary marker has an explanatory text. At the same time, the horror of what is actually being recalled—the fact that this building was one step on the forced journey to Auschwitz or another camp and to death for so many people—is still difficult to understand when confronted with this modest stone. That is not to say that the memorial should be more sensationalistic, but rather more a commentary on the inherent abstraction of memorialization. The grief, fear, and brutality that transpired at this particular set of geographic coordinates are diluted by the passage of time and the process of representing them to later generations. (See Figures 3.1–3.3.)

When the Wall fell, this small memorial soon found itself in the heart of one of Berlin's most dynamically changing neighborhoods, the Spandauer Vorstadt.[21] The neighborhood quickly changed from a sleepy quarter housing artists, outsiders, and elderly longtime residents in dilapidated buildings to a center of Berlin's gallery scene and nightlife, full of pristinely renovated apartments and expensive restaurants. The memorial

FIGURE 3.2. Große Hamburger Str. Photograph by Jennifer Jordan.

abuts one of the most sought-after pieces of real estate in the area, the Hackesche Höfe. This is a massive Art Nouveau building with eight court-yards packed full of galleries, restaurants, and increasingly exclusive apart-ments.[22] When this memorial was built, there was no market. Yet when a market rather suddenly arrived after unification, although property values skyrocketed, and buildings, clubs, restaurants, high-end shops, and condos sprang up all around, the site remained.

Adjoining the memorial site is a much larger lot, set back from the street and used today as a park. This plot on Große Hamburger Straße is the oldest Jewish cemetery in Berlin, and the resting place of the remains of twelve thousand Jews buried between 1672 and 1827.[23] The SS laid waste to the cemetery during the war, and the East German government removed what was left of the headstones in the 1950s.[24] The site is further compli-cated by the fact that not only was the cemetery destroyed in 1942 and lev-eled in 1970, but it was also a burial site for more than 2,400 victims of the bombing in the last two months of World War II, including members of the SS.[25] Few people venture into the green expanse or along its paths, but it does provide a reservoir of leafy green in one of the most densely built sections of Berlin, and it is the view out of the windows of many of

FIGURE 3.3. Große Hamburger Str. Photograph by Jennifer Jordan.

the residents of the neighboring Hackesche Höfe. It is no longer an intact cemetery, but is still untouchable by the real estate market, and it is still difficult to envision a day when it might be opened up for development, despite the new development taking place on all sides.

The persistence of both the cemetery and the memorial site is tied, in part, to the issue of ownership. The property records for East Berlin show a curious ripple in late 1961. In the months following the building of the Berlin Wall, the authorities sifted through the property registries and converted many properties into *Volkseigentum*, or people's property. On October 10, 1961, this was done with Große Hamburger Str. 26, which was thereafter administered by the Parks Department. (Until 1961, the owner was still technically Reichshauptstadt Berlin, the capital city of the Third Reich, as a result of the confiscation of Jewish property by the Nazis.) Once the Wall fell, this lot was clearly going to have a restitution claim placed on it. In 1992, the lot was first transferred to the state government of Berlin, and it was restored to the Jewish community on September 11, 1998.[26] The site is further guaranteed by the fact that it is now under historical preservation.[27] Its status as a space of memory is never called into question, at least not in any way that appears in newspapers or public political discussion.

Unlike most of the pre-1989 sites, Große Hamburger Straße has since then become an important site of periodic collective remembrance and public discussion. The wording and imagery used there are not overtly socialist, so the content and aesthetics do not appear to have met with official or popular disapproval after unification. This memorial ensemble is also a stop on organized tours of the city, and many tourists find it on their own because of its location in the heart of a well-visited area. Since 1989, it has been one of the more visible and widely used memorial sites in Berlin. Dedication ceremonies and anniversaries in general, anchored to particular places, provide opportunities to renew the meaning of a place, to gather people together, and also for the press to repeat the stories of these places to a broader public. In 1998, on Holocaust Remembrance Day, for example, volunteers stood in line in the cold to read the names of all Berlin Jews killed in the Holocaust. As the speakers read out the names in the growing darkness, neighborhood residents walked past the very small crowd that had gathered, walking their dogs or going around the corner to pick up something for dinner.

Various levels of government and community organization anchor acts of remembrance at interconnected sites throughout the city.[28] Another date that often anchors such public ceremonies is the anniversary of the pogroms that took place across Germany and Austria in November 1938. Like other anniversaries, this day is often marked with marches, gatherings, and speeches at synagogues, monuments, and cemeteries.[29]

The Große Hamburger Straße site is also ignored by many and has even been vandalized repeatedly since 1989. On the night of December 30, 1998, for example, vandals overturned the memorial stone and broke the nearby plaque.[30] The stone was replaced and rededicated in February, in a ceremony attended by around two hundred people, including politicians from the Social Democratic party, the author Christa Wolf, the Israeli consul general, and other dignitaries. Vandals damaged the monument again a week after its rededication, prompting Andreas Nachama to call for an all-night volunteer guard.[31] Vandalism has continued (at this and many other sites) in subsequent years. One side effect of the watch, in both its official and volunteer forms, was to spark discussion with people walking by, as one newspaper reported: "Tourists stumbling through the East Berlin bar scene suddenly become aware of this historical place and start asking questions, school groups fooling around begin serious conversations."[32] The central location of Große Hamburger Straße means that many people take notice of it each year, unlike so many other markers throughout Berlin.

Overall, this site clearly continues to resonate with a broad public. The site must also be seen as connected to the thousands of places from which entire families were taken to Große Hamburger Straße, where they were held until being sent to a train station like the Bahnhof Grunewald or Anhalter Bahnhof and transported to distant death camps. These small stones in oases of urban greenery trace parts of the interconnected geography of Nazi violence—not systematically, and not comprehensively, but as pieces of a much larger picture and nodes in a much larger system, in ways that are not always immediately apparent in the urban landscape.

Memorial Stones

Scattered throughout eastern Berlin are dozens of individual memorial stones placed in the cityscape over the course of decades, many recalling resistance to or persecution by the Nazi regime, many focused on anti-fascist resistance. Some are in "authentic" locations, while others are in central locations that could serve as the sites of public ceremonies and centrally organized demonstrations. Since 1989, few of these stones have appeared in public discussions or events, but most have remained in place.[33] These stones scarcely convey the intensity of the events they recall, a terror, courage, or brutality that is difficult for many of us to imagine, who have not experienced it ourselves. Even memorial stones that have so far received little attention may nonetheless be noticed by locals passing by, and they may also act as future anchors of memory if they are threatened in some way. Perhaps a local school group might take an interest in the history being recalled, or a threat of removal might provoke a renewed interest in the history embodied in the stone. Such sites of memory do flare up at times, even after decades of fading into the background. These stones, as with all of the places discussed in this chapter, are wrapped up in multiple layers of interpretation, so that they recall both particular events during the Nazi era, the ways in which people interpreted this history in the GDR, and the ways in which people interpret them now in the post-1989 era. Obviously, such interpretations are potentially quite heterogeneous. The stone itself conveys a particular message, sanctioned by the authorities at the time, but the original message is not necessarily identical with the way that a given passerby, or an eyewitness, might experience the site and the message, and might encounter these instances of courage or persecution memorialized by a piece of rock.

Looking through newspapers and state assembly records, memorial stones rarely surface as objects of discussion. Most have received little or no attention. Any given stone was important to someone sometime, and may still be, but they clearly bring up issues of audience and intention. A handful of stones have disappeared since 1989, but most remain in place.[34] Yet, as noted above, persistence does not guarantee resonance. What, then, might be the implications or consequences of these kinds of sites, and this use of a site? Such stones can act as lightning rods for potent political messages, and can mark sites of violence or courage. Yet they may also become increasingly invisible over time. Perhaps the initial act of marking needs to be separated from the later influence of a memorial stone. Without a political apparatus in place to support recurrent ceremonies centered at these sites, they may fall out of use and awareness. (See Figure 3.4.)

FIGURE 3.4. Memorial Stone in the district of Köpenick (in the center right portion of the photograph). Photograph by Jennifer Jordan.

How (and why) certain moments get marked and certain moments do not is in part a result of the vagaries of funding and historiographic trends. While most stones have remained quietly in the background, I begin here with a discussion of the Herbert Baum memorial stone, one of the few markers that has become the subject of some debate.

The Herbert Baum Gedenkstein

At one corner of the Lustgarten, a sweeping plaza in the heart of the eastern half of Berlin, stands a small stone cube that might be easy to overlook. The Herbert Baum Gedenkstein is one of the few memorial stones to have figured in discussions in the city's daily papers in recent years. It marks the site where, in 1942, members of the Herbert Baum Resistance Group set fire to an anti-Soviet exhibition the Nazis were staging in the Lustgarten.[35] Baum and other members of the group were later murdered, some while in Gestapo custody, others at the nearby Plötzensee prison, and still others in concentration camps.[36] The horror of these deaths can hardly be conveyed by a memorial stone, so perhaps this stone has to be understood as connected to the memorial at Plötzensee and the memorials at concentration camps, a web of remembrance laid over the geographical web of Nazi violence. The stone does serve as a reminder of resistance that took place in the middle of the city, but it does not necessarily evoke either the initial events—the efforts by young Jewish men and women to set this anti-Soviet propaganda exhibition on fire—nor the resulting murders. The original stone, designed by Jürgen Raue, was placed on the square in 1981. Helmut Caspar writes:

At the edge of the Lustgarten stands a memorial stone originating in the GDR era, with the motto "Bound in friendship with the Soviet Union forever." (The rest of the inscription reads: "Unforgotten the courageous deeds and the stead-fastness of the anti-fascist resistance group led by the young Communist Herbert Baum.") The cube recalls the Jewish resistance fighter Herbert Baum (1912–1942). . . . On the night of May 17–18, 1942, the young men and women tried to set on fire the "Soviet Paradise" exhibition that the Nazis had built in the Lustgarten. . . . Some time ago the stone cube became the subject of debate, [and] its removal was even demanded in conjunction with the renovation of the Lustgarten. This did not occur; on the contrary, this rather unobtrusive monument received additional plaques, on which the background of the actions against the Nazi exhibition is explained.[37]

Many people, including a surviving member of the Herbert Baum group, Gerhard Zadek, felt that the existing inscription did not adequately convey what had taken place in 1942. Rather than removing the stone, which some people saw as dated, two Plexiglas plaques were added in 2001, making clear the layers of history and interpretation.

A broader public gradually became aware of the stone, first as a result of the suggestions that it be removed, and then through the debates in the district city council over the possibility of reframing its message. The stone also received attention through a variety of ceremonies, as well as newspaper coverage. The *Berliner Zeitung* reported on the dedication ceremony, for example: "The memorial stone in the Lustgarten for the members of the Herbert Baum resistance group was rededicated yesterday: Two additional panels with Plexiglas layers now explain the text on the stone. Because in the view of the local politicians in the district of Mitte the original inscription was, until now, incomprehensible."[38] One of the new panels lists the names of thirty-four people who participated in the group, and the other panel offers more historical detail about the original events. These

FIGURE 3.5. Herbert Baum Memorial Stone on the edge of the Lustgarten. Photograph by Jennifer Jordan.

modifications occurred in part thanks to Gerhard Zadek, who approached the District City Hall with the idea of updating the stone. "The President of the Federal Parliament, Wolfgang Thierse, welcomed the idea for the memorial stone," the *Berliner Zeitung* noted. "He described it as a successful effort, combining the original stone inscriptions with text on Plexiglas, 'in order to make transparent the different historical dimensions of the memorial stone on the Lustgarten.'"[39] (See Figure 3.5.)

The Herbert Baum Gedenkstein continues to anchor memorial activity. It was the site of a public ceremony in March 2003, for example, marking the sixtieth anniversary of "the murder of the members of the Herbert Baum resistance group and 500 unconnected Berlin Jews murdered as an act of retribution by the Nazi regime."[40] The land on which the stone stands is state property, and the presence of the stone did not conflict with the planned renovation of the park. At the same time, the message and intentions of the cube *have* changed, and a new political era has infused the same place with new meaning. Even a granite cube can become a dynamic element of contemporary interpretations of a city's history.

Marzahner Parkfriedhof

In the district of Marzahn, on the eastern edge of the city, stands a cemetery housing a range of different memorial sites, including many that treat resistance to or persecution by the Nazi regime. The cemetery is technically defined as a "Parkfriedhof," a park cemetery, because of the beauty of its landscaping. Full of imposing old trees and evoking a sense of being deep in a forest, the cemetery offers a profound contrast to its surroundings—sprawling train tracks, light industrial areas and small machine shops, and high-rise, prefabricated apartment buildings constructed in the 1970s and 1980s. Few people from other parts of the city, and even fewer tourists, find their way to this district, much less to the cemetery next to the S-Bahn station. But the cemetery is rich in memorials, and despite being off the beaten path, it has remained a salient part of the commemorative landscape (Figures 3.6–3.7). The local district museum and local politicians have taken an active interest in it, pre-1989 memorials have remained in place, more information has been provided, and new memorials now include efforts to recall the sufferings of forced laborers and of the Sinti and Roma.

FIGURE 3.6. Memorial in the Marzahn Park Cemetery. Photograph by Jennifer Jordan.

FIGURE 3.7. Memorial for the "Victims of Fascism" in the Marzahn Park Cemetery. Photograph by Jennifer Jordan.

The district office that oversees the cemetery has produced an informational pamphlet describing the cemetery, including the following listing of memorial stones and plaques:

Several memorial stones recall victims of the First and Second World Wars. A [stone] hand is raised in an oath near the entrance. Here 3,330 victims of the bombing terror warn us, the living: never again! In the Soviet memorial grove [*Ehrenhain*] rest 285 soldiers and officers who fell in the area of Landsberger Allee. Their ashes are held in a shell limestone urn. Other stones recall the victims of Nazi power: One memorial stone is dedicated to the Sinti and Roma victims. The monument of the United Nations recalls the people who were deported to Germany from occupied countries and who died here, of whom 6,000 rest in this cemetery. The OdF [Victims of Fascism] memorial stone on the main path of the cemetery was erected for 46 people, primarily young people, who actively resisted fascism and were executed or died as a result of torture.[41]

The cemetery is laden with extremely complex elements of Berlin's Nazi past.[42] Interpreting it requires a fair amount of preparation—at the very least, one needs the descriptive pamphlet available from the district Heimat-museum, but probably a fairly thorough background in German history and memorial practices as well. Periodically, an article about the cemetery appears in one of the Berlin daily papers. In 1997, for example, the *Berliner Morgenpost* noted:

Soldiers killed in action in the First and Second World Wars, bombing victims, deportees, resistance fighters, Soviet soldiers, Sinti and Roma: in the Park Cemetery on Wiesenburger Weg, the victims of war and National Socialism are remembered—as a warning to the living. Whoever wends their way here is met with an impressive testimony to contemporary history, whose care nonetheless threatens to overtax the district of Marzahn. . . . the attentive person out for a stroll must be surprised. Why are there no plaques with more detailed explanations of the many memorial stones? This question was put to the district city planner, Wilfried Nünthel (CDU), in a recent district city council meeting. His answer: "For that, first of all, no funds are available—unfortunately."[43]

In addition to the lack of funds, the cemetery is simply known to a relatively small number of people.

Not surprisingly, the cemetery was preserved after 1989. It is public land, designated as a cemetery, under historic preservation, and in a district with little demand for new construction. It also fits the pattern of sites marking the Nazi past being located on land that is already publicly owned and does not involve competing uses. It may be difficult to imagine converting a cemetery to real estate, but certainly in other settings and other cities, cemeteries, as well as unmarked burial grounds, have been obliterated by development. The site is also highly "authentic," in that it contains the remains of people who died at the hands of the Nazi regime and its supporters. Hans Maur speaks of "the urns of 46 brave anti-fascists, executed by the fascists in the years 1939 to 1943 in the Brandenburg an der Havel penitentiary, [that] were laid to rest [here]. Against the fascist orders, cemetery employees placed the urns on a separate spot."[44] The stone reads "ODF [*Opfer des Faschismus*, Victims of Fascism]. 46 people died so that we may live."[45] The relative continuity should not be so surprising, in part because a cemetery remains a cemetery, but also because the people involved have not really changed. It is important to remember that the people working on this site, and living near it, are many of the same people who were there before 1989. The political context has changed, but many of the actors are still the same. This is true for much district-level memorial work. While certain eastern districts (primarily Mitte, Prenzlauer Berg, and Friedrichshain) have experienced a significant influx of people who grew up in the

West, this is much less the case in many districts farther out from the city center and some with less older housing and more prefabricated housing blocks. This means that memorial work at the district level is not being shaped by newcomers so much as by longtime district residents.

One part of the cemetery that has received more attention in recent years is a small complex located at the edge of the cemetery, at the end farthest from the entrance, dedicated to the Sinti and Roma deported from Berlin.[46] The first element of the ensemble, a large engraved stone designed by the sculptor Jürgen Raue, the same sculptor who created the Herbert Baum stone, was placed there in 1986 at the insistence of religious groups and a local writer, Reimar Gilsenbach.[47] The text reads: "From May 1936 until the liberation of our people by the glorious Soviet Army, hundreds of members of the Sinti suffered in a prison camp not far from this site. Honor the victims." A memorial tablet was added to the ensemble in 1990, which reads: "To the Berlin Sinti, who suffered in the Marzahn 'gypsy camp' and died in Auschwitz. May 1936–May 1945." In 1991, an informational plaque was also added that reads as follows (Figure 3.8):

In a former sewage field to the north of this cemetery, in preparation for the Olympic games of 1936, the Nazis constructed a "Gypsy Campsite" in which hundreds of Sinti and Roma were forced to live. Crowded together in dismal barracks, the camp residents led a miserable life. Hard labor, sickness, and hunger claimed their victims. People were arbitrarily deported and arrested. Humiliating "racial hygiene examinations" spread fear and horror. In the spring of 1943, most of the prisoners were deported to Auschwitz. Men and women, the elderly and children. Only a few survived.[48]

This ensemble has since been the location of various public ceremonies. In 2001, Bundestag President Wolfgang Thierse, the Catholic bishop of Berlin, and the head of the Berlin-Brandenburg Roma and Sinti organization, Otto Rosenberg, were among those who attended a ceremony at the site.[49] In May 2002, the vice president of the Berlin parliament gave a speech in the cemetery, where she drew clear connections between the persecution of Roma and Sinti by the Nazis and contemporary xenophobic violence, concluding by saying that "in light of contemporary attacks with racist, xenophobic, and anti-Semitic backgrounds, all responsible societal powers must keep alive the memory of persecution and injustice during the Nazi era. This is the lasting responsibility of our country, in which the Roma and Sinti suffered so terribly."[50] In June 2002 and 2003, there were memorial ceremonies in the cemetery marking the anniversary of the forced relocation of Berlin's Roma and Sinti to the nearby camp in 1936.[51] The idea of a central memorial to the murdered Sinti and Roma, in addition to these memorial sites on the edge of the city, has been under discussion (often in conjunction with the activities focused on the Marzahn site) since at least the 1980s.[52] It now appears certain that a central memorial will in fact be built across from the Reichstag in the city center.[53]

More recently, other new memorials have appeared in the cemetery, including a memorial for forced laborers, unveiled in January 2004, on the annual Holocaust Remembrance Day. (The issue of memorials dedicated to forced laborers is addressed in greater detail in Chapter 5.) For a range of different groups of people, the Marzahner Parkfriedhof contains material traces of a significant past. Its continued use by groups of activists, educators, politicians, and survivors means that the site continues to

FIGURE 3.8. Memorial for the Sinti and Roma in the Marzahn Park Cemetery. Photograph by Jennifer Jordan.

be a dynamic element of the city's memorial landscape, albeit for a more limited cross-section of the population than some of the other sites discussed in this book—more local than national, more neighborhood residents than tourists, but also connected to memorial projects at citywide and national levels as well.

Memorial Plaques

Here I turn to the question of a rather different kind of memory site, the memorial plaque. Contrasting plaques with the more permanent memorials in the rest of this book helps to demonstrate the centrality of ownership and land use. Plaques do not alter land use directly. They are also highly subject to issues of ownership, given that since 1989 in the East (and long before in the West), no property owner can be forced to maintain or accept a plaque on his or her property. It is also simply much easier for vandals, construction crews, or building owners to take down a plaque than to remove an engraved fieldstone or metal column. The two primary factors shaping the landscape of memorial plaques in the 1990s were the generally unofficial disappearance of plaques, on the one hand, and the relatively cautious official treatment of the symbolic remnants of the GDR, on the other. The layering of the landscape of plaques in the central district of Mitte (discussed in greater detail below) is due in large part to the decisions by a local district commission not to remove GDR plaques, but rather to leave them as witnesses to the complex history of eastern Germany. In the meantime, more than eighty new plaques have been placed throughout the district by the Memorial Plaque Commission since its formation.[54] In other districts, decisions were made by the district city planner (*Baustadtrat*) or someone in a similar position. The fates of plaques after 1989 received extensive attention among researchers and activists who grappled with the consequences of 1989 for exhibits, as well as symbolic replacements of plaques that had disappeared. For this analysis, I rely in part on the extensive publications recounting resistance and Nazi persecution, as well as the various catalogues of memorial plaques produced in the 1980s and 1990s in both East and West Germany.[55] A variety of books and newspaper accounts examine the landscape of memorial plaques, some focusing specifically on plaques dedicated to the commemoration of resistance to and persecution by the Nazi regime, others treating plaques more generally. There are more than six hundred memorial plaques in the eastern half of the city, nearly half of which recall resistance to or persecution by the Nazis.[56]

In 1997, Holger Hübner brought out what was, at the time, the most complete catalog of Berlin's memorial plaques, which spans a much broader spectrum than those discussed in this chapter. He began from the premise that "a great city like Berlin is a living history book. In nearly every building, on every corner, something took place, someone important lived or worked." He was inspired to write the book in part by visits to East Berlin, where he saw many plaques to resistance fighters and Nazi victims, at a time (the 1970s) when such markers were "almost entirely missing in West Berlin." Hübner points to the early 1980s as a time when "people in the West also turned to a stronger *Aufarbeitung,* or processing, of recent German history, and noticed gaps that one wanted to close." When he began his research, Hübner found that neither East nor West had a complete listing of its memorial plaques. In Hübner's account, there were a total of 212 plaques in Mitte, 61 of which were dedicated to events that occurred during the Nazi era. Hübner claims that most plaques for socialists or resistance fighters disappeared "quickly" after 1989, but other accounts indicate that many such plaques remained.[57]

In his 1994 volume on resistance in Mitte and the nearby district of Tiergarten, Hans-Rainer Sandvoß lists thirty-two plaques or places recalling resistance in Mitte. Of these, most are on the façades of buildings, and a few are on interior foyers or courtyard walls.[58] In 1996, Hermann Zech found seventy-six plaques in Mitte that had been mounted between 1945 and 1990, and forty-three since 1991. He also found forty-two missing plaques from the period between 1945 and 1990. "This overview," he cautions, as do many who write about plaques, "makes no claim to be complete."[59] Indeed, it is difficult to find a precise accounting of plaques, which come and go. In early 1992, the Active Museum published a small book by Martin Schönfeld cataloguing the memorial plaques in eastern Berlin, and in 2002, it released an updated listing of the plaques in Berlin containing references to resistance or persecution during the Nazi era.[60] In a clear differentiation between authentic and inauthentic sties, Schönfeld distinguishes between memorial plaques and remembrance plaques. The former are placed on the actual site where the subject lived or worked, or where a particular event occurred, whereas the latter involve sites named for important figures, but without any direct connection between the place and the figure. Schönfeld also divides East German remembrance plaques into two main categories. The first is those connected to the naming of public facilities, schools, and factories for resistance fighters who were in some way connected to the site, thus instilling this memory into daily life. The second category consists of the naming of streets, squares, bridges, and other sites in conjunction with the placement of a memorial plaque on the site.[61] This decoupling of the marking from the authentic or original site also plays an important role in memorials using urban land.

The stock of memorials in a city, including plaques, may partially indicate official priorities concerning the collective identity of a given place. However, the number, location, and content of such markers are significantly shaped by other factors as well. Money is a primary factor determining whether or not a plaque or memorial will be installed. Prior to the question of money there must first be an active group of individuals, inside or outside the government, who designate a site as worthy of marking. But without funding, nothing more will happen. A typical bronze plaque, for example, may cost a few thousand euros.[62] During the 1980s, public funds for memorial plaques in both East and West Berlin were concentrated in certain districts, resulting in a distribution of plaque sites that does not directly reflect the stock of potentially memorializable events. By the 1990s, however, much of this government money had dried up. Activists had to seek funding from private groups and individuals, and from a much smaller pool of state funding. In addition, in the West, and after 1989 in eastern Berlin as well, no plaque could be mounted on a building without the agreement of the owner. Municipal or even federal impulses to attach plaques to buildings could no longer, as they could in the GDR, override the interests of the property owner. Hübner recounts at least twenty building owners in both East and West who reject plaques tied to the history of the Nazi era.[63] In May 1996, the Active Museum and the state Green Party questioned Culture Senator Peter Radunski as to whether he was aware of the disappearance of memorial plaques. He responded that he and the Berlin Senate were aware of the phenomenon, but that it was the right of an owner to remove a plaque, as long as the plaque itself was not under official historical preservation or part of a designated monument.[64] Since 1989, the newspapers have also reported cases of property owners resisting the placing of plaques recalling events from the Nazi era on their buildings, in both eastern and western Berlin.[65] One way for activists and officials to circumvent the owners' wishes is to place a marker on the sidewalk in front of the building, beyond the property limits. This option, however, can be far more expensive than attaching a plaque to the wall of a building, and, until recently, it was used only very infrequently. (A new series of memorial projects involves placing much more inexpensive "stumbling stones" in the paving stones in front of a given building, outside of the property, which is a more affordable alternative, but not without controversy. I discuss them at greater length in Chapter 6.)[66]

After 1989, some plaques were vandalized, and others were removed in the process of renovating façades and simply not replaced, or taken down by the owner or property manager out of a desire to avoid any association with either the Nazi era or the East German government. The activist Christine Fischer-Defoy points out that is difficult to tell whether there is a "clear political reason" behind every vandalism and removal.[67] Another observer wrote that "it is unclear whether this has to do with the deeds of people hunting for souvenirs of the German unification process, or with politically motivated forms of the radical working-through of GDR history."[68] In August and September 1990, the Active Museum and the New Society for the Fine Arts held an exhibition of East Berlin monuments and memorial plaques, including those that had already been removed. The Active Museum reported that by May 1991, sixteen plaques had been secretly removed in eastern Berlin, none by official decree.[69] In 1991, Schönfeld tallied twenty-four missing plaques, all of which had been stolen. Schönfeld and many others saw these physical remnants of East Germany as "acutely endangered" and fought actively to ensure the preservation of those that remained.[70] In addition, they engaged in symbolic remounting of plaques that had disappeared. In May 1993, the Active Museum mounted eight replacement plaques in four eastern districts of the city, replacing plaques memorializing anti-fascist resistors and victims of the Nazi regime that had been removed.[71] By that point, thirty-three plaques had disappeared from building walls in the eastern part of the city since 1989, according to the weekly *taz*, which cited the *Village Voice* referring to the Active Museum as memorial plaque–guerrillas (*Gedenktafel-Guerillas*).[72] On the forty-sixth anniversary of the German capitulation, the Active Museum remounted five plaques that had been removed recently by unknown vandals.[73] One of the plaques that has disappeared and been replaced many times hangs beneath an overpass of the Friedrichstraße train station, where Friedrichstraße passes beneath the elevated station and train tracks, marking the site where two young German men were executed by the SS in the last days of the war for refusing to fight. The plaque disappeared, was replaced, disappeared again, and was replaced yet again.

One category of plaques did disappear by official decree. Shortly after the falling of the Wall, and before unification, the East Berlin magistracy ordered the removal of all monuments and plaques bearing specific references to Erich Honecker and to the Communist Party (SED). Most of these objects were sitting in the basement of the Märkisches Museum in the center of Berlin by 1992.[74] But aside from those explicitly political plaques, there was much agreement that the rest should remain. One reason so many monuments and plaques remained may be because the regime they represented was so discredited that its symbols represented no viable threat. Many residents also certainly wanted the plaques to remain as historical artifacts, and of course as memorials to those who resisted and suffered at the hands of the Nazis.

Mitte's Commissions

Each district has its own approach to the memorial landscape, both the markers in place when the Wall fell and the new projects that have emerged in the intervening years, but the district of Mitte found itself in a unique position due to its centrality, as well as the concentration and quantity of markers. In Mitte, the bureaucratic framework for dealing with memorial plaques actually has its origin in the controversy surrounding street names in the first few years after the Wall came down.[75] As early as July 1990, a Christian Democratic city council member asked the magistracy, which governed the former East Berlin until unification in October 1990, what it had in mind with regard to "the renaming of streets and squares, made necessary by the fall of socialism in autumn 1989."[76] It responded that it had no plans of its own to do anything about the street names, and that eventually responsibility for street names would rest not with the citywide government (eventually the all-Berlin Senate) but with each district government. In November 1990, the Social Democratic faction in Mitte successfully passed a measure to form a "Commission on the Renaming of Streets and Squares in the District of Mitte." The party justified the commission in the following way: "With the renaming of streets and squares of our district, whose names symbolically stand for the Stalinist and totalitarian-influenced GDR heritage, a service to the confrontation of the past in a public, democratic space should be rendered."[77] Fourteen streets and squares were renamed in Mitte in the early 1990s.[78] This renaming commission clearly illustrates one aspect of memorial construction in a more democratic setting, where official collective memory appears not necessarily as the result of a top-down decree but also as a combination of citizen activism, political pressure, and funding. It is also important to notice that only the street names, monuments, and plaques in the eastern half of the city were being systematically evaluated. In the western half of the city, 1989 brought with it neither the same political and economic changes nor the same scrutiny of the existing memorial landscape. Many observers felt that the memorial landscape of the West should also be reexamined in light of unification and found it problematic that only eastern markers would be called into question.[79] The process in Mitte, however, was initiated by longtime residents of the district and resulted in a comparatively careful treatment of this memorial landscape.

In late 1991, the district city council voted to establish a temporary commission named "Monuments in Mitte" to review the district's collection of plaques and monuments.[80] Every party represented on the district council had one representative on the commission, as well as one expert citizen. The Monuments in Mitte Commission made very clear that it saw an open confrontation with these monuments as an important way to begin helping the city to grow together, and it did not directly assess either artistic or historical preservation value, but focused rather on monuments and plaques that "in their statement or the occasion of their mounting had unequivocal political and ideological functions and thereby served the one-sided historical understanding of GDR ideology and the justification of the leadership claims of the Socialist Unity Party, or justified or glorified violence, or that, in their message, violated basic human rights."[81] In addition the commission discussed markers of the "anti-fascist resistance" and images of socialism, ultimately deciding that all but a few of the existing monuments, and all of the plaques, should remain. In June 1992, the commission accordingly recommended that all forty-one GDR memorial plaques on buildings in the district of Mitte should remain.[82] "Like the readable rings [of a tree], memorial plaques should remain signs and documents of a past epoch that through event, wording, and the style of the text actually speak for themselves."[83] They decided that some plaques might require the addition of the date on which they had been put in place, assuming that the date alone would make clear that the plaque was a product of the SED and allow it to act as a "readable ring." While plaques disappeared unofficially, no plaque was removed officially in Mitte after 1990.

In May 1992, the Commission concluded its work, but it urged the district to establish a longterm memorial plaque commission, which was done later that year.[84] This new commission's work was restricted only to memorial plaques, as the construction of new monuments fell under the jurisdiction of the state government, the Senate.[85] The district council approved the commission indefinitely in 1994, assigning it the following tasks: "The primary goal of this commission is to bring together suggestions for new memorial plaques into a memorial plaque program; to clarify content, historical, and aesthetic questions in relation to memorial plaques and monuments; and to deliver suggestions as to the realization of these projects to the district administration."[86] In most other districts of Berlin, decisions about memorial plaques are made by appointed rather than elected officials, and often simply by individuals. In Mitte, such decisions are made by the commission, with city council members from every party represented in the district council. The plaque for Otto Weidt, discussed in greater detail in the next chapter, was the first result of the plaque commission's efforts. By 2003, the commission had already initiated or mounted eighty plaques.[87]

The commission almost always succeeded in putting forth its policy of leaving old plaques in place as historical evidence not only of the original event, but also of the way in which East Germany represented its past. In November 1996, the Senate did forbid the district council and the citizens' group "Luisenverein" to restore a plaque on the Institute for Tropical Medicine in the district of Mitte. The Senate was administering the building at the time, and rejected the return of the plaque due to its socialist content.[88] That is, the words "with revolutionary and strong unions for peace, democracy, and socialism!" were objectionable to the Senate. The district council had proposed, with unanimous consent from all parties, to remount the plaque, with the addition of the year in which it had originally been placed there, 1983.

The plaques are part of a moral project that presumes that marking the past will, ideally, have preventative effects. These sites are, in part, about attempting to convey a moral message to people who encounter these places. There is an admitted pedagogical content to memorials, both those related to the Nazi era and of other times as well, and this was the case in the GDR as well as the Federal Republic. Artists, educators, and public officials often assume that marking these sites will help to prevent the recurrence of similar events, or at least that such marking is a necessary, if not sufficient, element of prevention. This moral content appears frequently in newspaper coverage. In August 1994, for instance, the city council for the district of Mitte placed a plaque on a former synagogue. The reporter interviewed a man from Denmark visiting Berlin with a group of other Jews who had fled Berlin during the Nazi era. He responded to the plaque in part by pointing to its historical importance, but also by linking it to broader and more international efforts: "In a united Europe there is a hope against growing German nationalism, a hope for democracy."[89] The question of the international gaze on Berlin is never very far away from discussions of Berlin's memorial landscape.

Why is it that unification does not entail the wholesale removal of the symbolic vestiges of communist power? One reason is that, as we have seen, plaques tend to be the responsibility of district governments, not the state government. The elected officials of the district governments are obviously district residents, and thus themselves either easterners or westerners even long after 1989, as there has been relatively little mobility across the disappeared Wall (with the exception of certain central districts). In addition, many western intellectuals involved in these processes, and already entrenched in public discussions of memorial practices, were also inclined to argue for the preservation of plaques. Finally, as others have also suggested, most of these symbols instantly lost much of their power, and posed little threat to the new institutions, because they were tied to a system that had been delegitimated. Memorial landscapes are one site for states to convey messages to their subjects and (especially in democratic settings) for various groups to convey messages to others.

Conclusion

These are some of the ways, then, in which memory gets concret-ized in the landscape. The appointment of committees, lengthy meetings, public spats, the press, and behind-the-scenes coalitions all leave their mark on the surface of the city. Both plaques and larger memorial sites constitute a form of collective memory refracted through bureaucratic and political processes, the work of activists and historians, and the actions of passersby, who may steal plaques, ignore them, vandalize them, place flow-ers on them, read them closely, or hide them in their basements. Plaques are clearly less permanent and far more subject to issues of private proper-ty and the opinions of a few than larger memorial sites. Still, the dramat-ic changes in economic and political structure have not produced equally dramatic changes in the memorial landscape of the city, as most pre-1989 memorial objects commemorating resistance to or persecution by the Nazi regime remain in place.

These sites have weathered at least two storms—the change in gov-ernment (and attendant shift in the ideological representations of the Nazi past) and a shift from communal, state-owned property (*Volkseigentum*) to private property. The ideological and political apparatus that supported the construction of these sites in East Berlin collapsed nearly overnight, and the pressures on the land changed dramatically over a matter of months, particularly in the center of the city, where many of these mark-ers are located. Neither a real estate market nor political delegitimation has led to the disappearance of most of these sites. At the same time, memo-rial landscapes are heterogeneous, and just because a given memorial or plaque remains in place does not necessarily mean that it occupies a prom-inent place on the calendar of public events or in the historical awareness of passersby. These sites are adapted, altered, reused, modified, updated, and renovated by a diverse array of groups and individuals, working in conjunction with officials (elected and otherwise). Some of these sites take on new meaning and new uses, and some are modified the better to suit contemporary memorial culture. Some are altered physically, have other elements of memory or ceremony added to them, or are incorporated into new memorial practices.

Much of this memory is also rooted in places where it is consonant with existing uses. Memory finds its niche in a way that is overdetermined by existing land use and ownership. A general lesson from all of these sites is that land can, and does, become infused with meaning. This is a social and linguistic process with material consequences that help these sites to remain off the real estate market despite skyrocketing property values. Turning any of the existing sites into real estate—developing them into shops, offices, or condominiums, or even government buildings—appears to be out of the question. But being located on undesirable pieces of real estate and plots of land already legally construed as open space also helps to keep these spaces off the market and laden with particular elements of the past. Existing land-use regulations also greatly hinder the development of many of these sites. In other words, most of these markers were placed on public land, in parks, cemeteries, traffic medians, public squares, or other kinds of spaces that, for a variety of reasons, were unlikely to become commercial, residential, or governmental construction sites after 1989.

One of these sites actually has become the subject of extensive controversy—the memorial ensemble in Köpenick (these sites are discussed in Chapter 5, as well, because they concern "wild" concentration camps and *Folterkeller*). The memorial, including a large stone fist with a socialist realist bas-relief behind it, is on public land, and set in a park, but it is the content and the symbolism that threaten the site, rather than any new demands for the land.[90] For many years, debate about the site ebbed and flowed. The solution proposed in 2004 was to surround the six-meter high fist with a transparent wall listing the names of the victims, as well as the history of the monument itself. Some who see the fist as a symbol of the SED argue for its demolition, while others want to leave it in place, while adding further commentary to it. As in so many other cases in Berlin, the debate seems all but settled (as can be seen in newspaper articles declaring that a compromise has been reached, only to be followed by an article proclaiming that the debate has begun all over again).[91]

But again, we should remember that few of these sites receive much attention from either tourists or residents. Certainly, many of these sites had begun to fade into obscurity long before 1989, a product of the indeterminacy of memorialization itself. We can ask the following questions of any memorial site: What are the intentions of its creators? Who is the audience? What are the consequences of a given site? Intentions, audiences, and consequences all change over time as well. A given marker may remain quietly unpublicized until someone tries to remove it, for example, at which point an individual or group may suddenly take up the cause and fight for it to stay. As James Young and others point out, "once created, memorials take on lives of their own."[92] Their creation is the subject of much supervision by artists, politicians, activists, and others. But in many cases, once they are built, this supervision falls away. Even without political and economic upheaval on a par with 1989, memorial sites do come in and out of public awareness, leaving us to wonder what this landscape of remembering and forgetting will look like once another generation or two has passed.

4

Changing Places:
New Memorials Since 1989

Once the Wall came down, the center of Berlin quickly became known (or at least advertised) as Europe's largest construction site.[1] New government buildings, corporate headquarters, and miles of underground tunnels for subways, trains, and roads were built. Whole new city quarters were constructed, and block after block of nineteenth-century tenements was converted into high-end apartments. The empty plain in the heart of the city, leveled by wartime bombing and postwar demolition, filled with massive construction sites that became tourist destinations in their own right. But other impulses were working to shape the cityscape as well in the 1990s. Alongside all of this other work, a host of people were engaged in producing memorial space marking resistance to and persecution by the Nazi regime, at times quite literally next door to governmental, commercial, and residential construction.

Figure 4.1 shows a particular juxtaposition of commercial development and memorial construction in the city. In the background stand the new buildings of Potsdamer Platz, a vast development, with offices, hotels, theatres, casinos, shopping centers, upscale apartments, and corporate headquarters now occupying a stretch of land that had lain vacant for decades. In the foreground lies the plot of land set aside for the Memorial for the Murdered Jews of Europe, the central Holocaust Memorial (Figure 4.1). This is a scene repeated on a smaller scale in recent years as people have continued to carve out new memorial spaces treating the city's Nazi past in the tumult of a nascent real estate market, a new political system, dramatic shifts in urban planning schemes, and the transformation of Berlin from a divided city into the capital of a unified Germany once again. Some projects are ambitiously central and the focus of international attention, while others are smaller and more modest, tucked into neighborhood streets, parks, or even the foyers of buildings. Thus while property values were fluctuating wildly and Berlin was being primed to be the capital of a unified Germany again, new memorial spaces appeared throughout the city. This public, material, official collective memory of the Nazi era occupies an important place in the project of transforming Berlin into the unified capital of a unified Germany.

FIGURE 4.1. The construction site of the Memorial for the Murdered Jews of Europe, with Potsdamer Platz in the background. Photograph by Jennifer Jordan.

It is one thing to leave in place memorial sites constructed by a fallen political system, as described in the previous chapter, most of which are located on land that is publicly owned and not likely to be developed. It is a very different process to carve out new memorial spaces amid rapid urban change. How, then, have these memorial sites actually come to be built? How does a particular moment in the history of a particular site materialize into a statue, an installation, a plaque, or a museum? And how have people gone about transforming seemingly anonymous spaces—whose history is remembered by eyewitnesses but by few others—into places of official remembrance, familiar to schoolchildren, tourists, and newspaper readers alike?

I turn in this chapter to five examples of new memorial construction in the eastern half of the city, where the new political and economic structures are felt with an obvious intensity.[2] Explaining the presence of such spaces in a city that has experienced such significant political and economic upheaval involves not only the memories themselves or the aesthetic form they may take, but also the land-use regulations and ownership patterns surrounding them. As Chapter 1 proposed, four elements in particular have shaped the process of memorial construction in unified Berlin: landownership, land use, the intervention of a memorial entrepreneur, and the resonance of the site with a broader public. Each example here highlights elements of these four factors, and the different ways in which they work to transform vacant lots and empty buildings into places vividly representing elements of the past. Nonetheless, the powerful events they recall—book-burning, protests, the hiding of friends and employees from the Gestapo—did not necessarily speak for themselves in the original sites without considerable work.[3]

Why, then, did *these* particular places become sites of official collective remembrance of the Nazi past? There are many reasons: because someone took up the cause, because land was available, because the land was publicly owned, because it could be politically difficult *not* to build a memorial at a certain point, because enough people supported its construction, because it resonated. This type of remembering is rarely a foregone conclusion, and while each memorial has followed a distinct path to completion, successful memorial projects do share some key elements. In the case of these new memorials, the actions of memorial entrepreneurs, coupled with land-use regulations and ownership patterns, successfully transformed these anonymous city lots into sites of concentrated collective memory, resonating at least with the relevant politicians and bureaucrats, and often with a broader public as well. Most land and buildings that become memorial sites follow similar trajectories, involving individual activism, political advocacy, and public resonance. Each factor alone is a necessary but not sufficient condition for transforming a building, square, or empty lot into a repository of widespread collective memory. The land has also become meaningful through the repetition of stories, the persistence of various groups and individuals, and now the presence of an array of interpretive materials retelling these stories. Furthermore, each case is very distinct, and, as James Young points out: "Memory is never shaped in a vacuum; the motives of memory are never pure. Both the reasons given for Holocaust memorials and the kinds of memory they generate are as various as the sites themselves."[4]

Over the course of the 1990s, the types of memorial construction prevalent in the West in the 1980s began to shape memorial practices in the eastern half of the city. Private property and a new set of urban planning visions coupled with new kinds of politics and media outlets to inaugurate a new era of memorial culture in the eastern half of the city. The democratization and decentralization of memorial practice (discussed at greater length in Chapter 2), as well as the heightened international attention being paid to the new German capital, significantly affected memorial processes in the 1990s. The role of the memorial entrepreneur, and of the resonance of a given proposal with a broader public, also grew significantly in the eastern half of the city in the 1990s (and had already been strong in the western half of the city in the 1980s). The physical work of clearing, casting, excavating, sculpting, and planting had to be done. Public meetings, letters to the editor, exhibits, and tours all serve to spread the word about the importance of preserving or modifying a given site. People have created these spaces and have made stones speak. But not all stones with stories actually do speak.

In recounting their emergence, I build on the analysis of specific sites in order to paint a broader theoretical portrait of the construction of memorials, and the crafting of a very particular kind of place in the urban landscape. Each of these sites went from being a vacant lot or empty room to being a full-fledged memorial site with state funding and public visibility. By observing these examples, it is possible to see the step-by-step process by which this occurs, and the central role played by factors not always associated with studies of collective memory and memorial work, questions of zoning, land use, and property relations, in conjunction with the more familiar elements of activists and powerful histories that come to resonate with broader publics. With a few exceptions, the memorial sites constructed after 1989 had a memorial entrepreneur. Frequently through the work of the memorial entrepreneurs, the sites treated here achieved enough resonance (sometimes simply with the local authorities, in other cases with an international public) to ensure their construction. Memorial entrepreneurs play a vital role in anchoring official collective memory in place, working in conjunction with the press, government bodies, educational institutions, and other actors. Their activities after 1989 also reflect a particular political and cultural moment. In less democratic settings, for example, when memorial culture is the domain of a single party or even a single leader, the memorial entrepreneur is far less important. Berlin's memorial entrepreneurs also help to shape understandings of official collective memory in the first place.[5] But (as discussed in Chapter 5 in greater detail) a memorial entrepreneur alone is not sufficient to ensure the success of a given memorial project. The examples treated here show that sites of official collective memory tend to arise, for a variety of reasons, on land that is publicly owned and that is not already being used in a way that is incompatible with memorialization.

Many of the places treated here are "authentic" locations—that is, places that were the actual sites of specific acts of heroism or cruelty in the Nazi era. The language of authenticity often proves to be a powerful argument for building a memorial, but, as Chapter 5 will demonstrate, it is not always powerful enough. Furthermore, despite the prevalence of a language of authenticity (in the press, among activists, researchers, preservationists, and educators), not all of the new sites are in "authentic" locations. Yet even these sites come to be treated as infused with a particular kind of official collective memory. A close look at these memorial projects thus yields important clues about the dynamics of memorialization, and about the contemporary construction of place. Each memorial object also has, for want of better terms, a prehistory and an afterlife (or simply a life—that is, its treatment following its construction and dedication), neither of which is very visible when simply looking at the memorial itself. Such places are dynamic, even when made of stone, bronze, or other seemingly permanent materials. The day of the dedication ceremony marks the end of this prehistory and the beginning of the memorial's active, material interaction with the urban landscape and the people who inhabit it.

This chapter turns, then, to the concrete processes by which people create such memorial places—the artistic visions, political debates, bureaucratic structures, and urban terrain that combine to create new memorial sites. Here I focus on the larger new memorials in the eastern half of the city in order to better understand the consequences of dramatic political and economic change for the memorial terrain of this half of the city. The examination of successful memorial projects undertaken here will also begin the process, continued in Chapter 5, of investigating why some sites become marked, while others fade into the cityscape. Berlin is a city full of places with difficult histories, but only some of them have become part of the official memorial landscape. These examples reveal some of the effort that it takes to turn a vacant plot of land into memorial space and help us to understand more clearly the juxtaposition of remembering and forgetting in the urban landscape.

Bebelplatz

On any given day, tour buses pull up alongside Berlin's Bebelplatz, a large, paved square, dropping off hundreds of pensioners, students, and other tourists. (Although the square dates from the middle of the eighteenth century, it received its current name in 1947 for one of the founders of the German Social Democrats, August Bebel [1840-1913].) A series of metal posts discreetly cordons off the square, leaving space for pedestrians but not cars, or tour buses, to pass through them. The tourists spill out into the square with their cameras, taking pictures of the Humboldt University across the street and the curious dome of the church at one corner of Bebelplatz. They find their way to the center of the square, toward a small glass panel set into the paving stones. People peer into this little window in the ground, take artful pictures of other people peering into it, and read the inscriptions on metal plaques set into the paving stones a few meters away. Clusters of tourists stand listening, with varying degrees of attention, to teachers and tour guides. Untold numbers of photographs of the square must end up in photo albums, across the country and across the globe. The square is also an outdoor space that people use as a shortcut to the university or as a place to enjoy the rare sun of a late winter day. Before 1995, however, few people would have stopped in the middle of the square, except to park their cars. (See Figures 4.2–4.3.)

Here, on May 10, 1933, "gangs of SA members and representatives of the 'German Students' group, celebrated or tolerated by a great crowd of people, rallied by marches [that had begun earlier in the day] and a speech by Goebbels, threw the books of numerous intellectually impressive authors into the flames of a gigantic pyre."[6] The initial event left no permanent mark in the landscape. The ashes were surely swept away at some point, either by the wind or by someone with a broom, and perhaps there was a charred spot on the square for a while afterward. At the time it was one event among many in the consolidation and intensification of Nazi power. After the war, no longer a site of fascist frenzy, the square became a public parking lot in the city center and the site of annual anti-fascist marches. Here, the façade of the Alte Bibliothek facing Bebelplatz looms above dozens of little Trabants, East Germany's primary car. In other words, decades passed in which this use of the square as a parking lot met with no lasting objections, and during which nothing marked the square's Nazi past or the

FIGURE 4.2. Bebelplatz. Photograph by Jennifer Jordan.

FIGURE 4.3. Bebelplatz. Photograph by Jennifer Jordan.

exact location of the fire. The fading of such locations into the landscape was common in both halves of postwar Germany. Without later interventions, many past events are illegible in the urban landscape for those who were not originally present. But at Bebelplatz and elsewhere, later interventions have occurred. Here the book-burning has emerged as a particularly significant event in the official memory of the Nazi era, both in the GDR and in a united Berlin, albeit with considerable effort.

The first official marker of the book-burning came in 1983, when the East German author Heinz Knobloch launched the first successful effort to permanently mark the site with a plaque mounted on the side of a neighboring building. The plaque, which remains there to this day, carries the following text: "In this square, the Nazi *Ungeist* [demonic or sacrilegious spirit] destroyed the best works of German and world literature. The fascist book-burning of May 10, 1933, is forever a warning, to be watchful against imperialism and war." As is the case with most memorial plaques, its presence reminded passersby of events that had transpired here but did not radically alter the use of the land itself. Indeed, life goes on around most memorial plaques. Larger memorial ensembles, on the other hand, frequently exert more influence on land use and on the kinds of activities that are appropriate on a given site. So, even when the East German authorities attached this plaque to a nearby building, the square continued to be used as a parking lot (Figure 4.4).

A few years later, in 1987, planning began for a larger monument to mark the site of the book-burning, one that would more extensively transform the use of the square. The suggestion came officially from the general secretary of the Central Committee of the Socialist Unity Party (SED).[7] The Council of Ministers of the GDR charged the Berlin magistracy with the task of choosing a "sculpture for a warning reminder of the fascist book-burning on May 10, 1933."[8] But the fall of the Wall significantly altered this plan. While the original plaque still hangs on a nearby building, the memorial that now occupies the center of the square differs distinctly from what the magistracy had originally envisioned.[9] Until the Wall fell, the East German government had planned to mark the square with an oversized heroic bronze figure intended to represent the socialist victory over fascism. The artist charged with the design of the memorial, the sculptor Siegfried Krepp, proposed the purchase of an Ernst Barlach sculpture, *Geistkämpfer*, "a sword-swinging human figure on an animal symbolizing the battle of the humanistic spirit against fascist barbarism."[10] The

FIGURE 4.4.   Bebelplatz, 1983. Photo: Landesarchiv Berlin.

meaning of the Barlach sculpture at Bebelplatz fell in line with the heroic anti-fascist narrative of the East German past. A bronze plaque measuring four meters across was also to be set in the ground on the precise site of the blaze, evidence of the importance of geographical authenticity for the GDR authorities (Figure 4.4).

Members of the district leadership of the Communist Party, the League of Fine Artists of the GDR, the Town-Planning Office, and Humboldt University all attended the meeting to plan the monument. They agreed that Siegfried Krepp should propose a statue near the existing memorial plaque, and they set a deadline, concluding that "there is unanimous agreement that the design of the monument should take place before the fortieth anniversary of the founding of the GDR on October 7, 1989." They also concluded that "pursuant to the monument regulations agreed on by the secretary of the Central Committee of the SED, this monument design should, in our view, be ranked as a monument of national significance," and thus overseen by national rather than local officials. Records credit the president of the Writer's League of the GDR (Schriftstellerverband der DDR), Hermann Kant, with the proposal, which also found agreement in the highest echelons of the Communist Party.[11] The funding for the project was to come from the budget of the Berlin magistracy (that is, the city). The Office for Architecture-Related Art in Berlin was supposed to purchase the statue for 1.5 million marks from Barlach's heirs, and the project was to be completed in 1990.[12]

Then, in the midst of these negotiations, on November 9, 1989, the East German government collapsed, and the existing plans for the square were quickly called into question. The figure was cast and purchased, the contract for the statue was actually signed in April 1990, and money did change hands.[13] But because the Wall fell before completion of the ensemble, it was never installed in the square. Instead, the statue ended up in the garden of the Gethsemanekirche in the eastern district of Prenzlauer Berg, marking a site of anti-government protests in the fall of 1989.[14] The aesthetics of the heroic bronze figure no longer fit in with the dominant aesthetic and historical approach to the city's Nazi past, particularly in such a prominent location and with regard to the book-burning. As with other memorial sites in the wake of the events of November 1989, little happened in the first years after unification. In 1992, the Berlin Senate began to develop a new plan for the site. While it

had scrapped the initial proposal, the government of united Berlin agreed
that some kind of monument should indeed be constructed on Bebelplatz. The Senate Committee for Cultural Affairs decided on September
21, 1992, that there was indeed "a need to commemorate the historical
event of the book-burning with a monument," but added: "The question
remains controversial, however, as to whether it would be appropriate to
place Ernst Barlach's sculpture *Geistkämpfer,* purchased under the GDR
[*zu DDR-Zeiten*], in the authentic location [Bebelplatz]. . . . [Indeed this]
would not do justice to the events of sixty years ago."[15] This emphasis on
the "authentic location" is a frequent refrain in discussions of memorialization both after 1989 and in some pre-1989 instances as well.

In April 1993, on the sixtieth anniversary of the book-burning, the
Senate and the district government of Mitte announced a competition for
a new memorial. Clearly, anniversaries repeatedly serve as memory flash-
points, and the Senate also asserted that "the goal of the competition is to
set an authentic sign of warning and remembrance of the book-burning
of 1933 on the historical location, what is now Bebelplatz."[16] The Senate
was well aware of the international visibility of the site, and of the opportunity to use it as a public and highly visible place to explicitly confront
Germany's Nazi past. It also saw this monument as an important statement against xenophobia at a time when there were increasing numbers of
attacks on foreigners in Berlin and throughout both halves of Germany.[17]
Finding the appropriate aesthetic representation to be placed on what the
Senate saw as an authentic site thus constituted a moral project embedded
in the urban landscape.

Over the course of the 1990s, parking came to seem increasingly inappropriate on such a site, even though it had been accepted for decades. One
of the artists who submitted a design for the 1993 competition, who spent
some time working on it seated on the actual site of the book-burning in
one of the parking spaces on Bebelplatz, declared: "French tourists recognized immediately that this place could be viewed with a special attention . . . [but German] drivers . . . were only interested in the parking
space I was blocking in the square! What the square needs most is a liberation from parked cars. . . . Here, cars displace access to history."[18] He did
not win the competition, but he was not alone in his feelings that parked
cars were intruding on a space whose past took from it the right to be a
mundane element of the urban landscape, and in 1993, the Senate decided

that "the current parking spaces are no longer acceptable in this context."[19] Around the same time, the Mitte city council also discussed eliminating parking from Bebelplatz.[20] Nothing had changed about the site physically or historically, but the context had changed significantly, and the idea of a memorial was resonating with a growing portion of the public and their political representatives.

In part in response to these changing conditions, work continued in the effort to find the proper aesthetic form for this square. The jury met in September 1993 and voted to approve Israeli artist Micha Ullmann's entry. The memorial would cost DM 450,000, according to the motion signed January 21, 1994. Ullmann opted for what he called a "nonsculptural solution" to the task set before him by the Senate,[21] and there is now a small square of glass set into the Bebelplatz cobblestones, revealing an underground room painted white and lined with empty shelves.[22] The artist described his work in the following way:

The work is composed of a subterranean, hermetically sealed room in the middle of Bebelplatz. It represents a library, whose walls are covered in shelves of white-plastered concrete. Twenty thousand books would fit here. . . . Einstein formulated that energy is matter times the square of the speed of light, or the opposite—matter (books) in connection with light (fire) is transformed into energy. . . . Only the spirit of the books and the people remains; they meet each other in the heavens (reflection).[23]

The winning entry fit the prevailing turn toward conceptual, rather than directly representational, monuments that had been developing in West Berlin in the 1980s (and indeed throughout the world).[24] The cornerstone was laid in July 1994, in a ceremony attended by Ullmann and state-level officials, including Culture Minister Ulrich Roloff-Momin and Building Minister Wolfgang Nagel, among others. Construction was finally completed in March 1995.

Such dedication ceremonies mark a divide between the prehistory of a memorial, and its transition into a living, dynamic component of the urban environment. Artistic visions and political intentions now face the weather, pedestrians, pollution, vandals, pigeons, street cleaners, and all of the other wear and tear of urban life. Two months after work on the Bebelplatz memorial was completed, the Mitte district council passed a measure expressing concern about the durability of the glass, as well as the lack of any informational signs to explain the underground library.[25] Because the glass is simply set into the ground, visitors were walking across it (as they were supposed to do—there was no intention of cordoning this space off from pedestrians). The glass grew increasingly scratched, so that it became difficult to see into the underground library. The district council also worried that the memorial site did not provide visitors with enough information to interpret the meaning of the library—a relatively common problem with conceptual monuments. Indeed, a variety of people were expressing such concerns before construction was even completed. Writing in the daily newspaper *Tagesspiegel,* Thomas Hahn (at the time a researcher with the Pedagogical Museum) insisted that "the observer must be helped to recognize the historical event in the first place," arguing that the underground library as originally proposed sorely lacked the necessary historical information to ensure that it would have the intended pedagogical consequences. He went on to proclaim it a "shame difficult to bear" that the authors, whose works were burned in 1933, and only partially "rehabilitated" after 1945, "would be humiliated a third time by not once in 1994 being allowed to be named in the area around the memorial devoted to them."[26] Bronze plaques were eventually set into the cobblestones a respectful distance away from the underground library to provide visitors with additional information about what they were seeing, including one bearing an eerily prescient line by Heinrich Heine, written in 1820: "That was merely a prelude; where books are burned, there in the end people will also be burned" ("Das war ein Vorspiel nur, dort wo man Bücher verbrennt, verbrennt man am Ende auch Menschen").[27]

All of this back and forth is a part of the afterlife of a memorial, when artists and administrators discover how the site actually works in space, and specifically how the public interacts with it. Thus, after complaints began coming in, the Senate modified the site with bronze plaques and more resilient glass, and the Bebelplatz memorial is now literally set in stone, a regular stop on the itineraries of tourists and school groups and in the memorial landscape of the city.

A significant controversy did emerge around the site, however, before construction crews even broke ground. In May 1994, shortly before construction of the monument was to begin, the director of the neighboring state opera house (Staatsoper) announced his intentions to build a parking garage underneath Bebelplatz, and thus objected to the construction of the monument.[28] The issue quickly took on a political hue, in part because the Free Democrats (FDP) asked the Senate to postpone construction until a decision about the parking garage had been made. "Does every bit of practical politics in Berlin have to turn into an ideological dispute?" one FDP official demanded.[29] Newspapers almost annually proclaimed that parking would be available the following year, and for a range of reasons (primarily how to pay for the expensive underground garage), the delays continued for years. Ullmann himself saw the prospect of a parking garage underneath the square "dishonoring" the memorial and "making [it] banal."[30] But in the end, the garage was built, opened in December 2004, and now offers space for over 450 cars.[31] During construction, the memorial was swathed in fences and black plastic, amid a sea of cranes, and the garage was built around it. Once the work was completed, the old paving stones were returned to the square. But Ullmann saw the "symbolism of his work disturbed" by the construction process. "In the view of the artist, the Berlin Senate lacks respect for this 'crime scene of 1933,'" reporter Ingeborg Ruthe noted. "How, then, can one create a peaceful coexistence between reminding [*mahnen*] and parking?"[32] The long-term effects of the new parking garage on the atmosphere of the memorial remain to be seen. Will it regain its necessary "emptiness and quiet," in Ullmann's words? Or will the incursion dilute the message of his empty library for the crowds of people who peer into it day after day?

Thus there is an interplay of permanence and change, as the site becomes irrevocable in some respects—ensconced, funded, politically viable, and officially acknowledged—but the city around it (and below it) changes. Once a monument is erected, even with some persistent controversy, it is in many ways a given, written into the landscape through legislation, funding, and tour guides, and an accepted element of the contemporary memorial landscape. But such places are also pieces of a larger urban fabric, alive and in flux. As fixed as this or any other memorial might feel to the observer, these sites of memory are dynamic. That is not to say that they are fluid, because that term belies the arduousness and solidity of the processes at work. But these memorials can be malleable, subject to change both through intentional actions and through the less intentional shifts in use, perception, and context that occur with the passage of time. What place will the Bebelplatz memorial occupy in the landscape of the city, and of collective memory, in thirty years, or sixty? For now, Bebelplatz and places like it do, however, anchor a particular element (and a particular interpretation) of the city's past in the landscape and in public awareness.

Koppenplatz

At Koppenplatz, a large square in the district of Mitte, children play at one end of the square, while at the other end sits an unusual bronze memorial. An oversized table and two oversized chairs perch on a bronze parquet floor. One of the bronze chairs has been tipped over, indicating haste or violence (Figure 4.5). The only text accompanying the memorial is a poem by Nelly Sachs, cast in the metal edges of the parquet floor, that begins "Oh, the houses of the dead . . ." No plaque announces the ensemble's meaning or origins. The memorial, erected in 1996, has not radically transformed the previous use of the land itself. The square has a long history of being an open, and even sacred, space in the city and of hosting both noncommercial and nonresidential uses. In 1705, the philanthropist Christian Koppe donated the land for a Christian cemetery for the poor, so that they could bury their dead within the city walls. In 1853, the cemetery was leveled, however, and a

FIGURE 4.5.   Koppenplatz. Photograph by Jennifer Jordan.

FIGURE 4.6. Koppenplatz, bunker construction by French prisoners, 1941. Photograph: Landesarchiv Berlin.

gasometer built on the site, and during World War II a bunker dug by forced laborers took up much of the square. In the early 1990s, the square was occupied only by a small, lackluster park and playground.[33] (See Figure 4.6.)

The monument that now stands on Koppenplatz was actually proposed and approved before the fall of the Wall. In 1988, the Berlin magistracy announced a competition for a small memorial in a neighborhood square in Mitte, in conjunction with the fiftieth anniversary of the 1938 pogroms. The call for proposals was officially titled a "Competition for a Monument Complex to Honor the Effects of Jewish Citizens in Berlin, to Remember their Persecution, and to Honor their Resistance."[34] According to Stefanie Endlich and Thomas Lutz, "it was the GDR's largest memorial project dedicated to Jewish citizens."[35] (In the same year the GDR also began the reconstruction of the New Synagogue on Oranienburger Straße). The magistracy asserted that "a monument complex should be dedicated to them all, the Jewish workers and clerks, the craftsmen, the intellectuals and the business people, artistically responding to the call to value and honor [them] in the designated urban space." In its attention to Jews and in the absence of any direct focus on anti-fascist resistance, the design of Koppenplatz differed significantly from other contemporaneous projects devoted to the effects of the Nazi regime. In July 1988, a magistracy committee met to settle on the details of this competition for a monument complex in "appreciation of the influence of Jewish citizens in Berlin and in memory of their persecution during Nazi rule." Originally, other sites were also considered, including Schendelgasse. The Koppenplatz location was justified as having an "important historical connection, because the center of the eastern Jews [*Ostjuden*] was once here." The committee asked that the monument conform artistically "to the established criteria of socialist realist art," yet it chose a surprisingly nontraditional entry.[36]

There was widespread interest in the competition, including 126 requests for the competition materials in 1988 and the first half of 1989. In July 1989, Karl Biedermann and Eva Butzmann won the competition, with a bronze sculpture ensemble that departed markedly from official East German aesthetics.[37] About his own work, Biedermann said, "the bronze sculpture is an appreciation of all Jewish citizens who lived and worked in Berlin over seven centuries. The sculpture should warn against the disregard of life and remind us of our humanistic heritage."[38] The committee awarded second prize to a proposal for a large Star of David, and third prize to a sphere with a large piece missing.[39] Both the second and third place entries were far more traditional than the winner. Given the official insistence of the East German authorities on socialist realist memorial aesthetics through the end of the 1980s, the chosen design was, perhaps surprisingly, in keeping with broader trends in memorialization at the time, particularly a turn to conceptual monuments that was also felt far beyond the borders of East Germany.

Unlike the pre-1989 plans for a sword-wielding figure in Bebelplatz, the pre-1989 design for Koppenplatz received widespread support in unified Berlin, and there was no substantive revision of the design after 1989. Aesthetically, it seemed to be in keeping with the sensibilities of the new unified Senate. However, while the design itself met with acceptance, after the fall of the Wall, the project stalled considerably. It was not clear in the early 1990s just who would pay for the monument and the park renovation. Money, rather than aesthetics, proved to be the primary obstacle to the completion of the Koppenplatz memorial, even though the land was already essentially vacant, and owned by the state. According to estimates from the district administration, the entire remodeling of Koppenplatz would cost two million marks, including 250,000 for the monument itself.[40] By March 1992, little had changed, and representatives of two different parties on the district council wanted to know why nothing had yet happened with Koppenplatz, despite the completion of the sculpture casting in the fall of the previous year. The Bündnis faction on the district council (a coalition that included the Greens and smaller, left-leaning parties) asked the council whether the memorial was even going to be realized, wondering "what is planned for Koppenplatz if the memorial ensemble is not going to be built?" Throughout the process there were tensions between the district council (Bezirksverordnetenversammlung, or BVV) and the Senate, a recurrent theme, not only in questions of memorial construction, with each expecting the other to shoulder financial responsibility for various projects in the district. This tension is especially acute in Mitte, where many of the memorials and much of the federal and state government are located. In May 1992, the same faction requested 2,250,000 DM to cover the costs of completion, arguing that "a further delay in the realization of the proposal for the design of Koppenplatz could give rise to many misinterpretations, which is the intention neither of the senate nor of the district."[41]

This concern about "misinterpretations" pervades discussions of sites dealing with the Nazi past, particularly with respect to how the international community viewed the reunited Germany and its reunited capital. Representatives in the state assembly (Abgeordnetenhaus) expressed similar concerns about the unseemliness of the delay in funding and construction. In the same year, a representative of the Christian Democrats asked whether the Senate felt that "a further delay in installing the already completed memorial was justifiable."[42] Clearly, the answer was no, yet delays continued, ascribed at least by the Senate to budgetary reasons. By 1994, Koppenplatz still consisted of nothing but, in one account, "old trees and a playground. And a boring field on the roof of a filled-up bunker."[43] Wolfgang Nagel, the Senate building minister, championed the construction of the memorial and promised the money for it from the Senate's coffers. The sculpture itself was finally dedicated on September 27, 1996, more than seven years after its initial approval by the East Berlin magistracy.[44] The activity surrounding Koppenplatz after 1989, then, was not about the design, but about generating sufficient political momentum and, in particular, finding funds in a new political and economic climate. These efforts succeeded—

in part because the meaning and aesthetics resonated with politicians and journalists (motivated by various factors, whether an interest in the history of the neighborhood or a fear of the kind of public embarrassment mentioned above), and in part because there were no conflicting uses of the land and the state already owned the square.

In some respects, Koppenplatz is not an "authentic" site per se but, like the Bayerisches Viertel in western Berlin (where two artists mounted signs on lampposts throughout a neighborhood printed with the laws that had systematically stripped Jews of their rights in the 1930s), it is tucked into a neighborhood, anchoring one element of a broader narrative of the Nazi past in the midst of the daily life of the city.[45] Like other projects in the West in the 1980s, and throughout Berlin in the 1990s, the Koppenplatz monument attempts to insert a reminder of the Nazi past—and here specifically the treatment of Jews—into an ordinary cityscape, recalling the lives lost right in the neighborhood. The Koppenplatz project inserted a story into public space, and thus became a potential (if not inevitable) node in a network of memories, reminders, and warnings. Like the next site to be discussed, Rosenstraße, the Koppenplatz memorial was built in an existing open urban space, so the transformation of land use in the wake of the memorial's construction was not as dramatic as it was at Bebelplatz or the Holocaust Memorial. Meaning was added to the site, but the basic land use was not dramatically altered. The case of Koppenplatz demonstrates the cementing of collective memory, but in a place that has been open space for hundreds of years. There is relatively little controversy, no obvious memorial entrepreneur, and no conflicting use. The aesthetics of the memorial are evocative and mournful, but not jarring. Turning this patch of park into a memorial still required years of planning and discussion, the outlay of public funds before and after 1989, and the agreement not only of the East German government but also of the democratically elected post-1989 Berlin governments.

As in the case of Bebelplatz and any other memorial, however, the story does not end at the dedication ceremony. The bronze statuary is now a part of the fabric of the city, with ensuing consequences. To begin with, vandals regularly spraypaint the ensemble. Furthermore, passersby do not always know what is being marked. An intern at the Historical Preservation Office, for example, mistakenly referred to Koppenplatz as a memorial to Nelly Sachs, the poet whose text lines the bronze floor. Many artists, intellectuals, and activists prize Biedermann's more conceptual style, but it may not always accomplish its pedagogical or moral goal. Many who know the ensemble's background find it stirring, but it is also not explicitly pedagogical. It is possible to walk past this outdoor "room" without reading in it the message intended by the artist and the various government offices supporting the memorial's construction. Passersby do not always easily interpret the memorial, and (unlike Bebelplatz, for example, or the Topography of Terror) the site is just off the well-trodden tourist paths. Koppenplatz reminds us that there can be discrepancies between the intentions and the outcomes of memorial construction. In this case, a public gesture, sanctioned by authorities and activists alike, is firmly ensconced in the urban landscape, but its success at communicating to residents and tourists can be difficult to judge.

Rosenstraße

Like Koppenplatz, the Rosenstraße memorial was also initiated under the East German government, but finally completed in the mid 1990s. The event it recalls is a protest that took place during the first week of March 1943. At this point, most Jews in Berlin had already been sent to concentration camps, but many Jewish men married to non-Jewish women remained in Berlin, as did their children. Most were forced laborers in munitions plants and other local factories. However, "in the first week of March 1943," writes local historian Gernot Jochheim, "hundreds of people, the vast majority women, protested day and night on Rosenstraße in Berlin-Mitte against the deportation of their Jewish spouses, children, and fiancés who were imprisoned in the former social administration buildings of the Jewish Community. This event, the so-called *Fabrik-Aktion* [factory action], began on February 27, 1943, and ended after a week on March 6, 1943, when the first prisoners were released."[46] The version of the story that inspired so much memorial activity (in which the protests of hundreds of women directly result in the men's release) has, however, been called into question, including by the historian Wolf Gruner in 2002. In early 1943, Goebbels ordered that the Jewish forced laborers remaining in the city be "deported"—sent to concentration camps-with the exception of the husbands and sons of non-Jewish women. According to Gruner, many of these male relatives were brought to a building on Rosenstraße formerly owned by the Jewish Community, where they were held until the deportations were over, after which they were to be reassigned to new forced labor posts. Götz Aly writes that "in fact approximately 150 Aryan wives protested against the arrest of their Jewish male relatives. Contrary to what was previously claimed, from the beginning the Gestapo had planned to release the approximately two thousand Jewish men in 'mixed marriages.' That does not diminish the courage of these women."[47] In a newspaper piece in response to Margarethe von Trotta's film *Rosenstraße* (2003), and in light of Gruner's findings, Wolfgang Benz writes

What really happened? In the *Fabrik-Aktion* at the end of February 1943, all of the Jews still living in the German Reich were arrested, with the intention of deporting them. Some of the German Jews were in "mixed marriages" with non-Jews. This group was detained in Rosenstraße, in the middle of Berlin. The women gathered in the street in front of the building, held out for days, fought for the freedom of their relatives, grew loud and refused to be driven away. They could not know that the men in the Rosenstraße were not meant for the concentration camps, but rather to replace others in specific jobs. This does not detract from the women's heroism, their admirable courage, the aura of the unconditional resistance of the weakest against the most monstrous regime.[48]

But the story that inspired most of the efforts to mark the site does not fit with Gruner's. The stories attached to places must be understood in part as the result of this push and pull of archival research, personal memory, and the lives that stories themselves seem to take on over time.[49]

For more than fifty years nothing marked the site. American and English bombs damaged the buildings at Rosenstraße 2–4 and Heidereutergasse during the war, but did not level them. The buildings were later torn down, leaving a vacant lot, which was eventually surrounded by highrise 1970s apartment blocks, which loom now on two sides of the small green plot of land where the buildings once stood.[50] But by 1995, things had changed, and this unique uprising had been officially marked in the cityscape. Today, the apartment building still casts its shadow over this small patch of grass, but now three large blocks of red porphyry statuary, carved in relief with various symbolic and narrative images indicating separation, resistance, courage, and other elements of the protest in 1943, stand not far from the dumpsters and delivery area at the back of the building. The only text on the sculpture reads: "The strength of civil disobedience, the strength of love vanquish the violence of the dictatorship."[51] A glass plaque hangs on a nearby structure, and two thick information columns display documents from Nazi offices and photographs of the street before the war. The foyer of a nearby hotel houses a small exhibition, with a stack of books about the history of the street for sale at the front desk. What caused this change? And why isn't this lot also a new office building or hotel, given its location in the city center? (See Figures 4.7–4.8.)

In early summer 1989, Dieter Klein, director of the Büro für architekturbezogene Kunst (Office for Architecture-Related Art) in East Berlin, wrote to the Ministry of Culture, saying that, since the previous year, the artist Ingeborg Hunzinger had been suggesting the idea of a monument "to remember and warn about the persecution and deportation of Jewish

FIGURE 4.7. Rosenstraße, with Ingeborg Huntzinger's sculptures. Photograph by Jennifer Jordan.

fellow citizens [*Mitbürger*] in Berlin during the time of fascism. . . . This event [the Rosenstraße women's protest] is assessed by the Jewish Community as particularly worthy of remembrance."[52] He suggested 1993, the fiftieth anniversary of the protest, as a possible completion date and supported the efforts of Hunzinger, who had planned and nearly completed an ensemble of sculptures intended to be placed on this vacant lot. This was a case where the original building was gone, but placing the memorial on the original (authentic) site was nonetheless important to its supporters. Even without the original structure, the artist and other advocates felt that this site was well suited to convey the story of what had happened there. As awareness of the site grew, the absence of a memorial seemed increasingly inappropriate. In a book of walking tours published in 1991,

FIGURE 4.8. Rosenstraße, with Ingeborg Huntzinger's sculptures. Photograph by Jennifer Jordan.

the description of Rosenstraße bemoaned the absence, not only of any plaque or statue marking the site of the protest in 1943, but also of any mention of this event in the histories of resistance to the Nazis.[53] In 1992, the reporter Ute Frings described Rosenstraße in the daily *Berliner Zeitung:* "In the landscape of the capital, Rosenstraße is a meaningless place. . . . While streets, buildings, and speeches recall the resistance of the Prussian elite, the uprising of these women is only a footnote for historians and not even worth a plaque to the city leaders."[54] Another account described this site in the mid 1990s in the following way:

Once a lively street, Rosenstraße is now cut off by the brutal construction along Karl-Liebknecht-Straße and has declined into a backyard situation. . . . [It is] an area in the heart of the city that misguided city planning has turned into a desolate dead end, with shabby sidewalks, broken benches, and trash and debris on a useless patch of green—an unworthy state of affairs for a place where Berlin's oldest synagogue once stood on Heidereutergasse, and the Community house on Rosenstraße 2–4.[55]

As with many of the other sites discussed in this chapter, the process of memorial construction stalled in 1989. Somewhat surprisingly, given the utter transformation of the economic and political arenas, the memorial was nevertheless constructed just as Hunzinger had originally envisioned it. But its completion was by no means inevitable. Years of discussion, planning, budgetary wrangling, and political negotiation were required before it was finally dedicated in 1995. One of the catalysts that renewed public interest in a memorial on this site appeared in 1992, at which point the lot was still vacant. To mark the anniversary of the protests that had occurred in this street nearly fifty years earlier, students of the Social Work College docent Gerhard Schumm erected a *Litfaßsäule,* or informational column, in front of the site, documenting the protest and the events leading up to it (according to the prevailing interpretations of the archival and oral history record at the time).[56] Traditionally, such columns have served as a place to hang movie or exhibition posters or other advertisements. The students took this familiar piece of urban furniture and turned it into a pedagogical vehicle. As other cases also demonstrate, the efforts of a group of students and their teachers can successfully anchor a given site in the city's memorial landscape. Students have time and incentive to engage in such projects and access to the skills and resources that can be helpful in memorial construction. At the same time that Schumm's students were busy with the columns, Hunzinger also continued to lobby for the construction of the memorial, and she and Schumm were thus two of the key memorial entrepreneurs for this memorial. As we have seen, Hunzinger herself pressed first the East German government and then the local and state governments of united Berlin to install the statuary on this site. She also continued work on the sculptures, completing them in August 1994, still unsure whether they would actually be installed.

One reason why it appeared the memorial might not be built is that the Jewish Claims Conference had placed a restitution claim on the land, which had previously been the property of Berlin's Jüdische Gemeinde. Unlike Bebelplatz or Koppenplatz, this site did not start out publicly owned. As of April 1994, it was still unclear what would become of the property itself, although it appeared likely that it would be restituted to the Jewish Claims Conference and then developed. In response to an inquiry from the Green Party in the state assembly, Building Minister Nagel said: "The Jewish Community intends, after its (not yet effectuated) restitution, to use the lot on Rosenstraße for its own building purposes. The Community only sees a monument in conjunction with such construction, which would conflict with the wishes of the artist for a 'protected' location."⁵⁷ On April 6, 1995, the Mitte district council requested that the district do all in its power to ensure that the planned memorial—"of citywide interest"— on Rosenstraße be built, arguing that "the meaning of the envisioned monument on the historic site is surely undisputed."⁵⁸ In addition to the historical meaning, the measure also pointed to the importance of green space here in the midst of the massive housing blocks along Spandauer and Karl-Liebknecht Straße. They also expressed concern that, if this lot were to be built up, the lower apartments in the existing building, which already received little sunshine, would then receive none. They urged the district to come to an agreement with the Jewish Claims Conference.⁵⁹ "The singular chance to preserve a significant monument [*Gedenkstätte*] of successful civil disobedience against Nazi barbarism, on the historical location in the middle of the city near the central Holocaust Monument, must not be thrown away."⁶⁰ The emphasis on the historical location—even in the absence of the original structures—is a familiar refrain in memorial projects, both in Berlin and elsewhere.

Six months later, in October 1995, the mayor and the vice mayor for health and environment finally responded. They reported that, although a contract had been signed in March 1994 between the district housing authority (WBM) and the district parks department (Natur- und Grünflächenamt), in the meantime, the Jewish Claims Conference had placed a claim on the land and expressed interested in using it for new construction. However, according to the city building code, the lot was technically an "unbuildable plot of the neighboring residential construction," and it would thus be transferred to the WBM.[61] Thus a compelling historical event was not sufficient in its own right to secure memorial status, but coupled with land-use principles and existing building codes (as well as behind-the-scenes negotiations in the city government impossible to uncover in the archival record), it was possible for those who supported the memorial to secure its construction.

Support for the monument also crossed party lines. Both the Christian Democrats (CDU) and the Democratic Socialists (PDS) pressed the mayor to expedite construction of the monument.[62] The district PDS wanted to know, in March 1995, "which position the district administration currently has, in light of the fact that in this densely built area, this lot is nearly the only green space, and therefore according to law must be secured as residential green space, and . . . that this has to do with the historical place that can be treated in a particular way by the monument?" The answer, in terms of the restitution claims, was quite simply that, according to the building code, the lot was not open to development. "The obvious interest in the utilization of the lot [for the restitution claimants, the Jewish Claims Conference] appeared to be linked to the possibility of construction."[63] In one of the political discussions concerning the memorial in April 1995, the PDS invoked the argument that not only was the monument "in its historical location . . . important beyond the borders of the city," but it was also a "small green oasis for the residents of" neighboring apartment buildings.[64] In the meantime, the district housing authority had been told by the district government "that the site will be designated as a residential green space and transferred to the district housing council."[65] On April 1, 1994, the lot was in fact transferred to the WBM. In 1995, the lot changed status, from public green space to green space with monument.[66] The argument about the need for green space prevailed, and the monument was dedicated on October 18, 1995. Several hundred people attended the ceremony, including Construction Minister Wolfgang Nagel, Roman Skoblo from the Jewish Community, and a handful of survivors who had participated in or been aided by the protests in 1943. Dedication ceremonies (in Berlin and elsewhere) can function as a kind of "consecration" of space. They are also one way of spreading public awareness and agreement about a site. The presence of high-ranking officials or well-known figures can prompt widespread press coverage as well, an integral part of spreading awareness of memorial landscapes.

The owner of an adjoining hotel and office building has also taken up the memory of the protest. Thanks to Germany's investment priority laws, the western investor Wolfgang Loock developed the building into a hotel and office complex.[67] Construction began in 1995, and the hotel opened in the summer of 1997. Loock has actively connected the hotel to its next-door neighbor in a number of ways. As noted above, an exhibition about the street itself, including the events in 1943, lines the foyer and a small book is for sale at the front desk detailing the street's history. Gernot Jochheim, author of this and other works about the Rosenstraße events, here tells us that, "the Hotel Alexanderplatz finds itself on a place where something unique in all of Germany happened during the Nazi era: here, in the heart of the imperial capital, in public view—hundreds of people protested . . . and the miraculous thing is, their protest succeeded" (again, the number of protesters is disputed in Gruner's article).[68] Recalling this version of the history of the street, from its role as site of the earliest synagogue in Berlin, to its rich manufacturing history, to the events of 1943 adds context to the hotel, and gives it an identity distinct from corporate chain hotels.

Loock also initiated a glass memorial plaque on one pillar of a new building erected between the hotel and the memorial site in September 1998. The president of the federal parliament, Rita Süssmuth, attended the dedication ceremony for the plaque, as did Ignatz Bubis, chairman of the Central Council of Jews in Germany, and eyewitnesses to the protests, including Hans-Oskar Löwenstein, who, at the age of eleven, was held in the building on Rosenstraße, and whose mother and grandmother demonstrated for his release.[69] Others present at the ceremony included Lea Rosh, the initiator of the campaign for a central Holocaust Memorial, and the district mayor. Such ceremonies serve to publicly assert the importance of a given site and to draw media attention to otherwise overlooked corners of the city. Newspaper coverage is a further step toward the inscription of such places in public memory. In every article concerning this monument, in both national and local newspapers, reporters recount the events of 1943 (including details that Gruner later called into question), quote eyewitnesses, and describe the proximity of this site to some of Berlin's most famous landmarks, including the television tower and Alexanderplatz. Such coverage both reflects and shapes popular understandings of these sites, and plays a central role in disseminating collective understandings of Berlin's memorial landscape (as well as making controversies public).

The collective meaning of this site, then, was significantly transformed in the course of the 1990s. An event that had gone unmarked for decades is now physically remembered in many different ways on this small street in the city center. The reasons for the success of the project certainly may be linked to the initial events themselves—the scale of the protest and the rare opportunity to tell a story of German resistance to the Nazis offer rich material for memorialization. In addition, the advocacy of a handful of people and the growing resonance of the meaning of the site drew in, not only those who had experienced the events of 1943 themselves and the artist proposing the monument, but also investors and international political figures. The fact that the lot was vacant and was designated as public green space also assisted in the success of the memorial project. The city was able to use the logic of *wohnungsnahe Grünfläche*—that is, preserving this small patch of green space in a densely built-up neighborhood—in order to keep the land from being developed. The value of public green space as a larger public good, as well as arguments concerning the authenticity of the site and its international resonance, helped to override development pressures and pave the way for the construction of a memorial.

Rosenstraße bears some similarity to Koppenplatz—it was initiated before 1989, finally completed (after some delay, and money problems, but without any aesthetic alterations to the original plan) in the mid 1990s, and built on a plot of land that was already vacant. Like Bebelplatz, Rosenstraße was for decades a site only of private memory (of survivors and of perpetrators) and a few historians. But through active memorial entrepreneurs, the resonance of the site with a broader public, and changes in ownership and existing land-use regulations, it became a place to remember collectively.

But the casual passerby also has to be somewhat attentive to really learn what happened on the site. On casual inspection, the statues might just seem like any public art, and from a distance the informational columns might just be assumed to hold the usual notices for upcoming concerts or movies. It is possible to walk past the figures without reading about the past of this site, and the information there in any case does not necessarily reflect the most recent research. This question of visibility and interpretation is an issue for many markers throughout the city, not only Rosenstraße and Koppenplatz. Before 2003, most Berliners I spoke to did not know the story of Rosenstraße unless they were actively involved in urban development and memorialization in Berlin.

The Holocaust Memorial

The central Holocaust Memorial, on the other hand, is known not only to Germans but in other countries as well. In January 2000, the *New York Times* reported on a dedication ceremony held at the site of the future Memorial for the Murdered Jews of Europe in the center of Berlin. "Most of the German government stood in icy winds beneath new billboards announcing the 'Memorial for the Murdered Jews of Europe' as Wolfgang Thierse, a Social Democrat from eastern Germany and the speaker of Parliament, explained that honor had to be accorded to the six million Jewish dead 'in the heart of our capital city.'"[70] A crowd of dignitaries, photographers, and police huddled beneath a temporary canopy that had been constructed in the northwest corner of the lot. The occasion was both the anniversary of the liberation of Auschwitz and the symbolic start of the construction of Germany's new central memorial for the murdered Jews of Europe.

A few days later, the canopy, the dignitaries, photographers, and police officers were gone, and the lot had returned to the same sandy state it had been in for nearly a decade. Today, of course, what had long been a controversial memorial is now completed and open to the public.[71] But how did a few scrubby acres shift from being an anonymous stretch of borderland, on the front lines of the Cold War, to a site fraught with so much of contemporary Germany's wrangling with its difficult past (and hopes for its future)? How did such symbolic weight come to be attached to this particular plot of land? And given that, in the mid 1990s, the massive construction sites of Potsdamer Platz and Leipziger Platz lay just beyond the memorial site, why is it that this lot was not also a sea of cranes and of slowly rising office buildings, shopping arcades, movie theaters, casinos, and high-end apartments?

Even on the day of this ceremony in 2000, "almost all [the] decisive questions" had yet to be settled.[72] Controversy surrounded nearly every step of creating the memorial. The intention of my analysis here is not to provide an exhaustive account of the debates about the memorial itself, as others have already done this.[73] The controversy surrounding the actual design for the memorial was extensive and is well documented. Rather, my intention is to highlight the contingency involved in the development of this memorial, and to emphasize what this project shares with other memorial projects of lesser renown. Specifically, the role of active memorial entrepreneurs and the eventual (but not immediate) resonance of the site with an international public distinctly resemble other successful memorial projects—as does the fact that its location on land that was vacant and owned by the government greatly increased its chances of being built.

The current site was not always the intended location of the memorial, and it was in fact still heavily patrolled no-man's-land between the two Berlins when public discussions of such a memorial first began in earnest. There were other potential locations, and it took some time for the current location to become cemented in public opinion and in the bureaucratic record as the future memorial site. In 1988, the citizens' initiative Perspektive Berlin e.V., headed by the television journalist Lea Rosh, first openly demanded a central memorial to the Holocaust. Her proposal was made public in the context of discussions about the fate of the Prinz-Albrecht-Gelände, the site of the former Gestapo headquarters.[74] James Young suggests that "the seeds of Germany's national Holocaust memorial were probably sown during President Ronald Reagan's disastrous wreath-laying visit . . . to the military cemetery in Bitburg, where the tombstones of Waffen S.S. soldiers lay side by side [with] those of Wehrmacht conscripts."[75] In part in the wake of this public relations fiasco, Rosh's proposal struck Chancellor Helmut Kohl and others as a way to create a central place to specifically acknowledge the Holocaust and the murder of European Jews during the Third Reich. Rosh was eventually able to secure "a promise from Chancellor Kohl of a hundred and forty million dollars' worth of Berlin real estate on which to build it—five acres of what was once a no-man's-land near the Brandenburg Gate . . . and is now the middle of town."[76] The granting of such a request does not happen out of the blue, however, but rather must result from extensive activity leading up to this point. Rosh has been a highly successful memorial entrepreneur, although it is also important to remember that memorial entrepreneurs differ dramatically in their motivations, their techniques, their interests (personal, professional, and otherwise), their expertise, and their approach to their work. Some, like Rosh, are media-savvy public figures themselves, while others toil in relative obscurity in the offices of neighborhood museums, or in their spare time after a long day of work.

The fall of the Wall opened up new possibilities for locations of the memorial and changed its political context as well. In the search for a new site, a wide range of suggestions was sent in to various government offices. In one case, an administrator from the district housing council, which administers the neighboring apartment buildings, offered a small patch of lawn in front of the complex's daycare center as a possible location for the memorial. This would have the advantage, according to the letter sent to the city council, of being "almost identical with the location of the former Reichskanzlei [Hitler's Chancellery] and the Führerbunker [Hitler's bunker]," and thus well suited to the purposes of the monument.[77] The district mayor and the city planning advisor responded in early 1992: "[S]uch a monument has citywide, national, and international relevance, so the preparation and coordination of the project is the responsibility of the Senate of Berlin. The city planning office of the district of Mitte points to the difficulty of finding an appropriate urban space on the suggested location, . . . because the land is occupied by apartment buildings and the Reichskanzlei and bunkers are neither architecturally nor materially in any way perceptible."[78]

An apparently more suitable location was found just south of the Brandenburg Gate, in the former no-man's-land. On June 2, 1992, the Senate decreed a competition for the memorial "in the area of the former Ministergärten."[79] Thus the location—in the form of a centrally located and state-owned vacant lot—was decided long before the actual shape of the memorial had been clarified. As Young writes, this lot was "bordered on one side by the 'Todesstreifen,' or 'death-strip,' at the foot of the Berlin wall, and on the other by the Tiergarten, the . . . site . . . was still a no-man's-land in its own right, slightly profaned by its proximity to Hitler's bunker and the Reichs Chancellery. But as almost five acres at the heart of a reunified capital, it would also become one of Berlin's most sought-after pieces of real estate."[80] The choice of this location (more than a decade of controversy notwithstanding) also has to do with the fact that the land itself was already categorized for low-density diplomatic construction (rather than high-density commercial construction, for example). One of the officials responsible for planning for the capital explained that the whole area was zoned for low-density diplomatic use. Because of its location between the green expanse of the Tiergarten (Berlin's equivalent of Central Park) and the densely built neighborhood of Friedrichstadt, the Ministergärten, including the memorial site, is intended to allow the fresh air of the Tiergarten into the dense city center. Indeed, this was part of the historical purpose of the Ministergärten. Demand for the land would actually be limited without a significant change to the city's land-use plan, so questions of land use clearly paved the way for memorial construction. Without changes to the city's land-use plan, this lot would not have been terribly saleable, given the relatively low demand for low-density diplomatic property. But construction of the memorial would not have occurred without the activities of a very visible memorial entrepreneur, Lea Rosh, and the profound resonance of the site, including the controversy, with a national and international public. The federal government, the state government, and Rosh's Förderkreis group, which sought a central memorial for Europe's murdered Jews, took joint control of the memorial design competition. Since that time, controversy over the actual shape of the memorial has raged, but the site itself has remained relatively fixed.

Were the dignitaries and reporters mentioned above standing on the site of an especially heinous atrocity or a place of remarkable heroism? No. The site is adjacent to the centers of Nazi power, but, unlike Bebelplatz or the "Blind Trust" exhibit, it has no direct, perceptible connection to the Nazi past. One critic found that "despite its proximity to political institutions, not being a historical site of the Holocaust it is unable to convey the authentic atmosphere of a memorial centre."[81] Authenticity also continued to be a prevalent theme in memorialization, and many people felt the central Holocaust Memorial diverted both funding and attention from "authentic" sites.[82] The debates about the monument also centered in part on whether it is possible, or even desirable, to use artistic means and a central (and inauthentic) site to memorialize the murdered Jews of Europe. Another early, and persistent, critique was that the exclusive attention to the murdered Jews of Europe excluded other persecuted groups, such as the Roma and Sinti.[83] Other controversies ranged from the departure of the artist Richard Serra from the project in 1998 to the use of an anti-graffiti spray on the final memorial that was manufactured by a company with ties to the makers of Zyklon B, used in the gas chambers.[84]

The actual shape of the memorial remained controversial, yet once this location was established there was no serious discussion of changing it. At the same time that the turn to conceptual monuments reflected a break with previous orthodoxy concerning the aesthetics, content, and siting of memorials, there also appears to be an unwritten limit to conceptual monuments as well. In Berlin in the 1980s and 1990s, many proposals were in fact rejected in part because they might be too disruptive to daily life or to central national symbols. A prime example was a suggestion for the central Holocaust Memorial that required grinding up the Brandenburg Gate. "The artist Horst Hoheisel proposed a simple, if also provocative, anti-solution to the [Holocaust Memorial] question: Blow up the Brandenburg Gate, grind its rubble into dust, scatter the remains over its former site, and cover the entire monument site with granite slabs. . . . Naturally such an intentional destruction could never be approved by the German parliament . . . and that too was a part of the artist's point."[85]

Throughout the planning process, many people involved have been acutely aware of the international visibility of the site. In 1994, in just one of many moments of controversy in the memorial's short history, there was discussion of reducing the area for the monument from 2 hectares to 1.2 hectares. In a motion proposed by the Social Democrats, the Mitte city council voted to do what it could to prevent this reduction, justifying the move in the following way: "In the construction planning for the area of the Ministergärten, the lot for the future Holocaust monument will have to be reduced from 2 hectares to 1.2 hectares for the benefit of the expansion of the gardens of the State Offices. That would be a scandal that would create an international sensation and would cast into doubt the credibility of the confrontation with the past [*Vergangenheitsbewältigung*] in Germany."[86] Thus local actors were acutely aware of the international audience for these few acres, and the stakes, in terms of Germany's international political legitimacy, were high. More than any other site discussed in this book, the Memorial for the Murdered Jews of Europe has captured public attention on an international scale. Public meetings, closed meetings, symposia, roundtables, international competitions, stacks of books, and countless numbers of newspaper articles have anchored this site in public (and international) awareness. One indicator of the visibility of this site is the plethora of published materials concerning its origins, the debate over the aesthetic form it would take, and the international political fall-out of these controversies. One activist group that maintains a clipping file on memorial issues in Berlin gave up on collecting all the relevant articles, since there was so much newspaper coverage of the debate over the memorial. James Young found the astonishing amount of debate about the memorial to be a kind of memorial in itself, and an important and beneficial result of the process, writing that, "in fact, the best German memorial to the Fascist era and its victims may not be a single memorial at all, but simply the never to be resolved debate over which kind of memory to preserve, how to do it, in whose name, and to what end. Instead of a fixed figure for memory, the debate itself—perpetually unresolved amid ever-changing conditions—might be enshrined."[87]

Just a few hundred meters away, gleaming new office buildings and shopping centers have shot out of the sandy soil of Potsdamer Platz since 1989. This square—really a former intersection—was essentially empty at the time the Wall fell, save for the Wall itself running along its eastern edge and a couple of buildings standing stranded among the weeds. In the first months after the Wall came down, suggestions poured in from investors, artists, and residents as to what to do with this vast empty space in the middle of the city, proposing everything from a new Autobahn to an open green space to affordable housing. Uncertainty about land use continued in the summer of 1990. The open expanses in the city center did not lie unused, however. A wide array of events took place on the former death strip, including circuses, a medieval village fair, the filming of a television game show, theater performances, and a meeting of the Volkswagen Bug Club (West Berlin).[88] Huyssen describes this area in the early 1990s in the following way: "For a couple of years, the very center of Berlin, the threshold between the Eastern and the Western parts of the city, was a seventeen-acre wasteland that extended from the Brandenburg Gate down to Potsdamer Platz and Leipziger Platz, a wide stretch of dirt, grass, and remnants of pavement under a big sky. . . . Berliners call it affectionately their 'wonderful city steppes,' their 'prairie of history.'"[89] In the end, this "prairie of history" was dedicated entirely to commercial development, now well patrolled by private security companies. At the dedication ceremony for the new Sony buildings, the mayor of Berlin, Christian Democrat Eber-hard Diepgen, gave a different spin to the site's past:

The wasteland in front of us is an ugly scar left over from the cold war, a tragic dis-play of the division of Germany. This segment of the death strip was once Europe's most heavily trafficked square. Before Potsdamer Platz, the dead heart of our city, fell into its dormant existence in the shadow of history, it had been an interface between east and west, a meeting place for Berliners and visitors from all over the world. . . . All of these are lost worlds. It cannot be our goal to reconstruct them, but we can be conscious of the fact that we are building upon historically fertile soil. This past can lend us wings as we set out to design our future.[90]

The investors were, of course, interested in the profitability of the space, but these interests were often discussed in a historical idiom, tapping into a positive, vibrant prewar urban tradition of entertainment, consumption, and administration.

Despite the intensity of development and the transformation of the city all around it, and despite years of uncertainty about the form the cen-tral Holocaust Memorial would eventually take, this plot of land so close

FIGURE 4.9. The Memorial for the Murdered Jews of Europe under construc-tion, 2004. Photograph by Jennifer Jordan.

to Potsdamer Platz and so much commercial development has in fact been devoted to exclusively memorial use. This former no-man's-land has been irrevocably infused with its role as the site for the monument for the murdered Jews of Europe, despite well over a decade of fierce debate (Figure 4.9). Now that construction is finally complete, it remains to be seen how the memorial will live in the city, change over time, be rejected or embraced, forgotten or reinvigorated.

"Blind Trust"

In light of the cases discussed in this chapter, I want to return to the "Blind Trust" exhibition discussed in Chapter 1. Like the other places treated here, the Blind Trust exhibition followed an uncertain path, but it seems to have succeeded in becoming a lasting element of Berlin's memorial landscape. How does a place like the site of the "Blind Trust" exhibition—forgotten by all but eyewitnesses for decades, and on a patch of potentially valuable real estate—become ensconced in public memory? To begin with, someone must be willing to argue on behalf of memorialization. There were (and are) active memorial entrepreneurs, working hard to ensure the permanence of the exhibit. In 1999, these efforts began to resonate with journalists, politicians, and growing portions of the public, thus securing (for now) the transformation of this site from a set of anonymous rooms to a locus of concentrated collective memory, and a place where nonmemorial uses are now difficult for many people to imagine. Somehow the thesis project of a handful of Berlin students—and the events and people it recalled—has captured the public imagination sufficiently to garner political, financial, and institutional support. But the property sits at one of the more valuable intersections of eastern Berlin. Throngs of tourists, shoppers, and movie- and theatergoers pass by every day, and the surrounding neighborhood has become one of the most popular destinations in the city.

Following a successful restitution claim, until its subsequent sale in 2004, this long, narrow building actually belonged to a group of more than two dozen heirs from three generations and scattered across five continents.[91] Because there were so many heirs, for many years no decision was made as to what to do with the building. The prolonged debate among the heirs themselves opened a window of opportunity for the meaning of the exhibition to become rooted in the building. In addition, if the rooms had already been in use as offices, for example, it is unlikely that claims about the significance of the site would have been strong enough to evict the office workers and put a museum in their stead. However, not only was there no conflicting use, but the vacant status of the rooms lent strength to arguments about the authenticity of the site, since these rooms had been essentially untouched since the end of World War II.

As discussed in the first chapter of this book, in the 1930s and early 1940s, these rooms had housed a small brush manufacturing company run by a German named Otto Weidt. One account describes the history of the building in the following way:

In the side wing was the brush factory of Otto Weidt, who provided protection from deportation to blind Jewish forced laborers through employment, and who, with a rare civil courage, successfully attempted to protect them from daily persecution and annihilation. After a long silence, a memorial plaque now recalls the inspiring story of a non-Jewish hero of everyday life. He helped at least fifty-six Jews, and twenty-seven survived thanks to his deeds.[92]

Much of the memory shaping the landscape of Berlin is not the recollection of eyewitnesses but the work of historians, activists, and politicians. In the case of the "Blind Trust" exhibit, however, an eyewitness has been directly involved in the creation of a memorial site. Inge Deutschkron was a key figure in bringing these rooms to public light, in conjunction with other actors. A few years after her successful efforts to secure a memorial plaque, work on an exhibition began. Initial impetus for the exhibition itself came in large part from Helen Adkins, an artist who runs a gallery and workshop in another wing of the building. She suggested the exhibition to students looking for their final project in a course on museum studies. The students contacted Deutschkron and began work. The exhibition was originally funded in part by the Neue Synagoge Berlin—Centrum Judaicum foundation, the Blind Assistance Project, the Museum of German Resistance, and the Schwarzenberg e.V. Berlin organization. It was extended beyond its first four weeks, until it was finally taken over as an official annex of Berlin's Jewish Museum. The building is now also partially protected under historic preservation laws, in part because of its connection to Otto Weidt. The authenticity of the site also played an important role in the students' interest in establishing an exhibition here. In 1976, for example, the district construction authorities concluded that this wing of the building was so dilapidated that renovation would be too expensive and recommended against any alteration of the building (and thus against renovating the rooms to a point where they might be habitable).[93]

The Blind Trust example makes clear how, step by step, accounts of the past become attached to places in ways that can profoundly shape their subsequent use. As noted in Chapter 1, one evening during the first month of the exhibit, Inge Deutschkron read from her book *Heroes* to a crowd of three dozen people, seated on folding chairs set up in two of the exhibition rooms. She read about the people who had worked in these rooms where the audience sat. After she had finished reading and the applause had died down, there was a flurry of questions from the audience, which made it clear that many of them had just had an experience that made these rooms real in a whole new way. A refrain that continued in the audience's comments for the next half hour concerned the authenticity of the site and the importance of preserving it. People's emotional reactions to Deutschkron's story and to the rooms quickly turned into a rapid discussion of what to do next. "What does the Senate think?" "Has Michael Naumann [the federal minister of culture at the time] been here yet?" "Someone should make a film . . . " Most of the question-and-answer session became brainstorming about how to turn this temporary exhibition into a permanent exhibition.

On a smaller scale, this brainstorming was going on a few weeks earlier after the breakfast attended by Deutschkron, Hobrack, and other people who worked for the marking of the site, and in countless gatherings afterward. That night was just one of many steps in the transformation of the meaning and use of these rooms, but it vividly demonstrates the way that talking about places in particular ways can dramatically, and seemingly irrevocably, change their meaning, and their use. The meaning and use of a place (a plot of land, a set of rooms, or any other site) *can be* (but are never destined to be) dramatically altered if an episode out of its past is attached to it in a powerful way, and in a way that resonates with a sufficiently broad base of people. For now, the status of the rooms of the Blind Trust exhibition as an official site of collective memory does seem to be secure. "Public action," in Rudy Koshar's terms, has invested these rooms with widely resonant meanings, and transformed their use.

The question has long been whether the interests in preserving the spaces are more powerful than the heirs' interests in developing these rooms into a more profitable venture than a small museum. Would newspaper articles, letters, personal visits, and pleas to the federal government succeed in keeping these rooms a memorial? Would it eventually be simply a matter of raising enough money to purchase or lease the rooms from the heirs or the corporation they sell to? Would the authenticity and resonance of the site help to guarantee its status as a museum, and as a site of concentrated collective memory? In the meantime, the neighborhood has changed dramatically as well, so that Rosenthaler Straße 39 is now one of the only remaining unrenovated buildings in the area. The crumbling façade is a stark contrast to the Starbuck's next door, and most of the rents in surrounding buildings would be unaffordable for the diverse array of artists inhabiting the building.

Around the exhibit, the artists inhabiting the mazelike building grew into an organized group, Haus Schwarzenberg e.V., fighting against the prospect of being evicted from their affordable space in the city center. Thus an entirely new controversy surrounding ownership of the site emerged in 2003. The building was finally to be auctioned off, with an estimated value of €3.4 million (if that price seems low for such a large building in such a prime location, it is important to remember that it has not been significantly renovated since at least the 1930s). The current renters, members of the Schwarzenberg e.V. group, launched a campaign to purchase the building themselves and to continue to use it for affordable artists' studios and other cultural projects, rather than having "a commercial investor renovate into oblivion this window on Berlin history." They are pushing not only for the preservation of the Blind Trust exhibit, but also, as they point out, "2,684 square meters of history, culture, and art . . . 8 years of financial self-sufficiency and cultural production without subsidies, 120 jobs." They also hope to maintain it as much as possible in its current state of decay, as "the building is the only remaining structure in [the neighborhood, Spandauer Vorstadt] that still shows traces of the 1930s and 1940s, as well as the state of decay AND conservation of the building's structure in East Germany, as well as traces of the post-1989 era . . . the building is a picture book of the history of the Spandauer Vorstadt."[94] After much back and forth, it appears that the building was successfully bid on by the district housing authority in 2005, and that the current occupants (including the exhibit) will remain where they are.[95]

Conclusion

Authentic and "inauthentic" sites with ties to the Nazi past became marked in the 1990s, even as the real estate market took off and the city launched a massive spate of commercial, residential, and governmental building. Although the new economic system means that land in the city center became extremely valuable, there was an increase in the amount of land devoted to memorializing, and existing memorials have not been turned into real estate. Theoretically, planning and market pressure might create less space for memorialization in an increasingly crowded field of real estate and urban development. However, precisely in the post-1989 era, new memorials are created and more urban land has been devoted to collective memory, in ways that are arguably a part of "building" a united Germany. The acknowledgement of elements of the Nazi past in the urban landscape became integral to urban development and to the political project of unification in the 1990s. Unification takes place in part on a bedrock of memorial sites treating the Nazi past.

But these new projects also frequently fit into the developing grid of the city, the ordering of private property, urban planning, and development that shapes so much of the urban landscape. Most new memorials fit into existing patterns of ownership and existing patterns of urban planning and land use. Memory has material consequences, but these consequences are often circumscribed by other concerns. Much of this particular form of collective remembering very often takes place on land owned by the state, and often on land zoned as urban green space. Memory does place limits on the market and on the reaches of urban planning, but the market and planning also place significant limits on memory, or, more precisely, the material manifestations of collective memory. No existing building has been torn down for a new memorial, no matter what has happened on the site. Privately owned sites are largely out of the running as full-blown memorial sites, no matter what occurred on them, as neither the state nor nonprofit organizations appear willing, or able, to buy the land or building from its owner and devote it to a purely memorial use.[96] In other words, in Berlin, memorials are far more likely to appear on public property than on private property.

Official collective memory emerges not of its own accord but through actions and practices of the kinds described here. This type of remembering is rarely a foregone conclusion. Such memorials result from lengthy and often arduous negotiations involving residents, activists, multiple levels of elected and appointed government officials, survivors, the press, and in many cases a larger international public of survivors, artists, and even newspaper readers. The efforts of memorial entrepreneurs must be filtered through the government, and in almost all cases examined here, there are local, national, and international interests at stake. The actions of district, state, and federal government bodies in Berlin (interacting with activists, artists, survivors, academics, and others) define and encourage the attachment of these kinds of meanings to plots of land and buildings, or parts of buildings. Here collective memory—if this is how we are to understand the uneven terrain of Berlin's memorial landscape—is thus not the precise sum of individual attitudes at any given point, but rather the set of institutions that enable the group to mobilize to recall the past, or the institutions on which the collective's most engaged agents of memory base their work. The physical markers discussed here comprise one result of the activities of such agents. Furthermore, once constructed, many then augment ongoing memory work, bolstering networks of activists and circuits of school tours, for example.

New memorials are generated in part by public discussion, and by often arduous bureaucratic processes. But they tend to hide their origins in the smooth surface of the finished memorial. There is rarely any sign in the bronze, stone, or glass of the political wrangling or budgetary back-and-forth that ultimately gave rise to these memorial sites. Yet these conflicts are not always put to rest by a monument or a ceremony. These sites and ceremonies are often compromises (especially in democracies—the situation is different in totalitarian states). To some extent, the material manifestations of collective memory are accidents of funding and political climate. Happenstance, timing, and contingency also play important roles in the on-the-ground processes of memorialization. Often, in Berlin and elsewhere, once a memorial has actually been built, it forms a more stable part, not only of the urban landscape, but also of shared understandings of the city and the past. Finally, despite the power of the language of authenticity in memorial construction, not all authentic sites are marked, and not all new memorials are on authentic locations. The next chapter addresses the counterparts to these projects, a range of sites that have, by and large, never been proposed as memorial sites, including many forced labor camps, damaged synagogues, and so-called "wild" concentration camps located within the city limits. Countless acts of persecution and resistance occurred during the Nazi era, but most remain only in people's memories or history books and are left unmarked in the cityscape.

5

Forgetting Places

Over the past six decades in Berlin, former synagogues have been demolished to make way for parking lots, playgrounds, or apartment blocks. Buildings that housed cellars and bars used by the SS and the SA as places to incarcerate, torture, and murder people have been reused as storage rooms, laundries, or restaurants. Barracks built to house forced laborers have been pulled down, abandoned, or used for other purposes. In a few cases, a plaque has been attached to a building façade to remind passersby of what once happened in one of these locations, and in even fewer cases, a larger memorial has been constructed to mourn the dead and warn against future violence and injustice. But many of these places have faded into the landscape over the intervening decades. This chapter turns to a more direct comparison of places that are officially marked with those that have disappeared into the landscape. The messages emanating from an existing memorial site may give the impression that the stones or bronze are themselves speaking, that there is something intrinsically communicative about such a site. But stones do not speak for themselves. Many places that should emit a sense of sorrow and warning, according to the prevalent logic of authenticity in German memorial culture, actually do not do so for anyone but eyewitnesses, without years of work on the part of survivors, historians, artists, politicians, and others. Contrasting marked sites with unmarked sites offers a way of thinking more broadly, and theoretically, about the infusion of land with meaning and memory, and of investigating what kinds of circumstances lead to the exposure in the landscape of a particular moment in a given site's history.

To better understand these processes I examine three categories of sites that are, all told, relatively numerous in the city, but only some of which are marked in any way. First, I examine the fates of synagogues in order to find out how many of these structures remain either as active places of contemporary Jewish life or as markers of the destruction of Berlin's prewar Jewish community. I then turn to a very different kind of place, the sites of so-called wild concentration camps and *Folterkeller,* literally "torture cellars," places of brutality set up in the early years of the Nazi regime throughout the city in pubs, laundry rooms, basements, and former prisons. Finally, I turn to the sites associated with forced labor, a category that incorporates a wide range of violence and exploitation.

Clearly, these are three very distinct kinds of sites. I have chosen these three categories of sites, not because they have much in common with one another, but because the majority of sites in each category have gone unmarked, and all three sets of sites have only recently become more broadly incorporated into memorial practices.[1] As Jochen Spielmann writes, "there were sites of historical events . . . that, until [the late 1980s], had either not been acknowledged or had been repressed. These included the subcamps of the larger concentration camps, industrial concerns, synagogues and the locations of synagogues that had been destroyed, public squares and train stations from which Jews had been deported, courthouses and execution rooms, etc."[2] At the same time, most of each of the kinds of places examined here remain unmarked. Within each category, there is also a tremendous range in physical form, visibility, and the scale of events being marked. Each of these categories involves a distinct set of historical events with its own contemporary implications for politics and education. These differences also mean that the potential moral and historical messages wrapped up in marking such sites also vary widely. But each offers the opportunity to return to a question highlighted at the beginning of this book: How do some places become central to official collective memory, while others are forgotten, or remembered only by eyewitnesses or diligent researchers? At least four lessons emerge from these examples. First, authenticity does not guarantee memorialization. Second, many sites only emerge into public awareness after many decades have passed, and in the wake of changes in political culture and historiography. Third, most larger memorials (as opposed to plaques) are built on public property. Finally, in many cases the most prominent sites (the locations of former *Gemeinde-synagogen*, or the largest "wild" concentration camps) do become marked, although this is not a hard and fast rule.

Extensive accounts exist of resistance activities, persecution by the Gestapo, the destruction of Jewish life, and forced labor camps,[3] and I have not sought to duplicate these. Instead, I set out to delineate the differences between those sites that emerge into official collective memory and those that remain out of public view. Interpreting the meaning, implications, and causes of memorialization efforts is difficult, in part because these results could change any day. In a sense, this is a necessarily inconclusive chapter. That is, when examining unmarked sites, there is always a possibility that things will change and that a given site will be marked in some way before this book is published. But it is also likely that such a change in status would have much to do with the factors I have found to be so integral to memorialization in Berlin—that is, the emergence of an active memorial entrepreneur, for example, or a shift in the resonance of a site.[4]

There is also a fundamental conceptual question at the heart of this chapter. Given the premise of authenticity so prevalent in recent memorialization in Berlin (and elsewhere), as well as the categories of sites that have come to be considered worthy of memorialization, there are numerous sites that could potentially be marked. The most isolated act of heroism or cruelty might be inscribed in the cityscape according to the logic behind many of the markers that already exist. According to the predominant approach of contemporary memorial culture in Berlin (and elsewhere), the material location of each act of resistance or persecution has in some way been altered by its past and conveys a potentially powerful moral message. But clearly most places are only altered in this way when people actively work to remind others of the history of a given site.

Much remembrance occurs in print, film, or other media of course, rather than in the built environment.[5] Survivors, students, amateur historians, professors, and curators at district museums all commemorate more in words than with stone or bronze, for obvious reasons. The history of one house or one street can occupy an entire book, or an entire museum exhibit, and indeed, particularly over the past two decades, just such careful accounts of individual places and experiences have made their way into growing numbers of exhibits, books, web sites, films, and other media. Kurt Schilde's small book *Erinnern—und nicht vergessen* (Remembering—and Not Forgetting), for example, traces the life histories of Jews in the single western Berlin district of Tempelhof before and during the Nazi era, listing pages and pages of places that might hypothetically be marked.[6] But most of these traces have vanished from view in the landscape itself. A violent past does not necessarily preclude mundane uses. A neighborhood synagogue, a building housing a *Folterkeller*, and Hitler's bunker, for example, respectively became a dental laboratory, a theater, and a parking lot.

A city cannot in any case be made entirely into a museum or memorial. Some people have even expressed concern that the existing memorial landscape threatens to overwhelm residents (and visitors) with a kind of inflation of memory of the Nazi past, provoking indifference or even active resentment.[7] Others express surprise that more marking has not been done. The number of potential sites is almost limitless, while the number of actual sites is inherently limited. These limitations include shortages of funding, the logistical impossibility of marking every event, political fatigue, and the possibility that a smaller number of powerful sites might be more effective (depending on how efficacy is measured) than scores of less powerful sites (or sites that lose their power because of repetition). The intersection of bureaucracy and politics with artistic and historiographic trends plays a fundamental role in bringing some sites to the fore, while others recede into the cityscape.

Even among those sites that are officially marked, there is substantial variation. A few places become exclusively memorial space, cordoned off from other uses. Many more places are marked with stones, statues, or columns set in traffic islands or small parks or patches of greenery. Even more places are marked with a plaque on a building façade or a stone set into the sidewalk, neither of which transforms the actual use of the land or building, but both of which may transform the experience of a given place in the urban landscape for some of the people who pass by, both through direct encounters with plaques and stones, and through coverage of dedication ceremonies and controversies in the media. While in the previous chapter I only examined cases where the use of the land was significantly shaped by the attachment of elements of the past, in this chapter, it also makes sense to include memorial plaques and other ways of marking that do not necessarily alter land use or preclude certain uses or activities. Thus in the cases examined here, many of these places may be marked, but life also goes on around them. Only in some cases is land cordoned off and, in general, in places where such delineation does not interfere with existing practices.

By pointing out the contrast between marked and unmarked sites, I am not necessarily advocating further marking, or condemning anyone for not marking. Rather, I am trying to understand what distinguishes places that do get marked from those that do not. One possible explanation is simply that the most powerful sites get marked. That is, places where the greatest number of people died, or the greatest number of deaths was planned, or places of particularly striking heroism, or of particular importance in prewar Jewish life, for example. There is also the possibility that the marking of some sites stands in for the marking of others. Scarce resources can be concentrated on a few places, referring to other similar locations throughout the city without stretching funds and skills thin. There is also the question of limited public receptiveness, noted above. Is there such a thing as too much memorialization—or too little? This chapter also serves as another reminder that, for many reasons, real estate and memory are not inherently at odds. The market and memorialization continued side by side after 1989. The real estate market in general, and the conventions of private property in particular, absolutely preclude some sites from memorialization without the consent of the owner. At the same time, even with the introduction of a real estate market to the eastern half of the city in the early 1990s, memorialization has also continued on apace, and new memorials have emerged alongside (and occasionally been incorporated into) new commercial developments or residential complexes. Finally, this chapter also addresses the transformation of specific urban spaces from the exclusive domain of private, personal memory to the province of official collective memorialization. This transfer of individual to collective memory in the landscape (bearing in mind Maurice Halbwachs's contention that individual memory also has deeply collective elements) happens only selectively, and in ways that have very varied relationships to the people involved in the initial events. As the number of surviving eyewitnesses dwindles, this transfer will become all the more pronounced and, eventually, total. Why, then, are some places remembered while others are forgotten? What distinguishes those that are marked from those that are not?

Synagogues

To begin with, I turn to Berlin's synagogues, places that potentially mark both the existence of robust Jewish communities before the war and their destruction by the Nazis. The structures ranged from small prayer spaces for newly immigrated Orthodox villagers to large synagogues designed by renowned architects that provided space for thousands of people. Of course synagogues (or the sites of former synagogues) are only one of a range of sites that could use the urban landscape to convey messages about the life and death of Berlin's prewar Jewish communities. The city is full of places that could be used to remind people of the Holocaust, and of the lives it destroyed. Apartments, restaurants, offices, or shops all witnessed both Jewish daily life and its systematic, utterly violent excision from the city.[8] There were an estimated 170,000 Jews in Berlin in 1933.[9] Official mass deportations to concentration camps began in October 1941, resulting in the murder of more than 55,000 of Berlin's Jewish residents. For some analysts, this fact alone was enough to transform the array of Jewish sites in Berlin into places that also marked the Holocaust. "Thus the un-places [*Un-Orte*] of Jewish life arose [*sind entstanden*], which can only be deciphered with great difficulty and regularly require new explanation."[10] The verb Ulrich Eckhardt and Andreas Nachama use here, *entstehen*, implies a process that takes place in both time and space, involving human activity changing the meaning of a specific site. Following their approach, the Holocaust irrevocably changed the meaning of even the most mundane sites associated with the Jewish past. As they point out, by the end of the twentieth century, most of the traces of this past had disappeared from Berlin's landscape, including the sites of former synagogues.[11]

Most of the original traces of Berlin's dozens of synagogues have indeed been removed from the cityscape. But this destruction actually happened in distinct stages. First, of course, were the pogroms of 1938, the most violent and targeted phase of this destruction. Second was the bombing during World War II, which inflicted further damage on many of Berlin's synagogues. But it is rare for either fire or bombs actually to raze a building, and in most cases quite substantial ruins remained in place for years after the end of the war. Most such ruins, however, were torn down in a third stage, the demolitions of synagogues (sometimes intact, but generally in various states of ruin) in the midst of the new urban planning schemes and economic recovery of the 1950s and 1960s. Decades later, a fourth stage began, particularly in the West in the 1980s, as many of the sites of former synagogues began to be marked with plaques or memorial ensembles. Different sources provide slightly different counts of the actual number of synagogues in Berlin in 1938, the year of the systematic "November pogroms." "No European city possessed as many synagogues as Berlin. . . . the Berlin *Gemeinde* alone had the use of twelve synagogues, which held on average more than two thousand people. . . . In addition, there were approximately seventy *Vereinssynagoge* and countless private prayer spaces. . . . With only a few exceptions, all [these] structures perished as a result of Nazi terror and war damage. Some of the ruins could have been rebuilt."[12] According to Adolf Diamant, relying heavily on Michael Engel's earlier account, there were approximately 115 synagogues and prayer spaces in Berlin in 1938.[13] Peter Reichel reports that out of a total of 50 synagogues in Berlin, 40 were set on fire by the Nazis in 1938.[14] Veronika Bendt and Rolf Bothe count 70 private synagogues and "numerous" private prayer spaces in addition to the twelve *Gemeindesynagoge*.[15] Many prayer services took place in rooms or structures that were not explicitly religious buildings, or at least not recognizable as such from the street.[16] Furthermore, some of these counts certainly include spaces in buildings that were not exclusively religious structures—small rooms in hospitals or orphanages, or within larger multifamily buildings.[17]

What, then, remains of Berlin's synagogues and other Jewish prayer spaces?[18] What does the topography look like today, as compared to 1938? There are seven synagogues in use in Berlin today, compared to over 100 before the pogroms of 1938. Few of the synagogues in use today are in the original main synagogue rooms that were used before 1938. Only six of the main synagogues remain standing, and only four of those continue to be used as synagogues. Furthermore, most of the larger buildings have disappeared, and many of the smaller ones that remain have been reused in other ways, such as for a dental laboratory or warehouse. These sites, marked and unmarked, carry with them messages (potential and actual) about both life and death. In many cases, particularly in the smaller spaces, the connection to the decimated prewar Jewish community does not preclude contemporary uses like office space. Today, there are approximately thirty-five markers of synagogues of some sort, ranging from small bronze or porcelain plaques to larger sculptural ensembles and displays of historical information. Five of the twelve *Gemeindesynagoge* were in the former East Berlin, and eight of the more than twenty-five marked synagogue sites are in the eastern half of the city. Most of the larger synagogues (almost all of which have been torn down) now have some kind of marker, at least a plaque, while most of the smaller prayer spaces have disappeared from the landscape. In most cases, these markers date from the past two decades. The forms these markers have taken range from simple plaques placed on nearby buildings to elaborate memorial ensembles such as the Steglitzer Spiegelwand.

Clearly, the pogroms of 1938 were a point of widespread destruction. On November 9, 1938, most of the prominent synagogues in Berlin (and indeed throughout Germany and Austria) were severely damaged. Most of the interiors were destroyed, and many of the buildings were set on fire by the SS and others, who also destroyed Jewish businesses, murdered dozens of people, and sent thousands of primarily Jewish men to concentration camps, many to their deaths. Because so many of the synagogues were damaged during the November pogroms, the memories of these places are intertwined with the conditions of their disappearance.[19] (Some of these structures also later served as so-called *Sammellager*, detention centers where Berlin's Jewish residents were held before being sent to concentration camps, including Mühlenstraße 24, in the eastern district of Pankow, and Levetzowstraße 7–8, in the western Tiergarten district.)[20] Despite the widespread and systematic destruction of both lives and property, few of the synagogues were actually fully demolished that night. The various accounts of synagogues in Berlin frequently list synagogues as having been destroyed either by fire in 1938 or by bombing in the early 1940s, but the term "destroyed" so often used to describe them is curiously imprecise. The synagogues were burned, plundered, ransacked, and desecrated, but in many cases they did not disappear from the urban landscape for many years.

By the end of the war, the Jewish communities had been almost entirely destroyed; the tens of thousands of people who had once filled Berlin's synagogues had been sent into exile or to their deaths.[21] A combination of the pogroms of 1938 and wartime bombing had damaged most synagogue structures. Throughout Berlin, in the years following the war people walked past ruins every day, including the crumbling shells of buildings that had clearly once been synagogues. Small survivor communities breathed life back into a handful of synagogues that were still partially use-able. But as the economy improved (particularly in the West), resources for rebuilding became increasingly available, which also meant that it became possible to remove existing ruins to make way for new construction.[22] These demolitions led, among other things, to the eradication of most physical traces of damaged synagogues in Berlin, in some cases removing burned out shells of buildings, in other cases removing fairly substantial structures.[23] These demolitions occurred for a variety of reasons, ranging from a lack of demand for an intact synagogue in the wake of the mur-der of most of Berlin's Jewish residents to the danger of collapse of exist-ing ruins.[24] The synagogue building at Münchener Straße 37, for example, was actually entirely intact at the end of the war, but was torn down in 1956, which one analysis finds "can only be explained by the assumption that a return of Jewish life was not expected."[25] The majority of the post-war demolitions of synagogues occurred when Berlin's Jewish population was far too small to fill existing synagogue seats, and when there was little of the widespread sense of the importance of preserving old buildings that is more prevalent today.

In the immediate postwar era, here and there a synagogue site was marked with a plaque or small memorial ensemble. However most of the memorials on the sites of demolished synagogues began to appear (again, almost exclusively in the West) in the late 1970s and 1980s, as many Ger-man historians and activists turned their attention to the fates of Berlin's Jewish residents under Nazi rule, as well as the importance of "authen-tic" historical sites that might be instructive to passersby, reminding them of the Holocaust and its roots in their own city streets, as well as recall-ing those murdered or sent into exile.[26] Thus only with the passage of nearly a generation did efforts to mark these sites become widespread, well after the visions of developers and city planners and demolition crews had removed most of the "authentic traces" from the landscape. Ruins gave way to demolition orders. Demolition orders were followed, in some cases, by excavations in the cityscape and in the archives, sometimes resulting in visible markers in the landscape, like those in Figures 5.1–5.4.

The synagogue sites remind us that time matters when examining the entrenchment of memory in the landscape. Berlin's landscape today is thus a mixture of erasure and of marking, reflecting, not only shifts in memorial culture and approaches to the Jewish past in Berlin and in Germany, but

FIGURE 5.1. Plaque for the former synagogue at Passauer Str. 2. Photograph by Jennifer Jordan.

FIGURE 5.2. Memorial stone for the former synagogue at Konrad-Wolf Str. 91. Photograph by Jennifer Jordan.

FIGURE 5.3.   Plaque for the former synagogue at Lützowstr. 16. Photograph by Jennifer Jordan.

also a broader, international shift in many of the basic premises of historic preservation, as Rudy Koshar, Diane Barthel, and others have pointed out.[27] This change has many causes, including an international (if particularly Western) turn toward authentic sites and *Spurensuche*, the search for traces of the past, as well as a changing political climate. It would be difficult today to walk through Berlin without noticing the sites where most of the main *Gemeindesynagogen* once stood, at least for the attentive pedestrian who might be inclined to look more closely at a porcelain memorial plaque or an abstract sculpture standing in a vacant lot that once housed a synagogue.

One step in the rediscovery of synagogue sites in West Berlin came in 1983, when the City Museum of Berlin sponsored an exhibition on Berlin's synagogues. Two large volumes were produced in conjunction with the exhibit on the architecture and history of many of Berlin's synagogues. One volume covers the *Gemeindesynagogen*, the other, the *Vereinssynagogen*, particularly those for which architectural and other records could be found. The exhibition and attendant catalogs clearly contributed to an increase in the public awareness of synagogues in Berlin's landscape. The curators clearly articulated their mission: "It is the goal of the Berlin Museum with this exhibition to recall a lost architectural style to public awareness." The project was inspired by the fiftieth anniversary of the opening of the Jewish Museum in Berlin's Oranienburger Straße and funded by the state assembly of West Berlin.[28]

The synagogue at Prinzregentenstraße is one example of this cycle of destruction, demolition, rediscovery, and remembrance. The interior and the roof were severely damaged, but the external walls were still standing after World War II. The ruins were torn down in 1956, and a home for the blind was built on the site. Today, a small plaque has been placed on the side of the new building constructed where the synagogue once stood: "On this site once stood the Synagogue of Wilmersdorf, built by A. Beer 1928–1930, dedicated September 16, 1930, set on fire and destroyed by National Socialists on November 9, 1938. The night of the Pogrom 'did not only destroy glass, but also our dreams and hopes, to be able to lead a safe life in our homeland.' Rabbi Manfred Swarsensky." The plaque itself was dedicated November 8, 1988, the fiftieth anniversary of the pogroms. Clearly, this rather unobtrusive plaque set back from the sidewalk would be relatively easy to overlook. And for decades there was no marker on the site at all. As a ruin, the building's message was unmistakable and "authentic" in ways that the small plaque hanging on the side of a new building cannot replicate. Some two dozen other sites underwent a similar transformation, and the process continues in both halves of the city today.[29]

Although it took decades to be renovated and refurbished, the Neue Synagoge on Oranienburger Straße 30, perhaps the most widely recognized synagogue in Berlin, never disappeared from the landscape, and today, its golden dome rises above the neighboring buildings, visible for blocks in any direction. The complex contains the partial ruins of the former synagogue building, as well as renovated and reconstructed rooms that now house exhibition space, offices, meeting rooms, and so on. This site is very much alive and constantly in use.

The renovation actually began in the 1980s, under the East German government, and was completed in 1995. The reconstruction of the buildings was overseen by the same architect who had rebuilt the cathedral a few blocks away, who thus had experience reconstructing Berlin's historic religious buildings. The Neue Synagoge survived the pogrom of 1938 thanks to a policeman who chased off the SS arsonists. However, it was heavily damaged by allied bombing toward the end of the war. The main synagogue was demolished in 1958, although at least one account questions whether this demolition was actually necessary.[30] The rooms may have been in poor shape, but much of the structure was still intact, and Hermann Simon finds that "demolition was, at least from today's perspective, hardly justifiable. It was a serious mistake that the ruins were not documented. The removal of the synagogue ruins was in accordance with the zeitgeist."[31]

In the early 1960s, members of East Berlin's Jewish community began to suggest to the East German authorities that the remaining structures be turned into a Jewish museum. In 1966, the Jewish Community placed a plaque on the remaining façade, which reads: "This Synagogue is 100 years old and was set on fire on November 9, 1938, in the Night of Broken Glass. During the Second World War 1939–1945 it was destroyed in a bombing raid in 1943 / The front portion of this house of God should remain for all time as a place of warning and remembrance. NEVER FORGET." Representatives of East Berlin's Jewish community periodically contacted various levels of the East German government over more than twenty years about the preservation of the buildings and the possible construction of a museum. It was not until 1988, the fiftieth anniversary of the 1938 pogroms, that the government finally lent its support to the project (albeit, according to some, largely for foreign policy reasons, including a desire on the part of East Germany to forge closer ties with Israel).[32] A resolution of the secretariat of the Central Committee of the Socialist Unity Party of June 15, 1988, notes: "The Chairman of the State Council [*Staatsrat*], Comrade Erich Honecker, as the first signatory, will transfer a donation of five million marks to the Foundation [Centrum Judaicum] for the reconstruction of the Neue Synagoge."[33] Honecker also appeared at the symbolic laying of the cornerstone. For the East German government, at least officially, "the sociopolitical goal [of the renovation was that] as the most important part of the 'Centrum Judaicum,' the Synagogue should be a center for the care and conservation of Jewish culture and tradition," as well as a national and international meeting point.[34] The Neue Synagoge Berlin—Centrum Judaicum was founded that year to oversee the reconstruction and the future creation of a center and museum. On June 10, 1988, the ownership of the Synagogue was officially transferred to the Jewish Community of Berlin.[35] By 1989, it was well on its way to becoming a permanent marker and an actively used social space, housing a museum, meeting space, and a small new synagogue. In October 1990, the reconstructed cupola was completed. Clearly, there were extensive physical remnants, left standing throughout the postwar period, that made it difficult to envision any other use of the land. This was also a part of town that, for all of its popularity and gold rush atmosphere after 1989, experienced very little new development in the 1980s, and indeed in the entire postwar era until the early 1990s. There is also little question as to the international resonance of this site, ranging from the use of foreign funds to begin the reconstruction to the crowds of tourists who visit the museum and the preserved ruins daily. Unlike other memorials, this site never actually lost its clear symbolism. There was no period of more mundane use or of a public forgetting of the past associated with this structure.

The Neue Synagoge stands at one end of a spectrum of contemporary uses and experiences of synagogue spaces in Berlin. The other pre-1933 synagogues that continue to be in use today are at Rykestraße (where the structure itself was not damaged), Pestalozzistraße 69–70 (where the building was only minimally damaged in 1938), and Kottbusser Ufer (today Fraenkelufer) 48–50. The synagogue at Kottbusser Ufer 48–50 was largely destroyed, but the part of the building that survived continues to be used as a synagogue. The building was damaged in November 1938, but was actually in use again by December of the same year. The Gestapo confiscated the building in 1942, and bombing heavily damaged the main building in 1944. In 1988, approximately thirty years after the main structure was torn down, a memorial stone was placed in front of the remaining synagogue building.[36]

Other synagogues have also remained standing but have been converted to other uses. The synagogue at Prinzenallee 87 still stands but has been used by the Jehovah's Witnesses. There is a plaque on the entrance to the courtyard, recalling the destruction of the interior of the synagogue in 1938 (although it simply reads "Destroyed 1938," which might lead the observer to conclude that the structure itself was demolished). The Synagoge Beth Zion at Brunnenstraße 33 was used as warehouse and office space for many years and is currently empty and the subject of much planning and discussion. There is a plaque on the exterior façade of the building that fronts on the street (the synagogue itself is in an interior courtyard), and preliminary studies of the building have been conducted in anticipation of preservation or renovation.[37] Local residents have been very active in calling attention to the structure and lobbying for its renovation and reuse as a cultural center. The private synagogue on Stierstraße, on the other hand, is still standing but is now apparently used as a dental laboratory.[38]

The small synagogue at Düppelstraße, Haus Wolfenstein, is also still standing, but it is inaccessible to the public, having been converted into privately owned office space. However, a larger memorial, the Steglitzer Spiegelwand (Mirror Wall), has been constructed nearby, which calls attention not only to the Düppelstraße synagogue but also to many others throughout the city. "The efforts of a citizens' initiative to turn the Wolfenstein Haus into a center for Jewish culture and an international meeting place had no success; instead, the lot was redeveloped by investors and otherwise used."[39] Memory of the history of the site has been shifted to the

FIGURE 5.4. Synagoge Beth Zion, Brunnenstr. 33. Photograph by Jennifer Jordan.

Spiegelwand, officially named the Denkzeichen Ehemalige Synagoge Haus Wolfenstein. The memorial consists of a stainless steel wall covered with the engraved names, birth dates, and addresses of Jews deported from the district, as well as other information about Jewish history in the neighborhood. Built in 1995 (after substantial controversy) on a small urban square near the former synagogue, the memorial provided occasion to refurbish a small patch of public space.[40] It also serves as a focal point for walking tours regularly held in the district.

The ruins of the Lindenstraße (today Axel-Springer Straße) 48–50 synagogue were torn down in 1956, despite the fact that enough of the building had survived the pogroms of 1938 for services to be held after that date and for the building to be used as a granary during the war. More recently, the owners of the new building constructed on the site have sponsored the construction of a new memorial:

For decades, this site held a parking lot and sheds. . . . In 1988, the district administration of Kreuzberg [one of the districts in West Berlin] . . . placed an informational sign on the street, with photographs and texts about the history of the synagogue. In 1997, the memorial project was finally realized, with which Zvi Hecker . . . along with Micha Ullmann and Eyal Weizman won a competition in 1995. Particularly noteworthy is the fact that the sponsors of the competition and the donors for the artwork were not public institutions, but rather the Barmer Ersatzkasse, owner and occupant of the old and new buildings on the historic site.[41]

Today, in the empty courtyard where the synagogue once stood, there are now rows of concrete benches, and two informational plaques have been placed at the entrance to the courtyard, one of the relatively rare instances of a memorial being constructed on private property.

One of the clearest examples of the change in official and popular attitudes toward synagogue ruins is the site of Berlin's first *Gemeindesynagoge* in the former Heidereutergasse, directly adjacent to the Rosenstraße site discussed in the previous chapter, and just a few steps away from the busy thoroughfare of Karl-Liebknecht-Straße. The synagogue was undamaged in 1938, but damaged by bombing in the early 1940s. The ruins—clearly visible in postwar photographs, and apparently intact enough for the synagogue to have been repaired—were torn down in 1968 to make way for a massive new construction project adjacent to the lot.[42] But a generation later the Berlin Senate approved funding for at least preliminary excavations and a nearby memorial plaque, dedicated 286 years after the synagogue was founded. "Senator Strieder [the senator for urban development] provided 250,000 DM for the archaeological excavations and the memorial plaque. The Mitte district city council, the State Historic Preservation Office, the Memorial Plaque Commission, the Centrum Judaicum, and the Jewish Community supported the project."[43] The outline of part of the synagogue has now been exposed in the grass of the small park that is now on the site. The political context has changed, as have expert and popular notions of what kinds of traces should be preserved, and the history of the synagogue is now incorporated into other markers of the history of this plot of land.

These examples show the range of activities, some by members of Berlin's Jewish community, others by non-Jewish citizens' groups and individuals, working to inscribe (or reinscribe) elements of Berlin's Jewish past into the landscape. The vast majority of these efforts have taken place since the late 1980s. Their physical manifestations range from a plaque on a nearby building to substantial memorial sites, such as Levetzowstraße, Lindenstraße, and the Steglitzer Spiegelwand. Given the count of more than one hundred synagogues altogether, approximately thirty-five of which have been marked, there are still dozens of synagogue sites that remain unmarked. In general, the larger structures more recognizable as religious buildings and once serving larger populations do have some kind of marking.

Throughout Berlin, smaller prayer spaces and a few larger synagogues have disappeared into the landscape, some because the original structures were demolished and no one has yet called successfully for some kind of marking, others because they are not immediately recognizable as synagogues or prayer spaces and are now used in other ways. One reason for the relatively sparse marking of private synagogues and prayer spaces may also have to do with the paucity of archival sources. The organizers of the 1983 exhibition on Berlin's synagogues at the Berlin Museum found the archival sources concerning private synagogues to be extremely sparse. "Questions of location, chronology, and building history hardly allow themselves to be clarified."[44] Walking down a single street in the center of the city, in the Spandauer Vorstadt neighborhood, you would pass by four former *Betstuben,* or prayer spaces, within just one or two blocks—but today there is no sign of their presence.[45] Here "the number of small prayer spaces simply cannot be reconstructed. . . . The traces of these people and their build-

ings are today almost entirely faded."[46] In another case, a building housing a former *Betstübe*, on the second floor of a courtyard building at Rigaer
Straße 27, was torn down in the 1990s.[47]

As in the other categories discussed in this chapter, there is great variation in the ways in which the sites are or are not marked in the cityscape. In
part because of these variations in physical form, there is also a wide range
of ways in which residents, tourists, and others perceive and experience
these sites. Clearly, sites on private property are most likely to fade into the
landscape. In addition, authenticity seems to have grown in importance
over time (although it is still by no means a memorial trump card). These
are the uneven ways in which this particular element of Berlin's Jewish past
and present are woven into the landscape, spanning the spectrum from
essential invisibility to the widely recognized dome of the Neue Synagoge.

Many observers of contemporary Berlin still find that, despite the
growth in shared ideas about historic preservation, the rapid urban development of post-1989 Berlin nonetheless resulted in the disappearance of important structures and other kinds of traces of the past. Decrepit façades and old
advertisements and other architectural evidence of prewar Jewish life have
given way to the pastel hues of new plaster and row upon row of restaurants and galleries. This phenomenon is particularly extensive in Spandauer
Vorstadt, a neighborhood in the heart of eastern Berlin that housed much
of the city's prewar Jewish population, particularly poor and relatively recent
immigrants. The unification of the two Berlins changed the economic,
political, and social context of this and other neighborhoods and certainly
led to a significant increase in the monetary value of these structures. Tour
guides and books alike point to the iconic images of the imprints of demolished buildings still clinging to the exposed brick of a neighboring structure.
These ghost images have a particular poignancy, both in their inscrutabil-
ity and perhaps in their difference, aesthetically, from the somewhat familiar
and less immediate aesthetic quality of memorial plaques and ensembles.

If, as I maintain elsewhere in this book, acts of remembrance in Berlin and elsewhere are often about visions of the future, it is also important to ask what these sites accomplish. Observed in conjunction with one
another, rather than as isolated elements of the urban landscape, they do
seem to constitute a coherent (if also highly heterogeneous) narrative. But
the range in backgrounds and motivations of passersby, the tools and pre-
conceptions with which they confront a given memorial project (ranging

from ignoring it to vandalizing it to being inspired to develop an exhibition or sponsor a plaque) make clear, among other things, the indeterminacy of memorial projects. Given that most of those who knew the destroyed synagogues personally are no longer alive, who are the intended witnesses to these plaques and sculptures, and what might be the consequences of these markers? Over time, more have appeared in the landscape. But many are easily overlooked, and it is also still difficult to read from the landscape both how entrenched and how diverse Berlin's Jewish population was before the Holocaust.

Some of these sites (particularly those in the city center) may appear on walking tours, and certainly many of them are documented in books like Eckhardt and Nachama's and other guides to Berlin's Jewish past, and some evidence still lurks in archives. Other traces are gone, like the people who originally created them, forever. Indeed, many traces of daily life were in fact removed—almost exhaustively—in the rapid urban redevelopment and renovation that took place after 1989, some of the most intense forms of it in the neighborhood that once housed so many of Berlin's Jewish residents.[48] Thus it is possible for many people to walk down a street, into a courtyard, or even into an apartment and not to know that they are passing by or through a former synagogue and the site of pogroms and deportations. In other places, it is still possible to walk past and not know, even if there is a marker or a monument—they are not always readily visible, and their messages are not always clear. Since the Wall fell, tourists, researchers, and others have begun to pay somewhat more attention to a few sites in the East. By and large the approaches to memorialization developed in the West in the late 1980s continue to hold sway, although they do take on new aesthetic forms and in some cases struggle for funding more than they might have in the 1980s, when subsidies flowed into both halves of Berlin as a part of the waging of the Cold War, including funds for historic preservation and memorial projects. Thus most of the larger sites have been marked, but the city still harbors many places that have stories to tell, even when these stories are difficult to discern in the contemporary landscape.

"Wild" Concentration Camps and *Folterkeller*

The so-called wild concentration camps and *Folterkeller,* or torture chambers, scattered throughout Berlin differ in obvious ways from the syn-

agogue sites. These are, first of all, places associated exclusively with violence and often death, flaring up briefly in the city and then disappearing
again. (Clearly these are not the only places in Berlin where people were
detained, tortured, or killed between 1933 and 1945.) After Hitler came to
power in 1933, the intensification of arrests and the systematic restricting of
rights led to prisons becoming overcrowded.[49] "The concept 'wild' concentration camp describes the holding, interrogation, and torture locations,
provisionally set up in the initial takeover phase when the Nazis came to
power [*Machtergreifungsphase*] by diverse SA and SS groups, that were not
legitimated or administered by any state authority, where Jews and [other]
anti-Nazis were carried off."[50] Researchers estimate that there were approximately 150 of these places. Most were quite temporary and only held a few
people, while the largest remained in place for months and held thousands
of prisoners.[51] The "wild" concentration camps and torture cellars only
existed in Berlin for a relatively short period of time beginning in early
1933, and most had been dismantled by 1934. The vast majority were dismantled after an order from Göring in October 1933, in part out of fear of
the unpredictable nature of the SA's actions in these cases.[52]

   With a few exceptions, these sites have remained unmarked. In 1987,
Helmut Bräutigam and Oliver Gliech found that the "places of horror that
found themselves in the middle of Berlin are by and large forgotten."[53] A
few of the larger and more sustained sites have been marked in some way
over the past two decades, but most of the smaller sites, and even some
of those that researchers list as having been some of the main locations of
early SA terror, are today being used in other ways, without any indication of what happened there in 1933 and 1934. The actual use of the sites
is altered in only a very few instances, while in the vast majority, life goes
on, despite widespread convictions among memorial entrepreneurs and
many members of the press and the public that the association with torture and murder pollutes or contaminates such spaces.[54] Out of 150 sites,
approximately 10 of the wild concentration camps are indicated by some
kind of marking.[55] This is a set of sites associated with incredible brutality,
and it is perhaps surprising that more of these sites are not cordoned off
from daily life. These acts of torture and murder were by and large integrated into the everyday urban fabric, in bars, former laundries, and basements in the heart of the city. Researchers believe that there was no way
for nearby residents not to have known what was going on, either from

hearing people's screams or from seeing the arrests and beatings in broad daylight.[56] Today people walk through or past these places without knowing about what once happened there, just as people walk through or past other places of great cruelty or violence around the world.[57] Of the five sites that Bräutigam and Gliech list as being most egregious, for example, only two are marked today.[58]

Relatively little research has been done on "wild" concentration camps and *Folterkeller*. One of the key pieces of research is Bräutigam and Gliech's 1987 essay "Nationalsozialistische Zwangslager in Berlin, I: Die 'wilden' Konzentrationslager und Folterkeller 1933/34" (National Socialist *Zwangslager* in Berlin I: The "Wild" Concentration Camps and Torture Cellars, 1933–34), which continues to be the authoritative preliminary investigation. Most of the other research about these sites has been done by lay historians through interviews with eyewitnesses, including a few perpetrators, but mostly victims. Part of the difficulty in studying these sites comes from the fact that they did not leave extensive archival traces, given that they were not systematically incorporated into the Nazi bureaucracy. Thus Bräutigam and Gliech see their account less as a conclusive analysis of wild concentration camps and *Folterkeller*, and more as an attempt to bring together the existing (and at times contradictory) literature and perhaps lay the foundation for a more detailed study.[59] In their opinion, at the time (1987), the definitive historical work on wild concentration camps in Berlin had yet to be written. This still holds true today, and that relative scarcity of substantive academic research also contributes to the relative paucity of markers of such sites in the urban landscape.

Like so many others who write about the material traces of the Nazi past in general, and memorial sites in particular, Bräutigam and Gliech also run into definitional difficulties, and the term "wild concentration camp" in particular needs to be used with caution. "While a few of the torture sites in bars, cellars, shops, halls, warehouses, sheds, former barracks, etc. appear repeatedly in contemporary reports and documentation, in others it appears that 'only' one-time abuses took place. Thus it is difficult to decide if a given site is a torture site or a 'wild' concentration camp."[60] These definitions continue to be the subject of academic debate in Germany, given the range in scale, permanence, and number of victims, so for this discussion I rely on the widely used term *Folterkeller*. Bräutigam and Gliech also provide a list—"for the time being"—of wild concentration camps and *Folterkeller*. By their provisional count, there were fifty-seven wild concentration camps or *Folterkeller* in the East, and ninety-two in the West.[61] Furthermore, they note, "the total number of those tortured and killed in 'wild' concentration camps is unknown."[62] The facts—the names of victims, the names of perpetrators, the number of murders, the exact location of *Folterkeller*—are often difficult to discern, which in turn affects how these places might be marked in the urban landscape. A central point to take away from these examples is the fact that some "authentic" sites are marked as such and others are not. This may sound obvious, but a closer examination reveals the layers of social, political, economic, and material processes so central to this book—and to the makeup of Berlin's urban landscape. Many—even most—"authentic" sites are absorbed into the fabric of daily life, in Berlin and elsewhere. Even when they are marked, the text may also be inaccurate, or at best vague—for example, contrast the extreme brutality of what happened in the basement of the Spandau district city hall with the bland texts of the memorial plaques on the building.[63]

By 2005, there were a total of ten marked *Folterkeller* sites in Berlin.[64] Five are in the eastern district of Köpenick, all put in place before the Wall fell, all treating a period of particularly intense violence in May 1933.[65] The physical forms of these sites throughout Berlin range widely. One is a small plaque placed on the entryway of a new building put up on the site of a demolished structure that once housed an SA hangout, or *Sturm-Lokal*. (See Figures 5.5–5.6.) Here the geographical coordinates of the original site still appear to be important, even if the actual rooms have disappeared.[66] This site and others where the original structures have disappeared prompt us to ask how memory happens when the building is gone—and either a vacant lot remains or something new is put in its place. Another site is a small museum in Köpenick, whose contents have changed in the wake of the falling of the Wall.[67] In some cases, the original structures have been torn down, in others, the original rooms remain. A handful of historians have engaged themselves on behalf of a handful of sites, so that the Columbia Haus, General-Pape-Straße, the Wasserturm, and the Amtsgericht in Köpenick are the subject of books, articles, exhibits, public gatherings, and other projects that anchor these sites in broader collective memory. Because so much of the violence in 1933 and 1934 was directed at communists and socialists, in the eastern part of the city much of the memory of *Folterkeller* is layered with East German and post-1989 approaches to this element of Berlin's past. This is particularly apparent in Köpenick, where the sites all refer to events that took place in May 1933, when the SA and SS brutally sought to intimidate and often murder the many socialists and communists in the district. As noted in the previous chapter, the content of the museum itself has changed, and the most prominent marker, a fist several meters in height, in familiar socialist style, has provoked extensive controversy.

Another case in which the original structure has since disappeared, but where physical markers of official collective memory continue to recall past events, is the Wasserturm (water tower) in the district of Prenzlauer Berg.[68] As Bräutigam and Gliech found with other torture cellars and wild concentration camps, Irene Mayer finds evidence in eyewitness reports that indicate that nearby residents must have known of the existence of a *Folterkeller* at the Wasserturm (not the round building today known as the Wasserturm, but a nearby building that has since been demolished).[69] Torture and murder were clearly taking place there. Eventually, the rooms that had served as the *Folterkeller* were turned into a cafeteria and recreation room for SA men living in the nearby buildings. The building itself was demol-

FIGURE 5.5.   Petersburger Str. 94. Photograph by Jennifer Jordan.

FIGURE 5.6. Plaque at Petersburger Str. 94. Photograph by Jennifer Jordan.

ished in 1935, and turned into green space.[70] In the 1950s, a playground was built on the site of the building. Various markers have been put up near the site, including a memorial wall erected in 1981, and a series of bas-reliefs on Schönhauser Allee in the same district. "The victims of the concentration camp were first publicly remembered in 1950 in the form of a memorial stone in front of the larger water tower. The stone was renovated in 1953 and the memorial altered into a memorial wall in 1981."[71] It is also likely that the forms of representation will change again in the near future as the history of the site (including the different political and aesthetic layers of remembrance) is reconsidered. (See Figure 5.7.)

The Columbia Haus and General-Pape-Straße sites are two of the most prominent memorial projects connected to wild concentration camps. Both of them were initiated in the 1980s, and both mark the sites of relatively large-scale actions by the SA. The two sites in question followed somewhat similar trajectories and even involved some of the same key actors. Both were comparatively large and located in Tempelhof. Columbia Haus was the only one of the wild concentration camps to be taken over by the administrative body overseeing concentration camps. Johannes Tuchel and Kurt Schilde estimate that the camp held a total of 8,000 prisoners, of

FIGURE 5.7. Memorial wall at the Wasserturm. Photograph by Jennifer Jordan.

whom they were able to identify 450 by name by 1990.[72] Clearly, the scale
here is very different from the torture cellars, where victims numbered in
the dozens rather than the thousands. This was "one of the worst torture
sites of the early Nazi era, in the middle of the city. Today, it is largely forgotten by the Berlin population. . . . Supposedly, almost 10,000 opponents
[to the Nazi regime] were incarcerated here. They were beaten, tortured,
some even murdered."[73] The site was forgotten for decades by average passersby, although obviously not by survivors or perpetrators. Schilde and
Tuchel found that it "was by and large stricken from collective and individual memory. . . . the acknowledgement of the former concentration camp
Columbia first resumed in the 1980s."[74]

However, "after four decades of being forgotten, the district research
project 'Memory Book for Victims of National Socialism from the District
of Tempelhof' (which also led to a permanent exhibition in the District

Museum) reawakened public memory."[75] A few isolated research efforts began to grow into larger projects. "On June 15, 1988, in order to recall the historical event, the Tempelhof district city council voted . . . to place a plaque or memorial [at the Columbia-Haus site] for the victims of the Nazi dictatorship."[76] In 1990, in anticipation of a memorial being constructed on the site, the Tempelhof district administration issued a book detailing the history of the Columbia-Haus concentration camp. There was also a competition to design a memorial, and Georg Seibert's prize-winning entry—a large structure that looks like a house, or possibly a headstone—was constructed across the street in 1994. It bears a plaque that reads: "Remember/Commemorate/Warn: The Columbia-Haus was, from 1933, a prison and from 1.8.1935 until 11.5.1936 a concentration camp of the National Socialist rulers. Here people were held prisoner, humiliated, tortured, murdered."

In the basement of the former barracks at General-Pape-Straße in the same district, approximately two thousand men and women were imprisoned and tortured between March and December 1933.[77] "After 1945, the place and the events fell into obscurity. Only in 1992 were the basement rooms of the prison . . . rediscovered through a tip from an eyewitness."[78] Other accounts also emphasize the decades in which the rooms were forgotten: "For a long time little was known about this SA prison. For decades the rooms remained undiscovered, and to this day their history has not been adequately researched."[79] "Until that point, this area (which is today a light industrial area) was not the subject of historical investigations. And it could have remained that way if Scholz [one of the artists] had not accidentally found swastikas and other signs in the cellar of his apartment building."[80] "For decades [the site had] disappeared from awareness or was hushed up, only recent publications of the Berlin History Workshop and the VVN [a victims' organization] point to this early torture site. The mounting of a memorial plaque on the building at Werner-Voss-Damm no. 62 in 1981 also contributed to the process of awakening memory about this place."[81] Note, as in so many other cases of memorial sites in Berlin, both the decades of silence and collective forgetting about a place and the importance of authenticity in the language of those working to bring the site back into public awareness. Since the early 1980s, there has been a plaque on the front of the building, now Werner-Voss-Damm, and there have been temporary exhibits in the original rooms, as well as exhibits elsewhere in the district referring to this location.[82] "In 1992, authentic cellar rooms could be found, on the basis of a witness's testimony and the fact that the rooms were never renovated. In early 1995, an exhibition took place there, with works by seven artists who live or work on the former barrack grounds."[83] Clearly, they played a major role in bringing this site back into public awareness. "The hobby-researchers have gathered together all of this information into an exhibition through their own efforts" (including financial contributions).[84] The exhibition definitely reached the public at large, as well as survivors. "The first exhibition on the history of this place found a lively echo: former prisoners, historians, and relatives all responded."[85] Around fifty visitors went through the exhibition each day.

The authors of one of the primary publications on the site, Kurt Schilde, Rolf Scholz, and Sylvia Walleczek, encountered difficulties in their research due both to the lack of archival information and the scant numbers of eyewitnesses still alive sixty years later.[86] In 1996, they published the results of their research as *SA-Gefängnis Papestraße: Spuren und Zeugnisse* (SA Prison Papestraße: Traces and Witnesses). The authors were hoping for a more permanent exhibition, particularly in light of the construction projects planned on the grounds. "With that [new construction], one of the few sites would be lost where the SA terror can be seen in its original state."[87] One Sunday afternoon in October 1997, in conjunction with Walleczek, who lived in the building at the time, the district *Volkshochschule* opened the cellars to the public. After an introduction covering the activities of the SA in the early years of the Nazi regime, visitors could see the "authentic location. In some places, traces are clearly still present, including messages scratched on the walls by prisoners." An eyewitness was present to give visitors a better sense of what had happened here. "After long negotiations with the building owner, it was settled that the character of the cellar would not be physically changed and that it could further serve as a museum."[88] These efforts are reported as a "rediscovery," yet the rooms were there all along, and memories of these events surely lingered among survivors and perpetrators. "Rediscovery" really means, perhaps, reminding, or even teaching. Through writing, tours, exhibits, plaques, and other media, particular moments in a given site's history help to convey this information to contemporary audiences. The Robert-Koch-Institut, located in the former barracks, sponsored an exhibition about doctors who were detained, tortured, and in some cases killed in the SA prison in General-

Pape Straße. Three years later, in May 2003, the exhibition was moved to the Tempelhof-Schöneberg District Health Department.

While these sites have been the subject of a range of public activities, most of the torture cellar sites continue to be "forgotten"—unmarked, used in a multitude of mundane ways, and silent with regard to this brutal portion of their history that is no longer visible to the casual (or even determined) observer. In books like Hans-Rainer Sandvoß's volumes on resistance, it is possible to read graphic firsthand accounts of the torture and murder that happened at places like Hedemannstraße 31.[89] In 2003, there was a restaurant in part of this building, with no visible indication of this aspect of the building's past.[90] Clearly, here these stones do not speak for themselves, and no one has made a concerted effort to speak for them, at least in memorial form. With the smaller torture cellars, there is also often a question of which rooms were actually used—sometimes that can be determined and sometimes it cannot, given the scarcity of archival sources. In another volume, Sandvoß lists three sites as having been particularly feared, and he again offers graphic eyewitness testimony of, in this case, the persecution of communist opponents of the Nazis: in the Karl-Liebknecht Haus, the barracks in the Kleine Alexanderstraße, and the *SA-Lokal* at Huttenstraße 3.[91] The Karl-Liebknecht-Haus is now the headquarters of the state Democratic Socialist Party (PDS). None of these sites is marked today, and this is the case for approximately 140 such sites throughout the city.

We can comb through survivors' testimony and the scanty archival record, scrutinize construction files, and sort through a handful of newspaper reports to find evidence of what happened in these places. But if we walk past them on our way to the greengrocer's or the train station, they do not stop us in our tracks and tell us what happened here, these unmarked places have no means of communicating to even the most interested pedestrian what happened within their walls. The outcroppings of memory that we do see in the landscape are worked on by economies, polities, and zeitgeists. They are shaped, but not determined, by these forces that alter the topography of the city. Sometimes such shaping happens slowly, sometimes abruptly, in anticipation of an anniversary or as part of a top-down nationwide scheme to imprint the landscape with a particular interpretation of the past in a way that is visible and legible to broad portions of the population. Obviously, this phenomenon is not limited to sites connected to Nazi crimes, or even to Berlin. The inherent silence of bricks and mortar is a rather fundamental fact of memorialization.

Forced Labor Camps

Historians estimate that there were between 700 and 1,000 forced labor camps in Berlin and its outskirts, set up primarily between 1939 and 1945, although they have struggled to establish an exact number, in part because of gaps in the archival record and in part because of the difficulty of defining forced labor and the great variation in the meaning of that term with respect to Berlin. Demps and Hölzer counted around 600 sites, and more recent figures range between 700 and 1,000.[92] As with many of the other places discussed in this chapter, for decades most of Berlin's forced labor camps were remembered (and indeed continue to be remembered) only by eyewitnesses, fading into the urban landscape without any official marking.[93] In January 1941, there were approximately 19,000 foreign laborers in Berlin, and one year later, there were 100,000. The number peaked in August 1944 at 381,147, not including prisoners of war.[94] Conditions in the camps varied widely. Some camp operators held Christmas celebrations and organized medical care and warm clothing for forced laborers, while other camps were designed "for the physical destruction of people [often Jews, Roma and Sinti, and others dubbed as racially inferior] through work and terror."[95]

Given the scope of forced labor in Berlin (and throughout Germany), there are relatively few permanent markers in the landscape. As of the early twenty-first century, fewer than a dozen permanent markers indicate the former presence of forced labor camps in the city. These include memorial plaques, larger memorial ensembles, and, most recently, museum exhibits. In addition, cemeteries throughout Berlin contain the graves of forced laborers, although they are rarely marked in ways that indicate the conditions of the laborers' lives and deaths (often they are simply listed as "civilian victims"). Following the premise that the original sites hold particular pedagogical, memorial, or even aesthetic properties, there are hundreds of places where forced labor sites could be marked. But official collective memory has settled in a comparatively small number of locations.[96]

Over the past two decades, in particular, historians, politicians, and the public at large have paid greater attention to forced labor sites, in part because of international struggles for compensation of forced laborers.[97] Through the local activism and the engagement of memorial entrepreneurs, these broader efforts have taken on more elaborate forms, including an exhibition that traveled around Berlin in 2002 and 2003 and ongoing efforts to preserve one of the remaining structurally intact forced labor camps in the city.[98] In addition, the tremendous variation in the consequences of forced labor camps for forced laborers themselves contributes to the heterogeneity of this memorial landscape. As noted above, these conditions ranged from the intentional working to death of groups identified by the Nazis as racially inferior to the use of foreign forced laborers as waitresses or nannies, settings in which workers were stripped of their freedoms and often subjected to many forms of abuse, but that were not as inevitably murderous as the conditions in work camps aimed at annihilation.

The immediacy of death helps to explain the markers in cemeteries, and isolated initiative may help to explain some of the plaques. The memorials in question emerge at the intersection of many factors, including international legal battles concerning damages to be paid to former forced laborers, and changes in academic approaches to historical research, such as the release of previously unavailable archival material. Some (but by no means all) of the larger and more egregious camps have in fact been marked. By and large, these sites were not studied extensively until the late 1980s and 1990s. Recently, particularly since the 1990s, historians as well as district history museums have paid increasing attention to the experiences of forced laborers.[99] The actions of district museum directors and curious students combine with international politics and historiography in ways that result in oral history collections, publications, public events, exhibits, and memorial plaques and statues. One result has been a series of new, in-depth publications including many photographs and personal recollections, as well as traveling exhibitions.[100] Inherent limits to this research include gaps in the archival record, the dwindling number of eyewitnesses, and the disjuncture between the *plans* for forced labor camps found in archival documents and actual *practice*, which is far more difficult to decipher from the remaining records.

In German historiography, the issue of forced laborers began to draw increasing attention in the 1980s, in both East and West. The historians working on these sites do not claim to have definitively analyzed all forced labor camps, but rather see themselves approaching an increasingly accurate understanding of this element of Berlin's Nazi past. Laurenz Demps and Reinhard Hölzer wrote one of the first major publications on the sites of forced labor in and around Berlin, *Zwangsarbeiter und Zwangsarbeiterlager in der faschistischen Reichshauptstadt Berlin, 1939–1945* (1986), relying primarily on archival sources available to them in the East, which only included material through 1942.[101] In another key academic analysis of forced labor sites in Berlin, "Nationalsozialistische Zwangslager in Berlin, IV: Fremdarbeiterlager 1939 bis 1945" (1989), Helmut Bräutigam observed that "the history of the foreign workers in Berlin during World War II and the camps where they were housed has so far belonged to the forgotten, barely addressed themes of the historiography about Berlin in the twentieth century." This was all the more astonishing, he noted, given that foreign workers had been such a visible presence throughout the city during the war.[102] Bräutigam drew on sources that had not previously been used in studies of forced labor, including Demps and Hölzer's 1986 study.[103] In 2001, the historian Rainer Kubatzki published his *Zwangsarbeiter- und Kriegsgefangenenlanger,* "the first inclusive account of forced labor camps for industrial production in Berlin and Brandenburg, especially for armaments," but this still only gave only a partial account of forced labor overall, excluding agricultural labor and forced labor used by churches.[104] Kubatzki also made it clear that there was much research left to do.[105] In his foreword, Wolfgang Ribbe also drew attention to the "contemporary political significance" of Kubatzki's study, given the ongoing decisions about the payment of damages to forced laborers.[106]

"Not every foreign laborer was always a forced laborer," Bräutigam points out, so that it is sometimes difficult to determine which foreign labor camps were also forced labor camps.[107] Furthermore, as mentioned above, the conditions for forced laborers differed dramatically from one camp to the next. Thus the numbers presented do not mean 1,000 places where people were stripped of all human rights and worked to death, for example. Such conditions did prevail at many of these sites, but because of the range in the conditions of forced labor, it is not a uniform category. Kubatzki acknowledges the extreme difficulty in developing precise definitions of forced labor camps and thus in achieving precise numbers of camps. In his analysis, this difficulty has many causes. The uses of the sites changed over time, multiple businesses may have used forced labor under the same roof, and a single company may have had multiple camps, for example. "In Falkensee . . . , a camp for civilian workers was converted into a prisoner of war camp, heavily guarded and surrounded by barbed wire. Renting space out, dividing up spaces, a change in owners, abandoned construction projects can be linked to specific sites, but do not allow for the calculation of a precise number of camps." Sites of forced labor, then, can include "apartments, entire floors of buildings, old warehouses, worn-out workshops and obsolete factories, dance halls, restaurants and bars . . . , pensions and hotels, [and] also barns, threshing floors, stalls, and deep cellars, as long as they were officially recognized [*amtlich genehmigt*], they housed prisoners of war or forced laborers, and their location was restricted and cut off from the public." Most camps held between one hundred and two hundred people, none were larger than three thousand (Adlershof and Falkensee), and some only had five to ten people.[108]

The material settings of the camps thus varied greatly, from large camps surrounded by barbed wire to a few rooms in an apartment. The historical processes of forced labor thus left behind a range of traces in the urban landscape. "The foreigner camps were distributed throughout the city. While in the city center there were predominantly so-called *Saallager* [literally "hall camps"] that were set up in already existing buildings (halls, hotels, empty rooms that were adapted for use as housing), the GBI [Generalbauinspektor für die Neugestaltung der Reichshauptstadt] built large barracks, often housing thousands of people [on the outskirts of town and in industrial areas]," Bräutigam notes.[109] Despite the massive presence of forced labor in the city, these material traces began to disappear relatively quickly. "Soon after the end of the war, the foreign workers returned to their home countries, leaving few traces behind. For the most part, the worn-out barrack towns in the outer districts disappeared very quickly, to the extent that they were not already destroyed by the effects of war or scavenging. Today, there are only a few traces remaining that might be recognizable as being former foreign worker camps." He points to one exception, the Arbeiterstadt Große Halle, which now belongs to the Evangelisches Waldkrankenhaus Spandau, a hospital (mentioned below).[110] The traces, then, were essentially forgotten (or ignored) in the landscape for decades, although remembered, of course, by the forced laborers who had survived and returned to their homes, as well as by those who oversaw the forced labor camps, ranging from SS officers to farmers. Needless to say, many Berliners must also have remembered the camps, because forced labor was all around them—most parts of Berlin were not far from at least one camp, and by 1944, the city housed hundreds of thousands of forced laborers.[111] But it was only very recently that these memories (and the information brought to light by historians) began to translate into material markers in the urban landscape. As Kubatzki describes it, in May 1945 "over the workplaces and residences [of the forced laborers] lay the ashes of the war, and grass grew quickly over them. Only in 1985, around forty years later, after politics, research, and public consciousness gave up the efforts at repression, did larger historical research projects about Berlin concern themselves again with these events." [112] And even with these efforts, fewer than a dozen of the hundreds of sites have been marked in any way. The juxtaposition of places that have been marked with those that have not, however, should not be seen as a call to mark all 1,000 sites. Rather, this comparison is one way to understand how official collective meanings settle into places differentially, and how archival research and claims for damages can also translate into visible markers in the landscape, albeit in a limited number of locations.

All of this academic work—the analysis of archival documents, the presentations at conferences and in academic journals—thus lays a foundation for further memorial activity. In the various accounts of different markers, authors bring up a range of inaccuracies that people have tried to rectify over the years—language on memorial stones that suppresses the brutal conditions under which forced laborers died, or inaccurate figures that lump forced laborers together with other bombing casualties in mass graves. But this activity settles on particular sites, in ways that are shaped by a constellation of bureaucracy, politics, economics, and memorial culture. In the decades following World War II, a few sites emerged that referred to forced labor, including memorial stones in cemeteries marking the sites of mass graves, as well as a few memorial plaques scattered around the city. More recently, efforts have become both more elaborate and more widespread.[113] Once the interest in forced labor sites began to grow—through international press coverage of legal battles, as well as the work of historians—curators and researchers in district museums reached out to survivors and collected oral histories, began to investigate concrete sites, and hosted public events with survivors as well. There are also now efforts under way to transform what is referred to as the only remaining forced labor camp (located in the district of Treptow) into some kind of documentation and education center (described in more detail below).

Relatively soon after World War II, there were markers connected to forced laborers, but these were generally stones in graveyards marking mass graves, which rarely made it clear that the dead were not only non-Germans but also forced laborers. In the St. Hedwigs Friedhof in the district of Hohenschönhausen, for example, there is an *Ehrenhain,* or memorial grove, established in 1954 to commemorate forced laborers. It includes memorial stones for 1,647 Soviet citizens and 297 Belgian and Dutch citizens, but Endlich points out the stones do not make clear the conditions under which the laborers were brought to Berlin or the conditions under which they died. Instead, the language of the stones treats them simply as other "civilian victims."[114] In a cemetery in the district of Marzahn (discussed in Chapter 3), there was also a marker for foreign forced laborers that was placed there in the 1950s, which also neglected to make it clear that these were in fact forced laborers. The original stone read: "Here lie 400 victims of the united nations [*vereinte Nationen*] 1939–1945 / They never saw their homeland again."[115] The number of victims was later corrected to 4,000, although a later source reports that "according to the most recent findings, at least 1,400 forced laborers are buried in the Marzahner Parkfriedhof."[116] The original burial site has also served as an anchor for more recent memorial efforts, culminating in the January 2004 dedication of a monument to forced laborers.[117] The monument was initiated by people from the district Heimatverein and the Marzahn-Hellersdorfer Wirtschaftskreis, and was paid for with donations adding up to €27,000. The monument was dedicated on January 27, 2004, in the presence of the mayor and diplomatic representatives of many of the countries in question. This new project is a reuse and updating of the Marzahn cemetery and a sign of the increasing attention being paid to sites of forced labor by a range of activists, survivors, politicians, and others.

In addition to the cemetery sites (which are not included in the figures given by the historians mentioned above, because they were counting places where forced laborers lived and worked), there are a few plaques scattered throughout the city marking sites of forced labor. A plaque at Gustav-Meyer-Allee 25 and Hussitenstraße, put up in 1995, "is one of the few examples of public remembrance of the large number of victims of forced labor in Berlin businesses."[118] The plaque is one of the official porcelain plaques from the Royal Porcelain Manufacturer (KPM), and reads, "At this factory site during World War II, the AEG employed [*beschäftigte*]

Polish forced laborers who had been deported to Germany. They, too, are victims of Nazi rule." The plaque was sponsored by the Wedding district city council. There are a few locations where there is a slightly larger memorial ensemble, but without any extensive historical information provided. One of the most brutal sites connected to forced labor was the Arbeitserziehungslager Wuhlheide, a camp to which forced laborers and others were sent as punishment. According to the historian Wolfgang Wippermann, "only a few Berliners in both halves of the city appear to know that on the site of what is today the East Berlin Zoo [*Tierpark*], there was a 'Work Training Camp,' in which an estimated 30,000 people from Germany and many different European countries were interned [between 1940 and 1945]."[119] Based on the relatively scanty sources available, Wippermann describes the poor conditions of Wuhlheide, including overcrowding and a lack of medical care, as well as torture and executions.[120] Since the mid 1980s, there has been a memorial stone at one corner of the former camp, marked with the red triangle and three different inscriptions about the history of the site.[121]

In the 1990s, in the wake of new historical findings and successful claims for damages on the part of forced laborers, there were also new efforts to create more in-depth exhibits concerning the history of forced labor in Berlin. There was an exhibition titled "Arbeit für den Feind" in 1998, and a book with that title was also published in conjunction with the exhibition. In 2003 and 2004, another exhibition, created in part by Bräutigam, traveled to thirteen different locations in Berlin.[122] One of the sites that has received the most attention lately is a former camp in the eastern district of Treptow, in the area of Schöneweide. In the district of Treptow alone, there were 82 forced labor camps, and "only one of these forced labor camps is by and large structurally preserved." As in other cases, there is a widespread language of rediscovery. The camp housed Italian, Belgian, and French forced laborers, among others, as well as female concentration camp inmates (primarily Jewish women from different countries) also being used as forced laborers.[123] In the wake of rediscovery, a study of the site was conducted, and an exhibition titled "The Forgotten Camp" was held in 1995. The structures were also placed under historic preservation in 1995. Since then, the site has become increasingly present in various memorial activities, but its future is not yet secure. The state Christian Democratic Party requested funding for a project on the site on September

16, 2002, with the following plea: "Despite structural changes, the character of the area (marked, since 2001, with a memorial plaque) is still clearly recognizable. As the last of the more than 1,000 camps in Berlin, the entire 3.3 hectare area has been under historic preservation since 1995; nonetheless the barracks are threatened with deterioration and demolition. . . . The establishment of an educational center, meeting place, and memorial site would therefore be a sensible use of the site."[124]

Thomas Flierl, the senator for science, research, and culture, responded in February 2003 that he had attempted to persuade the Regional Finance Office (OFD) to sell the federal property for a "symbolic sale price" to the Sozialpädagogisches Institut (SPI) for the creation and development of a memorial and meeting place, but the OFD had rejected this proposal, saying that it would seek to sell it for its full market value.[125] By June 2003, the OFD had come to an agreement about a sale price, and negotiations continued about who would be responsible for a possible documentation center.[126] In the debate in the state assembly's cultural committee, the senators and assembly members repeatedly referred to the authentic character of the place, one emphasizing, for example, that "here is an almost entirely authentically preserved camp. Furthermore, nowhere in Germany is there a documentation of forced labor such as that to which this site so lends itself."[127] The relatively transitory use of the land, negotiations over ownership, and the presence of a committed group of advocates have all further helped to secure this site in the city's memorial landscape.

In another case, a single letter from a former forced laborer, Maria Derewjanko, addressed to the school where she had once been forced to live, inspired an ever-expanding set of projects at the school. The letter describing her memories of life as a forced laborer led to a visit by Derewjanko and other members of her family, and eventually to an exhibition and a memorial plaque, "one of the few existing signs of remembrance for the more than 700 forced labor camps in Berlin."[128] This has turned into an expansive set of projects for the students, ongoing since Derewjanko first wrote to the school. Research projects, the recording of oral history, and meetings in Berlin and the Ukraine and in other towns where Derewjanko and her family were forced to work have all ensued. There is also currently a plan to create a memorial "on the authentic site" in the school.[129]

The issue of authenticity, then, appears frequently in discussions about marking the sites of forced labor. In the district of Spandau in 2003, there was a dispute in the district city council over the proper location for a memorial to the district's many forced laborers. There were close to fifty forced labor camps in Spandau alone, and the extensive industry (including armament production) there led to a large number of forced laborers living, and dying, in the district.[130] The dispute centered around the question of whether to place a memorial for the 40,000 forced laborers who worked in the district in a central location near the city hall (a plan favored by some Social Democrats and a group called Bündnis gegen Rechts, owing to the centrality and visibility of the site) or on an "authentic" location in front of a hospital on the western edge of the district, the Evangelisches Waldkrankenhaus Spandau.[131] The district city council finally decided that "the Waldkrankenhaus is an authentic site, because it was the location of the Arbeiterstadt Große Halle, in which around 3,000 forced laborers lived."[132] The choice is difficult to interpret—is this an attempt to keep this cruel chapter of Spandau's history out of plain view (and the town square), or is it a careful treatment of a pedagogically significant authentic site?

Even with the greater attention paid to forced labor sites recently, only about a dozen sites have been marked, and there are thus hundreds of other places where people walk by (or work in or live in) former forced labor sites without even knowing it. One factor contributing to this state of affairs is that comparatively little is known about many of these sites, because of the sketchy archival record. One such site is the Zwangsarbeiterlager Schönholz, "about which only very little information is to be found, and about which so far nothing has been published, [which] supposedly was located in the area of the Volkspark Schönholzer Heide . . . but there is even contradictory evidence concerning the exact location of the camp."[133] It is very possible that more markers will be erected commemorating sites of forced labor in light of new research, court decisions, and the last efforts to collect oral history and other information from the remaining survivors.

Today's landscape does not extensively convey how utterly interwoven forced labor and forced labor sites were in the city. But these sites are increasingly the subject of research and publications, and of exhibitions in local museums (*Heimatmuseen*) and other venues. The places that do get marked come about sometimes because of resonant claims about authenticity, because of the perseverance and engagement of a memorial entrepreneur, through chance, and sometimes (although never exclusively) through the gravity of what occurred on a given site. Shifts in historiography and the publicity surrounding forced labor clearly contributed to a growing number of efforts to mark sites of forced labor in the landscape, often in ways that filter national and international shifts in the historical and political understandings of forced labor through the efforts of local students or district city council members or district historians. These memorial projects are by no means exclusively top-down expressions of an official party line on forced labor. They vary broadly in scope and in audience. There is little doubt that local history projects—and memorial entrepreneurs— have played a very significant role in bringing these events into public memory. Certainly, markers appear on some of the larger and more egregious sites, but they also appear in places where people have (for various reasons) taken an active interest, such as the school to which Derewjanko wrote. Many historians and activists (and lawyers, victims, and corporations) see this as a history that was long forgotten, and that only started to gain more attention in the 1980s and especially the 1990s. In January 2000, for example, an article appeared in the *Berliner Zeitung* detailing Kubatzki's research, and offering specific addresses of forced labor camps throughout the city, as well as the names of companies that had used forced laborers.[134] As such research expands, it seems safe to assume that more memorial sites will appear in the future. This landscape of sites connected to forced labor is, and will continue for some time to be, dynamically intertwined with legal and historiographic processes, as well as an array of activism.

Conclusion

As one administrator pointed out to me, there is a more or less infinite pool of events that could be marked and remembered. Yet for reasons both obvious and obscure, only a finite pool of events is actually officially marked. The process of "rediscovering" places that had been collectively (if not individually) forgotten also leads to the question of what places, or what kinds of places, will be rediscovered in the future. It is entirely possible, even likely, that any of the hundreds of unmarked places referred to in this chapter may come to be marked. I would predict, however, that in those cases where any memorial more elaborate than a plaque or a stumbling stone is put into place, it will be on land that is publicly owned and vacant (or at least used in a way that is compatible with memorial use, or relatively easy to transfer to a different location), and that a memorial entrepreneur or group of memorial entrepreneurs will succeed in conveying a content and a meaning that resonate widely enough to generate both funding (whether public or private) and official approval. One area where there may be more extensive marking in the next few years is sites associated with "silent heroes" (*stille Helden*) who hid Jews or aided Jews in hiding, who have been the subject of increased attention in recent years.[135]

These memorial categories also overlap and are potentially intertwined. The destruction of Jewish life, for example, is by no means entirely separate from the issue of forced labor. Many forced laborers were Jewish, some of whom were married to non-Jewish women, others of whom performed forced labor in concentration camps or in urban subcamps of nearby concentration camps.[136] Similarly the people persecuted in "wild" concentration camps and torture cellars were often Jewish and/or political opponents of the Nazis, who (if they survived) may have later ended up as forced laborers. Thus the stories of persecution anchored to these sites are frequently connected to one another, albeit not always explicitly. Another form of interconnectedness that affects these sites is the fact that the persecution of any one individual actually took place in many locations—from the centers of Nazi power to the apartment from which a single person was hauled away to the distant concentration camp where she or he was killed. The marking of one site may bring multiple other places in the city (or the country or the continent) into awareness without the people engaging in the marking feeling compelled to mark all such sites. In reading through the texts of memorial plaques connected to resistance to or persecution by the Nazi regime, it is clear that the plaques (many of which were mounted in the 1970s and 1980s in the East, under the auspices of marking sites of anti-fascist resistance) heavily emphasize the dwellings of victims and resisters. Many plaque texts begin with the phrase "Here lived . . . ," so that people are often honored with a plaque on the building where they lived or were born, even if the place where they were tortured or killed is unmarked. So, there is a kind of triangulation of locales, which may partially explain why some places are not marked. In a sense, they may already be incorporated into other markers.

It is clear, then, that only some places get marked. Even with similar histories and similar claims to authenticity, only relatively few of the kinds of places examined here emerge into public awareness in ways that lead to official marking. Marking happens at these intersections of academics and laypeople, museums, political watersheds, anniversaries, and legal decisions. All of these elements combine and act on the landscape in uneven ways—calling some places and events "back" into public awareness, while leaving others behind. Because memorialization happens in both time and space, things change. New categories of sites emerge as worthy of research and, later, of marking. Furthermore, the meanings of past markers may change as well. New research may reveal past inaccuracies, and new generations may embrace or reject existing memorials in new ways. Certain issues, phenomena, and specific places may also fade from the public view or interest—they cease to be mentioned in newspapers, to appear as stops on walking tours, or to be the sites of visible public ceremonies where survivors or foreign dignitaries may gather to mark anniversaries. There are many active ways to forget, from noisily demolishing a building to simply ignoring a particular site, just as there are active processes of remembering.

6 Berlin and Beyond

I began this research wondering how people create memorial spaces in the middle of bustling cities. I wanted to know how patches of urban land are transformed from anonymous parking lots or vacant buildings into places of wide-ranging collective meaning where people might lay wreaths, hold ceremonies, or simply pause and take notice as they walk past. I wanted to find out what happens to places of great cruelty or great heroism as the decades go by. Digging into the archives, assembling stacks of before-and-after photographs, walking through the city, talking with architects, bureaucrats, and volunteer historians, and combing the pages of published catalogs of memorial sites have yielded a pattern I had not expected. Beneath the surface, I discovered a complex interplay of factors in which neither the market nor memory appeared singularly destined to prevail. I also found that the original event and the supposed authenticity of a site played only a partial role in shaping whether a given site became an officially designated element of the memorial landscape. While few markers disappeared after 1989, and considerable numbers of new markers emerged throughout the 1990s, many of the new and existing sites are located on officially designated public space rather than private property—traffic islands, green space, cemeteries, or sidewalks. In addition, despite the power of claims of authenticity, and the widespread emphasis on preserving authentic sites, not all places tied to the Nazi past become officially recognized sites of memory. Acts of individual courage or systematic terror that took place sixty years ago do not necessarily haunt these spaces to the point of precluding mundane uses like apartments or government offices. People may feel a chill down the back of their necks, or be deeply saddened by a given site, but at least seen from a sociological perspective, this troubling atmosphere or powerful feeling frequently emanates, not from the site itself, but from the social activity poured into the place and reminding those of us with no firsthand experience of the events what exactly happened there.

Based on this research, I argue that inquiries into urban landscapes and the social forces that intersect with them should combine an attention to memories and artistic representation with a close analysis of bureaucratic, legal, and material contexts. We can neither presume the exclusive dominance of market-driven land-use policy, for example, nor assume that very powerful collective memories like those associated with the Nazi past will necessarily become permanent parts of the urban landscape. What appears literally on the ground is the result of a negotiation between these different approaches to the cityscape. Rather than being a done deal, a city—any city, not only Berlin—is a conglomeration of happenstance and intention, inertia and upheaval. But it is the particular mixture of these forces that gives a city the shape we see as we walk its streets, plan its future, and face its problems and possibilities.

To understand cities and how they change over time, it is, of course, necessary to understand supply and demand as well as interest groups and growth machines. But if we limit ourselves to these arenas, we struggle to tell a complete story. Symbols, international politics, accident, moral visions, and the mechanisms through which these elements interact are also fundamental aspects of urban change, in Berlin and elsewhere. The theoretical framework running through this book comprises one way to incorporate historical and symbolic factors more systematically into analyses of urban change, and to bring legal, political, and economic concerns to bear on questions of aesthetics and the representation of the past. Spaces of concentrated collective memory rarely emerge in the urban landscape of Berlin as victors in a sharply drawn battle between market and memory, but more frequently at the intersection of art and recollection with bureaucracy and politics, as well as land use, landownership, the resonance of the site's meaning with a broader public, and the presence or absence of a memorial entrepreneur.

Examining these four forces and their broader structural contexts is one way to better understand the creation of the markers and erasures that shape the terrain of the city alongside the projects of residents, corpora-tions, real estate developers, government officials, and others. Private prop-erty, buildings already in use, places whose meanings do not resonate with a broader public, and sites without a committed advocate generally do not become memorials. In most cases, a site can meet three out of four of the above-mentioned criteria and still fade into the cityscape. In general, only when these conditions are met can a site with a close connection to resis-tance or persecution actually be transformed into a memorial or marker of some kind. I do not mean this framework to serve as a rigid model of urban memorial production, but rather as a schema of core processes inte-gral to the production of spaces of concentrated collective memory. This schema can serve as one approach for exploring how polities, communi-ties, neighborhoods, and states impose their visions of the past and of the future on the built environment. This framework is built on the case of Berlin, but I also mean it to be a useful starting point for the study of other places as well.

In addition to factors like memorial entrepreneurs, broader struc-tural conditions also play important roles in shaping these landscapes of memory. Politics and economics shape memorial construction profoundly, as do deeper habits and practices, and passing trends. Over the course of the 1990s, the types of memorial construction prevalent in West Germany in the 1980s began to shape memorial practices in the eastern half of the city too, for example. Private property and a new set of urban planning visions, combined with new kinds of politics and media outlets, led to a new era of memorial culture in the eastern half of the city (and to a lesser extent in the West). The democratization and decentralization of memo-rial practice, as well as the heightened international attention being paid to the new German capital, significantly affected memorial processes in the post-Wall era. The role of the memorial entrepreneur, and of the resonance of a given proposal with a broader public, also grew significantly in the eastern half of the city in the 1990s because of the new political structures. Indeed, the processes described here function primarily in democratic set-tings. In nondemocratic societies, memorialization is more likely to be more top-down, orchestrated by a central elite with a clear vision of how it wants to represent its past. In the case of Berlin, many (although not all) suggestions for memorial sites come from private citizens and civic organi-zations, even if they are then put through the filter of official approval. A parliamentary democracy offers far greater responsiveness of government to pressures from constituents than does a state socialist system dominated by a single party. But either way, states shape landscapes of memory. "In every sovereign country of the modern world, the workings of the state have set their mark upon the land," and Germany is no different.[1] On the other hand, much memorial work in a variety of political and economic systems (beyond Berlin as well) is more bottom-up, and more impromptu and impermanent—flowers left at a roadside cross, surreptitious markers placed at sites of state-sanctioned violence, or the leaving of objects and notes on chain-link fences surrounding the sites of recent tragedies.[2]

In Berlin and elsewhere, patches of land have become meaningful through the repetition of stories, the persistence of various groups and individuals, and now the presence of an array of interpretive materials retelling these stories. The closer we look at memorial production, the more these symbolic sites fall apart into the countless individual stories of bureaucratic happenstance, individual engagement, and being in the right place at the right time. But can we put these pieces back together again and see patterns? Indeed, the whole can tell a story of underlying norms, and of their production in committee meetings, newspaper articles, classrooms, and street corners. These memorials are perhaps what Michael Schudson refers to as a unity "whose origins are lost in time."[3] Memorial entrepreneurs both produce and reflect collective memory, and cultural conceptions of place and of history are both the impetus and the product of these actions. Public meetings, letters to the editor, and speeches in government committees may be the actions of individuals, but they also come together to define the boundaries of memory and the limits of the material representation and transmission of certain elements of the past.

Nearly every site examined here was years in the making. The web of building codes, government budgets, legislative process, and activism contributes to the slowness. In many cases memorials result from the attempts of citizens (often historians, artists, or archaeologists) to mark sites they deem particularly powerful and instructive. These civic efforts must be filtered through the government, and in almost all the cases examined here, there are local, national, and international interests at stake. The actions of district, state, and federal government bodies in Berlin (interacting with activists, artists, survivors, academics, and others) define and encourage the attachment of these kinds of meanings to plots of land and buildings, or parts of buildings—and not only when it comes to sites of resistance or persecution during the Nazi era. During one of our first conversations, I asked Volker Hobrack whether the presence of a memorial plaque might affect the value of a given property, and specifically whether there was a difference between positive and negative events being remembered. He quickly corrected me, telling me that for his purposes, it is wrong to think in terms of positive and negative events. For him, what I was referring to as "negative events" are simply aspects of Berlin's overall historical landscape. "It's all history," he said, and the goal of the commission that he heads is "to reinstate traces, [to work] against forgetting, to honor, to hinder forgetting, to awaken curiosity, to enrich the city." This means creating markers reminding people, not only of Nazi crimes, but also of a range of other eras and figures. Many people involved in creating markers commemorating resistance to and persecution by the Nazi regime are also involved in other aspects of marking the past in the built environment. Collective memory rears up everywhere in the cityscape—in equestrian statues of Prussian leaders, in popular struggles to prevent the demolition of East German buildings, and in plaques and statues honoring the scores of scientists, philosophers, and writers who have lived and worked in Berlin. The meanings treated in this book constitute only a small portion of Hobrack's efforts and of the total memorial landscape of Berlin.

These processes of investing urban land with powerful symbolism clearly occur in places very different from Berlin as well. For decades, scholars of the city have explored the anchoring of memory and meaning in a range of urban landscapes. Nearly sixty years ago, the sociologist Walter Firey looked at the symbol-drenched landscape of Boston and found a pattern of significant but economically unviable sites that could "only be understood in terms of the group values that they have come to symbolize."[4] In particular, he found that the obtrusive open spaces of Boston Common and three colonial burial grounds that stood in the way of retail expansion and smooth flows of both pedestrian and car traffic were impossible to explain using more conventional ecological models of urban growth. The colonial burial grounds, which interrupt the continuous line of storefronts, "have become invested with a moral significance which renders them almost inviolable."[5] Firey also concluded that, in the case of the Boston Common, it "has thus become a 'sacred' object, articulating and symbolizing genuine historical sentiments of a certain portion of the community. Like all such objects its sacredness derives, not from any intrinsic spatial attributes, but rather from its representation in people's minds as a symbol for collective sentiments."[6]

But how do such places emerge? The oppositions present in that long-ago article have continued to appear in the intervening decades.[7] The kinds of sentiments invoked by powerful symbols may also serve to boost tourist dollars, draw consumers, and encourage nearby investment, even if they may keep certain patches of urban land out of the real estate market or interrupt flows of traffic.[8] In the case of Berlin, overall memory does not trump the market, and the market does not trump memory. Politicians, activists, students, property owners, and others do devote urban land to memorialization despite dramatic fluctuations in property values and the demand for land, but frequently in places where the market is not very interested.

It is also important to remember that collective memory and its material manifestations are not the precise sum of individual attitudes at any given point. Instead, such memory results in part from a set of institutions that enable a group (a neighborhood, community, nation, or something even broader) to mobilize to recall the past, or the institutions on which the collective's most engaged agents of memory base their work. The physical markers discussed here are one result of the activities of such agents. Furthermore, once constructed, many then augment ongoing memory work, bolstering networks of activists, circuits of school tours, or series of publications, for example. Memorials happen only if they are approved, but they then can and do affect public opinion and deeper-seated ideas about history and ethics. The reception of the meaning of a given project can also range from near apathy to passionate enthusiasm. Opposition can also occur in the form of noisy protests against monument projects on the floor of the Bundestag or in editorial pages. Memory shapes the landscape through the day-to-day practices of memorial construction, which range from international debates about art and history to the offices of local parks departments, the meticulous pages of property registries, and colorful land-use plans.

One of the key issues in contemporary memorial practice in Berlin, and in these kinds of representation and transmission in general, is certainly the question of authenticity. Most of the places discussed in this book are what people would consider "authentic" sites, markers built on the sites of specific events that happened during the Nazi era. Authenticity can be very powerful. Many of us have had the experience of going somewhere where something "really" happened: a battlefield, Ground Zero at the former site of the World Trade Center, or the Anne Frank house, for example. Relics of human suffering and material damage clearly do transform the experience of a place, and places with such visible scars may seem to speak for themselves. But for those who did not experience the original events, and who encounter such sites when the most obvious evidence of destruction has been cleared, this intensity is largely created by people talking about a place, learning about it, researching its history, and conveying that history to other people, rather than by the site itself, especially in the middle of a dynamically changing city.

In Berlin, many authentic places do become memorial sites, but many fade. Arguments of authenticity appear across the board, but only some authentic locations are devoted exclusively to memorial use. Because the city experienced twelve years of Nazi rule, the stock of potential markers is nearly limitless. Theoretically, no part of the city remains untouched by some range of activity from that era, whether bureaucratic complicity, illegal pamphleting, or torture and systematic murder. Most of these actions and events are preserved only in the memories of those who experienced them. Other events are less fleeting, widely recorded, and firmly situated both in the collective memory and in the built environment.

While the language of the sacred is problematic in this context, in part by implying a positive connotation that does not often fit the sites being treated here, if we approach it carefully, it may provide a useful theoretical tool for understanding how a given plot of land may be infused with meanings that distinguish it from the rest of the urban environment. Particularly if we follow Émile Durkheim's understanding of the construction of the sacred, no place acquires this sort of untouchability of its own accord, and yet such places can be experienced in very powerful ways.[9] Both pilgrimage and tourism, for example, indicate a widespread desire to touch or be near authentic places or relics, even to be transformed by a wall, a pool of water, or a patch of earth. In the case of Berlin and other places of violence and suffering, sometimes elements of the past seem to inhere in the physical landscape, threatening to rise to the surface at any moment. But inhering is complicated. Accounts of persecution or resistance appear to cling to specific places, but this inhering is actually the result of extensive social activity that exposes and builds the past of a place. Durkheim writes that "by sacred things one must not understand simply those personal beings which are called gods or spirits; a rock, a tree, a spring, a pebble, a piece of wood, a house, in a word, anything can be sacred."[10] Rather than rocks, trees, and springs, in Berlin, we see vacant lots, parking lots, and abandoned buildings infused with properties that connect them to a very difficult past and sometimes set them apart from the meanings and rhythms of daily life. Often this happens in places with "authentic" connections to particular events.[11] These sites exhibit some of the properties of sacred places in the ways that they are cordoned off from other elements of urban life, and infused with meanings that set them apart from other plots of urban land. The sites treated in this book are infused with violence and sorrow rather than the kinds of meanings generally associated with the sacred. Thus it may be inaccurate to refer to these sites as sacred, but Durkheim's conviction about the social origins of the unique properties of sacred spaces may help to illuminate the unusual power of authentic sites in Berlin's material and political landscape.[12]

Material practices are fundamental to the creation of such places, as the play of language solidifies into buildings, lawns, and monuments. Mary Douglas finds that "most pollutions have a very simple remedy for undoing their effects. There are rites of reversing, untying, burying, washing, erasing, fumigating, and so on, which at a small cost of time and effort can satisfactorily expunge them. . . . The social consequences of some offences ripple out in all directions and can never be reversed."[13] In the case of Berlin, "pollution" by the Nazi past is often reversed by use. The finance ministry moved into Göring's air defense ministry, and Sony built its European headquarters atop the site of an infamous Nazi court. At the same time, however, activists, residents, eyewitnesses, and politicians fight to preserve the traces of certain pollutions (and also the more positive meanings associated with resistance), in part for their moral and pedagogical effects. This maintenance of the traces of "pollution" requires much time and effort if they are to "ripple out in all directions." Thus the language of pollution and of the sacred does not map perfectly onto Berlin's memorial landscape but offers ways to more clearly understand the production of intensely symbolic spaces in the midst of the city. Many of these spaces, in turn, have a kind of moral narrative attached to them.

In his study of the White Mountain Apache, Keith Basso also recounts the power of the landscape to act as an anchor of moral tales. Specific mountains, rivers, and trees, as well as the names they are given, remind White Mountain Apache of proper ways of living. The model for Western Apache storytelling "holds that oral narratives have the power to establish enduring bonds between individuals and features of the natural landscape. Furthermore, as a direct consequence of such bonds, persons who have acted improperly will be moved to reflect critically on their misconduct and resolve to improve it."[14] Basso charts the attachment of these narratives to places as a highly social and linguistic process, achieving its authority through public, if often subtle, retelling and recurrent personal remembering. Thus Basso makes clear not only the causes but also the effects of the moral tales inscribed in the Arizona desert. The process is executed collectively, but directed at and experienced by individual wrongdoers. The landscape instructs, warns, and reminds, but through social activity. Basso also draws on Bakhtin's notions of chronotopes, which might offer a model with which to think about these punctuating sites in the landscape of Berlin, despite the obvious differences between the recollection of Nazi crimes in Berlin's landscape and the infusion of the desert with moral lessons among the Western Apache.

Geographical features have served the people [the Western Apache] for centuries as indispensable mnemonic pegs on which to hang the moral teachings of their history. Accordingly, such locations present themselves as instances of what Mikhail Bakhtin calls *chronotopes*. As Bakhtin (1981:7) describes them, chronotopes are: "points in the geography of a community where time and space intersect and fuse. Time takes on flesh and becomes visible for human contemplation; likewise, space becomes charged and responsive to the movements of time and history and the enduring character of a people. . . . Chronotopes thus stand as monuments to the community itself, as symbols of it, as forces operating to shape its members' images of themselves."[15]

In both Berlin and the Arizona desert, it is not only time that takes on flesh, but also a moral vision. In the case of the memorials examined here, this moral vision is a mixture of atonement, recollection, mourning and warning literally embodied in the landscape. Such sites became the kind of "mnemonic pegs" to which Bakhtin refers, concrete places and symbols enmeshed in webs of memory, political legitimacy, and moral instruction.[16]

Beneath the often garrulous processes surrounding the creation of such memorial sites, then, lies a widespread agreement about the terms of debate. Most parties involved seem to agree that the city's land can be cleanly classified into authentic and inauthentic sites, and that places that witnessed Nazi violence have a potential moral volatility that sets them apart from places less charged with the Nazi past. One example is a museum developed in western Berlin in the 1990s in the Wannsee Villa in a wooded upper-class district of West Berlin, where a meeting to organize the systematic destruction of Europe's Jewish residents took place in 1942. For decades after World War II, the villa was used as a day camp for school outings to the lakeside, but in 1982, on the fortieth anniversary of the Wannsee Conference, groups of citizens including victims' leagues, the Jewish Community, and the League for Human Rights developed an initiative to set up a museum (*Gedenkstätte*) in the building. In 1986, the West Berlin Senate began supporting the initiative.[17] The Gedenkstätte was dedicated on the fiftieth anniversary of the Wannsee Conference, January 20, 1992.[18] "The authentic rooms, with a few historical wall-, ceiling-, and ground-traces exposed in the process of restoration, serve to some extent as 'environment' for the documentation exhibit," Stefanie Endlich and Thomas Lutz, two active participants in Berlin's memorial culture, note in their guide to memorial sites in Berlin, *Gedenken und Lernen an historischen Orten.*[19] Here the term "authentic" conveys a sense of the wallpaper, paneling, and floorboards as in some way witnesses to the original events, and their exposure in the restoration process as apparently contributing to the mood, and perhaps power, of the exhibit.[20] Brian Ladd concludes that, "the single terrible day in this house's history denied it the right to be a normal place in the city." But in fact this house spent decades as a "normal place" and was only denied that right once a combination of activists and officials envisioned the space as determined fully by its "single terrible day."[21] Old flooring tiles, prison walls, or wallpaper are themselves rarely capable of communicating the events that they witnessed. These events may have been seared into the public memory and into the landscape, but not of their own accord.

One kind of authenticity seems actually to preclude the construction of any kind of memorial space or museum. Public controversy has repeatedly flared up about different portions of the bunker complex around Hitler's chancellery, most built in 1938, along with the Neue Reichskanzlei

itself (a massive building constructed adjacent to the existing chancellery), and each time, the city authorities and many city residents have
flatly rejected any kind of preservation. Every few years, a new construction project seems to expose another corner of the complex, provoking
another round of public debate. This kind of authenticity appears to be
so potent, and so likely to attract right-wing extremists, that the favored
option is to cover these places over again with gravel and sand. Clearly,
these are singular sites, the centers of Nazi power, their ability to capture
the public's fascination evident in television documentaries, films, walking tours, and years of newspaper coverage. Even with state ownership, no
competing land use, and, in many cases, a committed memorial entrepreneur, no portion of this complex has yet been placed under historic preservation. Various prominent figures have worked to have various elements of
these bunkers preserved as witnesses to the city's Nazi past, but all without
success. While these efforts have failed so far, until the last remnants are
removed, there is still the possibility that their official status might change.
Will they be treated differently once another generation has passed?

In 1988, the GDR built high-rise apartment buildings on top of the
former chancellery and parallel to the no-man's-land along the Wall. The
East German government made no effort to indicate what had previously
been on the site, or to preserve Hitler's bunker, which was largely destroyed
in the process of laying the foundations for the new buildings.[22] The rest
of the bunkers remained untouched beneath the Berlin Wall and the no-
man's-land that ran its length. Within days of the fall of the Wall, however,
discussion began about what to do with these vast empty spaces deep in the
heart of the city, which had tremendous development potential. Throughout 1990, different portions of the bunker complex were uncovered accidentally, including the *Fahrerbunker* used by Hitler's drivers. In each case,
the bunkers were covered up again.[23] In the case of the *Fahrerbunker*, however, the sealing of the bunker was the point at which the debate began.

In January 1991, Alfred Kernd'l, at the time scientific director of
the State Archaeology Office, wrote an opinion piece in the Berlin daily
Tagesspiegel arguing in favor of preserving the newly rediscovered drivers'
bunkers.[24] He felt that conservatives kept quiet on the subject, while the
"liberal-progressive camp" was arguing for the removal of the bunkers. "It
may be painful to us," he wrote, "but the bunkers here are the only physically perceptible coordinates of the historical topography. Simply for that

reason they must be preserved in situ as an accessible [*begehbare*] monument."[25] In another piece, Kernd'l called the bunkers "authentic witnesses of their time, which, through a simple presence here and now, can make historical remembering comprehensible and perceptible. Their historical substance in a constantly changing and renewing cityscape [*Stadtbild*], precisely in a capital city with its particular demands, secures both profile and singularity." Thus Kernd'l emphasized the intrinsic historical value, authenticity, and instructive properties of these bunkers as justification for their preservation. In 1992, the State Archaeology Office, under Kernd'l's direction, was fighting for the "preservation of the last material fate-traces [*Schicksalsspuren*] in an otherwise faceless wasteland."[26] In March of that year, the state assembly took up the issue, with the Greens authoring legislation to support the documentation of the site. All parties on the culture committee of the state assembly unanimously supported this move. The Social Democrats even tacked a suggestion about a possible *Gedenkstätte* onto the legislation, but later that same year, at another public forum, it was clear that the planning for this area was still up for grabs.[27] Today, none of the bunkers have been placed under historic preservation, and much of the land housing the bunkers is either already slated for construction or on the market. What happened?

The area simply appears to be too politically toxic for any kind of official marking. Opposition to any official designation of this "historically contaminated" land was expressed by historians, officials, and leaders of Berlin's Jewish Community, among others.[28] Many archaeologists and historians may argue that some portion of the bunkers should be preserved so that the blunt material remnants of the center of Nazi power confront people in the new German capital. But opponents counter that the sites are not worthy of preservation, that they have no right to official acknowledgment so close to the center of a unified Berlin and the new Holocaust Memorial, and that officially sanctioned markers would run the risk of becoming pilgrimage sites for neo-Nazis.

There have been years of tug-of-war about the various bunkers stuck in the sand south of the Brandenburg Gate. On July 1, 1992, Kernd'l called for the drivers' bunkers to be placed under official historical preservation, "integrated into the foundations of any new construction such as state offices or ministries," and made accessible to the public.[29] Kernd'l estimated that the restoration and preservation of the bunkers could be completed within two or three years.[30] The day after Kernd'l's plans appeared in the newspapers, a wide spectrum of groups spoke out against the plans, including Berlin historians and leaders of Berlin's Jewish community.[31] Kernd'l's boss, Culture Senator Ulrich Roloff-Momin, who appears to have been a key figure in the bunkers not being placed under historical preservation, said by July 4 that the issue was not whether to make the bunkers publicly accessible but to "secure these traces in light of the dynamic planning and construction precisely in this area."[32] A few days later, Roloff-Momin officially denied that the bunkers would be opened to the public. At this point, he still left open the option that the bunkers might be placed under historical preservation, but by October 1992, he had backed away from wanting to preserve them at all. "I defend myself against the levelers [*Glattmacher*] of history," Kernd'l proclaimed.[33] Other prominent figures did indeed argue for "leveling," claiming the best solution to this increasingly thorny problem was to document the contents, then fill up the bunkers, seal them, and build over them.[34] In the Senate's view, the authenticity of the site clearly posed a risk of attracting neo-Nazis, and it was thus left unpreserved and up for sale. Years later, neither the drivers' bunkers nor any other remaining bunkers in this area are under historic preservation. Even a site so "polluted" by its association with the Nazi past can become a regular piece of real estate if other forces do not intervene, and in this case, even relatively prominent memorial entrepreneurs and an obvious international fascination with the sites have not been sufficient to lead to any of them being placed under historic preservation. The architecture critic Michael Mönninger wrote in 1999,

every time construction crews begin digging in the area between the newly routed Behrenstraße and the disappeared Voßstraße, they scratch some corner of the extensive bunker system. . . . Must we now stop the new rebuilding of the Ministergärten for years and turn it into a *Gräberfeld* of Nazi archaeology? . . . Anyone who rigorously answers this question "no," and like Andreas Nachama, already speaks of "archaeological environmental pollution," overlooks the difficult ripening process that this sunken toxic waste [*Giftmüll*] will undergo. Even in the distant future, not enough grass will grow in the gardens of the State Offices to make us forget the carefully documented caverns. And upon entering the *Stelenfeld* of the Holocaust Monument on the corner of Behren- and Ebertstraße, only the most clueless person will be able to ignore [the fact] that they are walking directly over the bunker of the Goebbels villa. Instead of a macabre reconstruction of the destroyed *Führerbunker*, the partially maintained sites of the Goebbels villa, the bodyguard [s' bunkers], or the Neue Reichskanzlei offer themselves to excavation.[35]

The discussion has often focused on the historical value of the site and on its instructional value and its ability to warn against a return of fascism— as well as the danger due precisely to its authenticity. These are themes that appear again and again in debates about memorializing resistance to and persecution by the Nazi regime. In August 1992, Kernd'l and others set up an exhibition of the drivers' bunker in the German History Museum on Unter den Linden, making the bunkers a topic of national discussion. Ostensibly, the Museum is a national museum, and its director, Christoph Stölzl, was appointed by Chancellor Helmut Kohl to oversee the official representations of the Federal Republic. Kernd'l, Roloff-Momin, and Stölzl held a press conference to open the exhibition. Here Kernd'l disagreed with the other two concerning the need for preservation of the bunkers as a reminder of the horrors of the Nazi era.[36] The organizers of the exhibition hoped to provoke some public debate, mainly in the form of a comment book designed to collect the public's opinion about what the fates of the bunkers should be. Stölzl suggested the removal of the objects found in the bunkers to an exhibition space in a museum, reasoning that the display of these objects—ranging from furniture to amateur Nazi-themed murals—in a museum might defuse the power of the site. The danger of neo-Nazi pilgrimages was, he felt, far greater if the objects remained in situ than if they were removed from their authentic location and placed within the confines of the museum.[37]

The issue arose again in 1995 when the state governments actually began the preparations for building their offices on the nearby lots. "The bunkers are in the way; not only in terms of construction, but also symbolically," *Der Spiegel* observed. By this time, Kernd'l had retired, but he continued his struggle to preserve the bunkers. The Green Party in the state assembly also took up the cause of preservation, seeking, not to prevent the construction of the states' offices, but rather to integrate the remnants of the bunkers into the new construction. A member of the Christian Democrats joined forces with the Greens on this issue, arguing that the bunkers should be like "thorns in the flesh of the place on which the federal states will soon reside. . . . National Socialism cannot simply be hauled off to the construction materials dump." New legislation had also shifted responsibility for the site from the Culture Ministry to the Urban Development Ministry. At this point, another round of controversy about the bunkers began. As *Der Spiegel* pointed out, it appeared the final decision concerning the bunkers—which it referred to as "contaminated catacombs"—would be made by the future property owners themselves, the state governments.[38]

By 1997, the states had still not purchased the land from the federal government, construction had not yet begun, and the question of historical preservation still hung in the air. The price of the land dropped to DM 5,000 per square meter (more than $300 per square foot), thanks to the designation of the plots as a special "development area" (*Entwicklungsgebiet*),[39] a designation that also required that the land be handed to its buyers free of physical, legal, or financial burdens (*Altlasten*), in this case potentially the remains of the bunkers. There was no question as to the salability of the land, only about the specific details of the sale.[40] In 1997, when the area of the Ministergärten was being prepared for the construction of the German states' Berlin offices, the new state archaeologist, Wilfried Menghin, vehemently rejected the proposals to demolish the remains of the bunker complex, warning that such a demolition "would generate a storm of international protest."[41]

Yet efforts to preserve any portion of the bunker complex have failed, despite extensive press coverage, the absence of existing buildings on the site, and the fact that the land was owned by the state.[42] The explanation for the failure of efforts to preserve the bunkers must, then, be the content and the lack of resonance. This site met three out of the four conditions— it was a vacant lot, owned by the state, and supported by an active and well-publicized memorial entrepreneur. In this case, however, it appears that a site is so polluted by its past, and apparently so at risk of generating contemporary neo-Nazi sentiment as well, that government officials like Roloff-Momin see it as preferable to return the site to "normal" use rather than to make its past visible. Today, there is no sign of such a project, the bunkers are not under official preservation status, and the land just to the north of the drivers' bunker has filled with the new offices of the federal states. Most parties involved operate under an assumption about the power of the authentic location and the moral content of this physical place, implying a belief in a kind of material transmission of evil. More important than the abstract location—the longitude and latitude of the site—were the actual physical remnants of the Nazi regime. This degree of physical connection to the Nazis renders it essentially toxic, at least in its original form. Kernd'l referred to the Reichskanzlei bunkers as "authentic witnesses of their time, which, through a simple presence here and now can make historical remembering comprehensible and perceptible," but it is also this authenticity tied to the Nazis, and specifically to the SS, that seems to pose the greatest threat of attracting neo-Nazis.[43] The discussion will likely continue to reappear as long as the remnants of these bunkers still lurk in the sand, if the past decade and a half are any indication. It may be the drivers' bunker or any of the other nearby bunkers, including Hitler's bunker and Goebbels's bunker, all located in an area of forty thousand square meters that *Der Spiegel* describes as "highly historically contaminated."[44]

The bunkers built for the Neue and Alte Reichskanzlei, Hitler's chancelleries, comprised an expansive complex. Hitler's bunker itself, the *Führerbunker*, warrants separate treatment here because its meanings and current use differ significantly from the rest of the bunkers. Hitler's bunker was located in the back garden of the Alte Reichskanzlei and was built both later and stronger than the rest of the chancellery bunkers. The chancellery itself was burned out in the war, but the façade remained. "In 1948, however, the Soviet occupation authorities closed the bunkers and then leveled the ruins of the chancellery and all the other buildings adjoining the ministerial gardens. . . . After World War II, the remains of the former government quarter were torn down, despite their partially rebuildable condition. Despite several demolition attempts, the 'absolute un-place' [*absoluter Unort*], the 'Führer's bunker,' was not entirely removed."[45] As late as 1959, large chunks of the bunker were still visible in the empty plains between Wilhelmstraße and Potsdamer Platz.[46] The area remained an empty wasteland along the eastern edge of the Wall until the late 1980s when, as has been noted, the East German government began building prefabricated housing blocks on top of the former old chancellery, including Hitler's bunker itself.[47] During preparation for construction, the bunker was opened and photographed, then largely removed.[48] In March 1992, the Free Democrats in the state assembly brought up the question of the Reichskanzlei bunkers and Wilhelmstraße more generally. "The history of this place must not be allowed to be suppressed, the remaining traces of history—and those include the remains of the *Führerbunker*—must be integrated into planning for the capital. . . . Demolition of the newly erected apartment buildings is out of the question owing to housing short-ages in the city."[49] Thus the land was already in use, and there was clearly insufficient public resonance that would support the preservation of the bunkers, much less the demolition of existing structures in favor of some kind of opening up of these "traces of history."

Authenticity is powerful in more than one way. On the one hand, many "authentic" sites appear to have an aura of instructive power, warning against the repetition of Nazi crimes. On the other hand, some authentic sites throughout Germany possess a different kind of aura, one that threat-ens to attract neo-Nazi pilgrimages. Just outside Berlin is another Nazi site where efforts to create some kind of *Gedenkstätte* have failed. The street leading up to the entrance of the former concentration camp Sachsenhau-sen is lined with houses built for SS officers. The question of whether to place the houses under historical preservation was hotly discussed in the 1990s. One concern expressed by residents was that if officially recognized, the houses might "become an El Dorado for radical right-wing youth," who might turn them into "cult objects and gathering points."[50]

Authentic ties to acts of great cruelty or great heroism are not, on their own, sufficient to bring a site into official collective memory and wide-spread public interest. Some authentic sites become real estate, and there are certainly instances of widely known memorial sites (including the cen-tral Holocaust Memorial) being constructed on "inauthentic" sites. Clearly, then, it is possible for potentially valuable urban land to be transformed into internationally known memorial sites side by side with some of the most valuable real estate in Europe. In the center of Berlin, for example, a parking lot has, as we have seen, been turned into a subtle marker of the Nazi book-burning at Bebelplatz, and a prime piece of real estate is now dedicated to the exclusive purpose of remembrance of the Holocaust. These sites have emerged alongside the burgeoning real estate market and the transfer of the German capital from Bonn to Berlin. Artists, survivors, activists, and politi-cians have continued to make powerful and successful arguments for mark-ing such sites. Such places take on meaning through a sequence of events that can happen over months or years, and that are capable of dramatically changing the meaning and use of patches of urban land.

Once constructed, memorials have a tendency to become uncontro-versial.[51] This type of remembering is rarely a foregone conclusion. But so often, in Berlin and elsewhere, once a memorial has actually been built, it forms a more stable part, not only of the urban landscape, but also of shared understandings of the city and the past. At the same time, urban landscapes are intrinsically in flux, and it is entirely possible, indeed likely, that the understanding and form of some of the sites I have examined will change. The official stance toward authentic sites has changed significantly in recent decades, largely in response to the actions of artists, historians, citizens' groups, and others concerned with memorialization. And in coming decades, new places will surely emerge as worthy of some kind of marking. The examples in Chapter 4, for example, only became memorials relatively recently. For decades, these places were used in other ways, and only with the intersections of the kinds of factors I talk about here were their meanings, and uses, transformed. Even as I write, once-forgotten places are being pulled into the public awareness. The physical remnants of Nazi forced labor camps are one example. When I began conducting this research, forced labor sites in general fell into the category of forgotten sites—they received little press, and few had been turned into any kind of memorial. By 2003, forced labor camps had become the subject of an exhibition that traveled to many of Berlin's local district museums, and proposals were afoot for turning at least one remaining camp (which still existed more or less in its 1945 condition) into a memorial site.[52] In this case, memorial entrepreneurs appeared on the scene at a time when forced labor sites had begun to resonate much more widely with the public, in part in light of recent court decisions concerning financial compensation of surviving forced laborers.

One of the new projects shaping the memorial landscape of the city is a series of hundreds of "stumbling stones" set into Berlin's sidewalks. In 2004, several U.S. newspapers ran stories on the subject. The *Boston Globe*'s Jefferson Chase reported, for example, "a 4-by-4-inch brass-plated cobblestone . . . the latest addition to the more than 3,000 'Stumbling Stones' that [the Cologne sculptor Gunter] Demnig has laid in cities and towns throughout Germany over the past decade. . . . Where the memorial stones are laid is determined not by governmental committees, but by history itself, as researched by Demnig, schoolchildren, or patrons."[53] The stones cost around $100 and recall a diverse array of Jewish residents killed by the Nazis, often placed in front of the buildings where the people lived or worked. Many Germans (and reporters) find the stones compelling in their simplicity and their immediacy, in contrast to the central Holocaust Memorial, for example. A Cologne homeowner, however, believed his rights to be violated by two stumbling stones that the sculptor had set in the sidewalk before his property and took Demnig to court in 2003; according to Demnig, he "threatened to take me all the way to the Federal Constitutional Court because the stones reduced the value of his property."[54] Sometimes objections to the stones were registered on a much larger scale. At least as of November 2003, the city of Munich had refused to grant Demnig permission to install stumbling stones in the city's sidewalks.[55] In Berlin, the move to place markers in sidewalks grew exponentially in the late 1990s and early in the 2000s. Between 1996 and 2004, 350 stones were set in the sidewalks of the districts of Friedrichshain and Kreuzberg alone, with the aim of eventually installing a stone for each of the 2,000 people from these districts who died at the hands of the Nazis.[56] "[T]he very nature of the project reminds us that history, like memory itself, is an ongoing process," Chase concluded in the *Globe*. (See Figure 6.1.)

The intense specificity of the sites of Nazi power in the historical imaginations of activists, European Community members, and readers

FIGURE 6.1. Four "Stumbling Stones," Oranienstr. 204, 2005. Photograph by Alexander Käsbohrer / Anje Werner.

of the *New York Times* may seem to contradict recent analytical assumptions that see the specificity of "place" receding in the face of homogenizing forces.[57] Yet this phenomenon, and other international aspects of collective memory, are difficult to interpret with the existing theoretical toolkit for the study of collective memory. Berlin is faced with the political, economic, spatial, and symbolic task of capital building at a time of expanding globalization, in which collective memory increasingly transgresses and adheres to national borders in uneven ways.[58] Berlin also evokes an international gaze like few other contemporary cities.[59] This international attention must push us to consider collective memory, material culture, and memorialization in international or transnational terms. Theories of collective memory in general and memorialization in particular have tended to remain resolutely located within national borders. But these theories need to expand beyond their traditional boundaries. Specifically, much of the study of collective memory and memorialization has presumed rather than investigated the role of the nation-state in defining the boundaries of collective memory. However, neither the creation nor the experience of memorial space happens exclusively within national borders. Rather, both take place in an increasingly transnational context.

From Cambodia to Berlin to South Africa to Washington, D.C., memorial projects and historic preservation efforts actually frequently operate in an increasingly international context, one in which artists, donors, historians, political officials, and even the people who visit sites of memory are often aware of the actions of their counterparts in far-off places. Yet little has been written about ways to theorize and investigate the international, transnational, or global quality of collective memory in general, and of memorialization and historic preservation in particular.[60] Much work has been done on the links between memory, territory, and the nation, but less on non-national forms of collective memory and connections to specific places.[61] Classical and contemporary analysts alike often presume that the nation-state is the logical boundary of collective memory—and of course they are frequently correct in doing so. But despite the fact that there are obvious (and possibly increasing) international aspects of memorial practices, the theoretical approaches to memory are largely silent when it comes to discussing the transnational aspects of memory.

Conclusion

The twin processes of remembering and forgetting, then, do need to be approached with a greater awareness of the potentially transnational properties of memory. They also need to be studied in ways that integrate structural and symbolic factors. Any memorial is wrapped up in questions of politics and economics, as well as in the memories of the actual events. When most of us walk past a given monument or memorial, if we notice it at all, we rarely think about where it came from or what it was supposed to accomplish, or alternative forms it could have taken or messages it could have conveyed.

A certain skepticism also exists concerning the direct effects of such memorializing, as even those who are directly involved are also aware of the uncertainty of the actual effects of a particular site on public awareness.[62] But even with this skepticism, efforts to mark the Nazi past in Berlin's landscape continue, as does the belief in the ability of these markers to shape future behavior. Sites connected to the Nazi past, and particularly places with "authentic" connections to that era, continue to carry a particular moral and political weight, even if it can be difficult to predict whether remembering will lead to prevention.[63] Furthermore, the use, experience, and interpretation of these sites will change over time. What will become of them in 100 years' time, or even in 20? None of these sites are as fixed in the landscape as they might appear. And new sites appear even after decades of silence about a particular site, event, or individual.

What are some of the consequences of remembering, and what are some of the consequences of forgetting? The ways in which people grapple with these questions refract broader debates in society, and controversies (or the absence of controversy) can serve as important windows into the way a contemporary polis confronts its past. Memorial sites often include messages about how people are supposed to behave, telling visitors about a shared heritage or warning them of the need to avoid a repetition of the crimes being remembered. Memorials are thus often ways of linking the past to the future, in Berlin and elsewhere.[64] This book suggests one way of analyzing competing visions of the future by investigating struggles over representations and interpretations of the past. Certainly, memorial construction follows different paths in different countries and in different eras. The precise constellation of these factors in Berlin may differ from the precise constellation in Buenos Aires, Rome, or New York. But the forces at work in Berlin can illuminate many of the forces at work in other places as well. Taking a closer look at memorial projects yields important clues about the dynamics of collective memory, and about the contemporary construction of place. The theoretical framework presented here illuminates the concrete processes of place making and memorial construction in Berlin, but speaks to the production of memorial spaces in other settings as well.[65]

Sometimes debates over sites of memory may be proverbial tempests in teapots or bitter battles over tiny patches of political turf. But debates over memorials may also be of dire urgency, not only for survivors, but also for broader formations of local or national identity, international political relations, urban development, and collective moral frameworks. Ultimately, these interpretations of the past of a given place (and of a given collectivity) are also intertwined with visions of the future. Plaques, sculptures, museums, and other memorial forms comprise one set of ways in which memory and politics settle into the social and physical terrain. By creating such places, people craft landscapes, conjure up selected elements of the past, and plot courses for the future.

REFERENCE MATTER

Notes

ABBREVIATIONS

AB   Abgeordnetenhaus von Berlin
BA   Bundesarchiv (Berlin-Lichterfelde)
BVV Bezirksverordnetenversammlung (district council)
DS   Drucksache
DW *Die Welt*
GDR German Democratic Republic (East Germany)
IHT *International Herald Tribune*
LB   Landesarchiv Berlin
NYT *New York Times*
SA   Sturmabteilung
SED Sozialistische Einheitspartei Deutschland
SS   Schutzstaffel
TLG Liegenschaftsgesellschaft der Treuhandanstalt mbH
VVN Vereinigung der Verfolgten des Naziregimes

CHAPTER I: LANDSCAPES OF REMEMBERING AND FORGETTING

1. The use of the term "entrepreneur" in this case is not entirely unproblematic, in particular in implying, incorrectly, that these actors might be motivated by financial calculation rather than the host of other motivations that I have found. I use the term here in a way that builds loosely on other sociological descriptions of actors engaged in particular transformative projects, marshaling resources and organizing supporters to achieve particular goals—in this case, the construction of deeply symbolic spaces in the urban landscape. Clearly, however, my use differs in important ways from Howard Becker's "moral entrepreneurs," who redefine the boundaries of deviance, or Paul DiMaggio's "cultural entrepreneurs." My use is much closer to Vered Vinitzky-Seroussi's "agents of memory." See Howard Becker, *Outsiders: Studies in the Sociology of Deviance* (New York: Free Press, 1963); Paul DiMaggio, "Cultural Entrepreneurship in Nineteenth-Century Boston, Part I: The Creation of an Organizational Base for High Culture in America," *Media,*

Culture and Society 4:1 (Winter 1982): 33–50, and "Cultural Entrepreneurship in Nineteenth-Century Boston, Part II: The Classification and Framing of American Art," ibid. 4:4 (Autumn 1982): 303–321; Vered Vinitzky-Seroussi, "Commemorating a Difficult Past: Yitzhak Rabin's Memorials," *American Sociological Review* 67:1 (2002): 30–51; Robin Wagner-Pacifici and Barry Schwartz, "The Vietnam Veterans Memorial: Commemorating a Difficult Past," *American Journal of Sociology* 97:2 (1991): 376–420.

2. Edward Linenthal, *The Unfinished Bombing* (Oxford: Oxford University Press, 2001); Michael Sorkin and Sharon Zukin, eds., *After the World Trade Center: Rethinking New York City* (New York: Routledge, 2002). Newspaper coverage of the debate over a memorial at the World Trade Center site consistently describes public conceptions of Ground Zero as sacred space that should not be profaned by commercial development. In his farewell speech, for example, Mayor Rudolf Giuliani said, "I really believe we shouldn't think about this site out there, right behind us, right here, as a site for economic development. . . . We should think about a soaring, monumental, beautiful memorial that just draws millions of people here that just want to see it" (Michael Kimmelmann, "Out of Minimalism, Monuments to Memory," *New York Times*, Jan. 13, 2002). At the six-month anniversary of the attacks, "relatives of the trade center dead and residents of the area ha[d] emerged as a powerful bloc intent on protecting the sanctity of the suffering as searchers continue to pull human remains from the grave that is ground zero" (Lynne Duke, "Six Months After: A Memorial Built on Beams of Light," *Washington Post*, Mar. 4, 2002).

3. See, e.g., Sorkin and Zukin, eds., *After the World Trade Center*; Judy Ledgerwood, "The Cambodian Tuol Sleng Museum of Genocidal Crimes: National Narrative," *Museum Anthropology* 21:1 (1997): 82–98; Andreas Huyssen, "Memory Sites in an Expanded Field: The Memory Park in Buenos Aires," in id., *Present Pasts: Urban Palimpsests and the Politics of Memory* (Stanford: Stanford University Press, 2003), 94–109.

4. When writing about "collective" memory in contemporary Germany, it is essential to ask just who this collective might be. While even in seemingly homogeneous settings, the notion of the collective needs to be called into question, Berlin in particular and Germany in general are also truly heterogeneous societies. More than 13 percent of Berlin's population consists of citizens of other countries. Furthermore, regardless of citizenship and country of origin, the extent to which a "collective" memory is shared by residents of a given city or country must vary significantly, in ways that problematize any direct correspondence between place of residence and shared connections to the past of a given place. See Rainer Ohliger and Ulrich Raiser, *Integration und Migration in Berlin: Zahlen-Daten-Fakten* (Berlin: Der Beauftragte des Senats von Berlin für Integration und Migration, 2005), and Yasemin Soysal, *Limits of Citizenship: Migrants and Postnational Membership in Europe* (Chicago: University of Chicago Press, 1994).

5. Wendy Griswold writes about these "economic, political, social, and cultural patterns and exigencies that occur at any particular point in time" as "the social world" in *Cultures and Societies in a Changing World* (Thousand Oaks, Calif.: Pine Forge Press, 1994), 15. To understand how cultural objects (which, I would argue, include memorial sites) emerge, she develops a "cultural diamond" to highlight the interconnectedness of audiences (intended and unintended), creators, objects, and contexts (ibid., 14).

6. Elements of this discussion also appeared in my chapter, "Collective Memory and Locality in Global Cities," in *Global Cities: Cinema, Architecture, and Urbanism in a Digital Age*, ed. Patrice Petro and Linda Krause, 31–48 (New Brunswick, N.J.: Rutgers University Press, 2003).

7. While the English-language materials produced by the museum refer to this exhibition as "Blind Faith," I believe "blind trust" is a more accurate translation of the German *blindes Vertrauen,* and I therefore use the latter translation here.

8. Her life in hiding in Berlin is well documented in her book *Ich trug den gelben Stern* (Munich: dtv, 1978). Unlike most of the other factory workers, Deutschkron is not blind, but for a while she was able to be exempt from harder labor (and be employed by Weidt) by claiming a knee injury.

9. As discussed in Chapter 4, the property was auctioned off to the district housing authority in 2005, further increasing the likelihood that the small museum will remain.

10. For more on restitution, see Bettina Reimann's *Städtische Wohnquartiere: Der Einfluss der Eigentümerstruktur: Eine Fallstudie aus Berlin-Prenzlauer Berg* (Opladen: Leske + Budrich, 2000).

11. Clearly, there is also a difference between "feeling" the authenticity in place—whether in Berlin, Cambodia, or Oklahoma City—and being exposed to historical narratives and artifacts in a museum context. Either way, such experiences of places and artifacts differ profoundly from the way that eyewitnesses and survivors would experience them. Allison Landsberg discusses elements of this phenomenon at length, with her concept of "prosthetic memory," which "emerges at the interface between a person and a historical narrative about the past, at an experiential site such as a movie theater or museum." The observer *feels* the memory through this experience, which Landsberg believes can "shape that person's subjectivity and politics." *Prosthetic Memory: The Transformation of American Remembrance in the Age of Mass Culture* (New York: Columbia University Press, 2004), 2.

12. Janrense Boonstra and Marie-José Rijnders, *Anne Frank House: A Museum with a Story* (The Hague: Sdu Uitgeverij Koninginnegracht, 1992), 78.

13. Ibid., 78–81.

14. James E. Young, *At Memory's Edge: After-Images of the Holocaust in Contemporary Art and Architecture* (New Haven, Conn: Yale University Press, 2000), 62;

David Chidester and Edward T. Linenthal, eds., *American Sacred Space* (Bloomington: Indiana University Press, 1995); Mircea Eliade, *The Sacred and the Profane: The Nature of Religion* (1959; reprint, San Diego: Harcourt Brace, 1987); Émile Durkheim, *The Elementary Forms of Religious Life* (1915; reprint, New York: Free Press, 1965); Pierre Nora, *Realms of Memory: Rethinking the French Past* (New York: Columbia University Press, 1996).

15. Rudy Koshar, *From Monuments to Traces: Artifacts of German Memory, 1870–1990* (Berkeley: University of California Press, 2000), 9.

16. Ernest Renan, of course, finds that "forgetting, I would even go so far as to say historical error, is a crucial factor in the creation of a nation." He adds that historical research can even be contrary to projects of national identity, because it might "bring to light deeds of violence which took place at the origin of all political formations, even of those whose consequences have been altogether beneficial." Renan, "What Is a Nation?" (1882), in *Nation and Narration*, ed. Homi K. Bhabha, 8–22 (New York: Routledge, 1990), 11.

17. See Edward Linenthal, *Unfinished Bombing* and *Preserving Memory: The Struggle to Create America's Holocaust Museum* (New York: Viking Press, 1995); Marita Sturken, *Tangled Memories: The Vietnam War, the AIDS Epidemic, and the Politics of Remembering* (Berkeley: University of California Press, 1997); Pierre Nora, *Realms of Memory: Rethinking the French Past*, trans. Arthur Goldhammer (New York: Columbia University Press, 1996). In his analysis of sites of memory in the United States, *Shadowed Ground: America's Landscapes of Violence and Tragedy* (Austin: University of Texas Press, 1997), the geographer Kenneth Foote develops an approach that incorporates both sites that are largely forgotten and sites that occupy central places in collective memory. See also Nuala Johnson, "Cast in Stone: Monuments, Geography, and Nationalism," *Environment and Planning D: Society and Space* 13:1 (1995): 51–65. One category of sites of great violence in the United States that have largely been erased from the landscape are sites of lynchings, the subject of recent works such as James H. Madison, *A Lynching in the Heartland* (New York: Palgrave, 2001); Laura Wexler, *Fire in a Canebrake: The Last Mass Lynching in America* (New York: Scribner, 2003).

18. This analysis builds on recent approaches to the study of memory in general. Influenced in part by Maurice Halbwachs and Pierre Nora, many sociologists, historians, geographers, and others have turned their attention to collective memory. See inter alia Jeffrey Olick and David Levy, "Collective Memory and Cultural Constraint: Holocaust Myth and Rationality in German Politics," *American Sociological Review* 62 (December 1997): 921–936; Jeffrey Olick and Joyce Robbins, "Social Memory Studies," *Annual Review of Sociology* (1998); Barry Schwartz, *George Washington: The Making of an American Symbol* (New York: Free Press, 1987); id., *Abraham Lincoln and the Forge of National Memory* (Chicago: University of Chicago Press, 2000); and John Bodnar, *Remaking America: Public Memory,*

Commemoration and Patriotism in the Twentieth Century (Princeton, N.J.: Princeton University Press, 1991).

19. Sharon Zukin, *The Cultures of Cities* (Cambridge, Mass.: Blackwell, 1995); Christopher Mele, *Selling the Lower East Side: Culture, Real Estate, and Resistance in New York City* (Minneapolis, University of Minnesota Press, 2000); Harvey Molotch et al., "History Repeats Itself, but How? City Character, Urban Tradition, and the Accomplishment of Place," *American Sociological Review* 65:6 (2000): 791–823; Chandra Mukerji, *Territorial Ambitions and the Gardens of Versailles* (Cambridge: Cambridge University Press, 1997); Richard Biernacki, *The Fabrication of Labor: Germany and Britain, 1640–1914* (Berkeley: University of California Press, 1995).

20. Robert Musil, of course, reminded us that "there is nothing in this world as invisible as a monument" (*Posthumous Papers of a Living Author* [Hygiene, Colo.: Eridanos Press, 1987], 61). He also adds that "you never know whether to refer to them as monuments or memorials," alluding to a definitional difficulty that persists to this day. Here I use the words "monument" and "memorial" relatively interchangeably, because they tend to be used in such varied ways by scholars, tourists, and memorial activists. The German equivalents—*Denkmal, Mahnmal,* and *Gedenkstätte*—offer slightly more nuanced definitions, but the uses are still not consistent within scholarship, memorial activism, or tourism. In *The Texture of Memory: Holocaust Memorials and Meaning* (New Haven, Conn: Yale University Press, 1993), James E. Young discusses the monument/memorial distinction, finding (at least for the purposes of his book) that it is best "to distinguish a memorial from a monument only in a broader, more generic sense: there are memorial books, memorial activities, memorial days, memorial festivals, and memorial sculptures. . . . Monuments, on the other hand, will refer to a subset of memorials: the material objects, sculptures, and installations used to memorialize a person or thing" (3–4). Thus, in his definition, the monument is the material object itself, while a memorial may be a set of practices or events, as well as objects.

21. Many of these activists are involved in much broader preservation and remembrance efforts than those discussed here, ranging from a plaque for an eighteenth-century scientist to placing 1970s architecture under historic preservation. For many, efforts surrounding sites connected to the Nazi past comprise only one aspect of their broader efforts to anchor memory in the urban landscape. In examining monument projects in the United States in *Nation into State: The Shifting Symbolic Foundations of American Nationalism* (Chapel Hill: University of North Carolina Press, 1988), Wilbur Zelinsky emphasizes that "with few exceptions, these costly projects were conceived, initiated, and funded mainly by the citizenry in grass-roots fashion rather than by federal or other governmental agencies. . . . patriotic associations, ad hoc organizations, public-spirited businessmen, and even schoolchildren have provided most of the cash and enthusiasm" (187).

Furthermore, the twentieth-century museumization of the American past, like the wave of monument building that preceded it, is mainly the work of the private sector and nongovernmental associations. "Federal agencies . . . may play a role, along with state and municipal governments, but the critical impulse flows from citizens' groups, voluntary organizations, philanthropists, and entrepreneurs, and government intervention is usually after the fact" (ibid., 194).

22. Chidester and Linenthal, eds., *American Sacred Space*, 16.

23. It is also important to ask when resonance might be something else. There are times when what appears to be resonance is actually better understood as an effect of power, marketing, guilt, or instrumentality. At times, memorial sites and their meanings may simply be tools used instrumentally by various groups, but distinguishing the intentions of people advocating a particular memorial project is difficult.

24. While the Wall began to come down on November 9, 1989, official unification of the two Germanys did not take place until October 3, 1990. In 1991, the Bundestag voted to move the German capital from Bonn to Berlin. See Hannes Bahrmann and Christoph Links, *Chronik der Wende: Die Ereignisse in der DDR zwischen 7. Oktober 1989 und 18. März 1990* (Rheda-Wiedenbrück: RM-Buch-und-Media-Vertrieb, 1999).

25. The articles that have appeared in the *New York Times* and the *International Herald Tribune* alone are too numerous to cite here, but include Roger Cohen, "Wiesel Urges Germany to Ask Forgiveness," *NYT*, Jan. 27, 2000; Roger Cohen, "Berlin Mayor to Shun Holocaust Memorial Event," *NYT*, Jan. 17, 2000; John Tagliabue, "In a New Battle of Berlin, Lines Drawn on the Capital Issue," *IHT*, Nov. 2, 1990.

26. Jeffrey Olick, "What Does It Mean to Normalize the Past?" *Social Science History* 22:4 (1998): 547–570; Andrei S. Markovits and Simon Reich, *The German Predicament: Memory and Power in the New Europe* (Ithaca, N.Y.: Cornell University Press, 1997).

27. Michael Bell writes about forms of authenticity that are much more familiar to many of us, such as his wedding ring, which he would not trade for an identical ring and a thousand dollars, or his own experience of a graveyard on an island where many of his relatives are buried, where he feels "some kind of sacred electric charge about the place" (Bell, "The Ghosts of Place," *Theory and Society* 26 [1997]: 813–836, at 819, 822).

28. Young, *At Memory's Edge*, 62. For more on the power of original historic sites around the world, see www.sitesofconscience.org/eng/index.htm (accessed Sept. 8, 2005) for the places belonging to the International Coalition of Historic Site Museums of Conscience, which range from the Lower East Side Tenement Museum in New York City to the Maison des Esclaves on the Île de Gorée in Senegal.

29. "Blindes Vertrauen," *nebenanders: Journal des Anne Frank Zentrums* 1 (1999): 23.

30. From the exhibition program for "Blindes Vertrauen: Versteckt am Hacke-schen Markt."

31. Durkheim, *Elementary Forms*. For a more in-depth discussion of the sacred, see Chapter 6.

32. For more on the connections between collective memory and the built environment, see, e.g., Diane Barthel, *Historic Preservation: Collective Memory and Historical Identity* (New Brunswick, N.J.: Rutgers University Press, 1996); M. Christine Boyer, *The City of Collective Memory: Its Historical Imagery and Architectural Entertainments* (Cambridge, Mass.: MIT Press, 1994); Fred Davis, *Yearning for Yesterday: A Sociology of Nostalgia* (New York: Free Press, 1979); David Lowenthal, *The Past Is a Foreign Country* (Cambridge: Cambridge University Press, 1985); Lyn Spillman, *Nation and Commemoration: Creating National Identities in the United States and Australia* (Cambridge: Cambridge University Press, 1997); and Daniel J. Sherman, *The Construction of Memory in Interwar France* (Chicago: University of Chicago Press, 2001).

33. See, e.g., Jeffrey Herf, *Divided Memory: The Nazi Past in the Two Germanys* (Cambridge, Mass.: Harvard University Press, 1997); John Czaplicka "History, Aesthetics, and Contemporary Commemorative Practice in Berlin," *New German Critique* 65 (Spring-Summer 1995), 155–187; Dominick LaCapra, *Representing the Holocaust: History, Theory, Trauma* (Ithaca, N.Y.: Cornell University Press, 1996); Harold Marcuse, *Legacies of Dachau* (Cambridge: Cambridge University Press, 2001); Markovits and Reich, *German Predicament*; Olick and Levy, "Collective Memory and Cultural Constraint"; Olick and Robbins, "Social Memory Studies"; Karen Till, *The New Berlin: Memory, Politics, Place* (Minneapolis: University of Minnesota Press, 2005).

34. Olick and Levy, "Collective Memory and Cultural Constraint," 922.

35. Olick and Robbins, "Social Memory Studies," 110.

36. Christhard Hoffmann, "Dilemmas of Commemoration: Introduction," *German Politics and Society* 17:3 (1999) reports that Germany is "now shifting from 'personal memory to 'history,' or, in the words of memory-theorist Jan Assmann, from 'communicative memory' (in which one can interview directly those with first-hand knowledge of events) to 'cultural memory' (in which memory becomes institutionalized through cultural means, such as commemorative rituals, memorials, museums, and archives" (4). Here, then, I analyze what Assmann would call "cultural memory."

37. I analyzed approximately two hundred sites in the city, focusing in particular on the eastern half of the city in order to capture some of the consequences of the fall of the Wall and subsequent political and economic changes. I analyzed all of the major sites in the city devoted to marking resistance to or persecution by the

Nazi regime (including sites that occupy measurable amounts of urban land and have consequences for patterns of land use, as well as dozens of sites marked with memorial plaques). The examples described in more detail in this book are, in many cases, particularly prominent sites, but the processes of memorial construction are similar for a wide range of projects. Achieving an exact count of memorial sites themselves can also be difficult, as evidenced by the discrepancies in the publications devoted exclusively to cataloging memorials. Definitional variations (some counts include memorial plaques, others focus only on larger *Gedenkstätten,* which often include both memorial and exhibition space) contribute to the challenges of establishing a precise count, as does the dynamic quality of any urban landscape.

38. These include (but are not limited to) the following: W. Barnack et al., *Denkmale und Plastiken im Stadtbezirk Berlin-Prenzlauer Berg* (Berlin: Rat des Stadtbezirks Berlin-Prenzlauer Berg, Abteilung Kultur, 1980); Berlin-Information, *Bauten unter Denkmalschutz: Berlin, Hauptstadt d. DDR* (Berlin: Berlin-Information, 1980); Annegret Burg, ed., *Kunst im Stadtraum: Denkmäler* (Berlin: Senatsverwaltung für Bau- und Wohnungswesen, 1994); Michael Cullen, ed., *Das Holocaust-Mahnmal: Dokumentation einer Debatte* (Munich: Pendo, 1999); Laurenz Demps, *Berlin-Wilhelmstraße: Eine Topographie preußisch-deutscher Macht* (Berlin: Ch. Links, 1994); Laurenz Demps and Reinhard Hölzer, *Zwangsarbeiter und Zwangsarbeiterlager in der faschistischen Reichshauptstadt Berlin, 1939–1945* (Berlin: Gesellschaft für Heimatgeschichte und Denkmalpflege Berlin im Kulturbund der DDR, 1986); Martina Düttmann and Felix Zwoch, eds., *Bauwelt Berlin Annual: Chronology of Building Events 1996 to 2001: 1996* (Berlin: Birkhäuser, 1996); Ulrich Eckhardt and Andreas Nachama, *Jüdische Orte in Berlin* (Berlin: Nicolai, 1996); *Vorschlag zum Umgang mit den politischen Denkmälern der Nachkriegszeit in Berlin* (Berlin: Arbeitsgruppe des Vereins Aktives Museum Faschismus und Widerstand in Berlin, 1993); Stefanie Endlich, *Gestapo-Gelände: Entwicklungen, Diskussionen, Meinungen, Fordergungen, Perspektiven: Eine Untersuchung mit Interviews* (Berlin: Akademie der Künste, 1988); Stefanie Endlich and Thomas Lutz, *Gedenken und Lernen an historischen Orten: Ein Wegweiser zu Gedenkstätten für die Opfer des Nationalsozialismus in Berlin* (Berlin: Hentrich, 1995); Stefanie Endlich and Bernd Wurlitzer, *Skulpturen und Denkmäler in Berlin* (Berlin: Stapp, 1990); Johannes Heesch and Ulrike Braun, *Orte Erinnern: Spuren des NS-Terrors in Berlin: Ein Wegweiser* (Berlin: Nicolai, 2003); Holger Hübner, *Das Gedächtnis der Stadt: Gedenktafeln in Berlin* (Berlin: Argon, 1997); M. Jeismann, ed., *Mahnmal Mitte: Eine Kontroverse* (Cologne: DuMont, 1999); Hans Maur, *Mahn-, Gedenk-, und Erinnerungsstätten der Arbeiterbewegung in Berlin-Köpenick* (Berlin: Bezirksleitung der SED, 1973) (as well as the volumes of this publication covering the other districts of East Berlin issued throughout the 1970s and early 1980s); Hans-Rainer Sandvoß, *Widerstand in Friedrichshain und Lichtenberg* (Berlin: Gedenkstätte

Deutscher Widerstand, 1998) (as well as volumes on the other districts of Berlin); Hans-Rainer Sandvoß, *Stätten des Widerstandes in Berlin, 1933–1945* (Berlin: Gedenkstätte Deutscher Widerstand, n.d. [198+?]); Martin Schönfeld, *Gedenktafeln in Ost-Berlin* (Berlin: Aktives Museum Faschismus und Widerstand in Berlin, 1991); Martin Schönfeld, *Gedenktafeln in West-Berlin* (Berlin: Aktives Museum Faschismus und Widerstand, 1993); Claus-Dieter Sprink, *Gedenkstätte Köpenicker Blutwoche Juni 1933* (Berlin: Bezirksamt Köpenick von Berlin, 1997).

39. In this book, I use the district names that were in effect when I conducted most of this research. Berlin's twenty-three districts were combined into a total of twelve districts in 2001. The minutes of committee meetings in the state parliament, where members heatedly debate proposed memorial projects, for example, are capable of showing, step by step, how a particular site emerges into (or, in a few cases, shifts out of) legislative favor. As I identified key sites, I then sought out property registries (indicating that the vast majority of memorial sites were on land that was in public hands), photographs, construction files, design competition brochures, and historic preservation records, the records of citizens' groups, land-use plans, the minutes of public meetings, maps, and stacks of secondary sources including guidebooks and pamphlets compiled by local museums and citizens' groups.

40. See, e.g., Gabi Dolff-Bonekämper, "Sites of Hurtful Memory," *Getty Conservation Institute Newsletter*, 2002, 11–16.

41. Tom Gieryn, "A Space for Place in Sociology," *Annual Review of Sociology* 26 (2000): 463–496, at 463. For further discussions of place (in addition to discussions later in the book), see Edward S. Casey, *The Fate of Place: A Philosophical History* (Berkeley: University of California Press, 1997); Bell, "Ghosts of Place"; and Rick Biernacki and Jennifer Jordan, "The Place of Space in the Study of the Social," in *The Social in Question*, ed. Patrick Joyce (London: Routledge, 2002): 133–150.

42. A central element of memorial culture after 1989 is neglected in this book and will be treated elsewhere. In addition to the confrontation with the Nazi past, both halves of Germany also grapple with the complexity of representing the East German past in the built environment. While occasionally some of these comparisons come too close, in my opinion, to equating the East German regime with the Nazi regime, there is no doubt that this complicated past must also be confronted, and that it also incorporates themes of resistance, loss, and state-sanctioned violence. Some of the key sites of this memory in Berlin include the following: the Wall monument, the few remnants of the Wall, and a strip of paving bricks running through the city to mark where the Wall ran (although even this is controversial, as the Wall itself was really a wide strip of land involving two walls, a no-man's-land, and other barriers, so that it is difficult to represent it with a strip of bricks a few centimeters wide); the prison at Hohenschönhausen, where politi-

cal prisoners were held and reportedly tortured; the Stasi headquarters at Normannenstraße; and an installation monument for the uprising on June 17, 1953. To date, little has been written about this, particularly in English and within sociology. See Annette Kaminsky, ed., *Orte des Erinnerns. Gedenkzeichen, Gedenkstätten und Museen zur Diktatur in SBZ und DDR* (Leipzig: Forum, 2004).

CHAPTER 2: BLANK SLATES AND AUTHENTIC TRACES

1. Jeffrey Olick, "What Does It Mean to Normalize the Past?" *Social Science History* 22:4 (1998): 553. Portions of this chapter appeared in my article "A Matter of Time," *Journal of Historical Sociology* 18:1–2 (March–June 2005): 37–71.

2. James E. Young, "The Counter-Monument: Memory Against Itself in Germany Today," *Critical Inquiry* 18 (Winter, 1992): 269. Young has written extensively on the German treatment of the Nazi past and on memorials in particular. He also participated actively in the discussions about the new central Holocaust memorial in Berlin. Also see James E. Young, *Mahnmale des Holocaust: Motive, Rituale und Stätten des Gedenkens* (Munich: Prestel-Verlag, 1993); id., *At Memory's Edge: After-Images of the Holocaust in Contemporary Art and Architecture* (New Haven, Conn: Yale University Press, 2000); and id., "Berlin's Holocaust Memorial: A Report to the Bundestag Committee on Media and Culture, 3 March 1999," *German Politics and Society* 17:3 (1999): 54–70, esp. 56.

3. These efforts have also arguably contributed to a particular kind of contemporary German national identity, one rooted to some extent in the public confrontation with the Nazi past. States have a long history of employing the landscape in the service of symbolic and material projects of legitimacy, representation, and control. For just a few examples, see the following: John Bodnar, *Remaking America: Public Memory, Commemoration and Patriotism in the Twentieth Century* (Princeton, N.J.: Princeton University Press, 1991); M. Christine Boyer, *The City of Collective Memory: Its Historical Imagery and Architectural Entertainments* (Cambridge, Mass.: MIT Press, 1994); David Jordan, *Transforming Paris: The Life and Labors of Baron Haussmann* (Chicago: University of Chicago Press, 1995); Chandra Mukerji, *Territorial Ambitions and the Gardens of Versailles* (Cambridge: Cambridge University Press, 1997); Robert Rotenberg, *Landscape and Power in Vienna* (Baltimore: Johns Hopkins University Press, 1995); Vera Zolberg, "Museums as Contested Sites of Remembrance: The Enola Gay Affair," in *Theorizing Museums: Representing Identity and Diversity in a Changing World*, ed. Gordon Fyfe and Sharon Macdonald (Oxford: Blackwell, 1996). Mukerji, *Territorial Ambitions*, argues that in Louis XIV's France the landscape of Versailles (and indeed much of France's landscape) was shaped from above—albeit meticulously on the ground—as one element of the consolidation of centralized state power.

4. Jeffrey Herf's discussion in *Divided Memory: The Nazi Past in the Two Ger-*

manys (Cambridge, Mass.: Harvard University Press, 1997) of the various eras of postwar German memory on both sides of the Iron Curtain provides a particularly in-depth examination of the political aspects of negotiating postwar memory of the Nazi era, tying the different eras more directly to political processes than specifically to memorial practice. Herf finds, for example, that "the public language of memory was related to occupation-era policies of denazification and judicial procedure" (72), so that memory was mediated through these broader political and institutional processes.

5. See Christhard Hoffmann, "The Dilemmas of Commemoration: Introduction," *German Politics and Society* 17:3 (1999): 1–8, 4.

6. These include Bodnar, *Remaking America*; Olick, "What Does it Mean to Normalize the Past?"; Olick and Levy, "Collective Memory and Cultural Constraint"; Jeffrey Olick and Joyce Robbins, "Social Memory Studies," *Annual Review of Sociology* 24: 1 (1998): 105–141; Barry Schwartz, *George Washington: The Making of an American Symbol* (New York: Free Press, 1987); and id., *Abraham Lincoln and the Forge of National Memory* (Chicago: University of Chicago Press, 2000).

7. Amy Adamczyk, "On Thanksgiving and Collective Memory: Constructing the American Tradition," *Journal of Historical Sociology* 15: 3 (2002): 343–365, reveals much layering of techniques and habits of memory (ibid., 352), although I think she could foreground this interesting finding even more.

8. Ibid., 350, 361.

9. Émile Durkheim, *The Elementary Forms of Religious Life* (1915; New York: Free Press, 1965); Maurice Halbwachs, *The Collective Memory* (1950; New York: Harper Colophon Books, 1980); Pierre Nora, *Realms of Memory: Rethinking the French Past* (New York: Columbia University Press, 1996).

10. In his study of public memory in the United States, *Remaking America*, John Bodnar takes an approach more focused on the conflictual elements of collective memory, asserting that the Vietnam Veterans Memorial results from two conflicting visions. He sets vernacular memory against official memory and asserts that official memory is inherently "distorted" and "ideological" (which might imply an "undistorted" source of memory somewhere else), asserting that "[p]ublic memory emerges from the intersection of official and vernacular cultural expressions" (13). Bodnar defines public memory as "a body of beliefs and ideas about the past that help a public or society understand both its past, present, and by implication, its future. It is fashioned ideally in a public sphere in which various parts of the social structure exchange views" (ibid., 15). For Bodnar, the three primary forces shaping this public memory are "elite manipulation, symbolic interaction, and contested discourse" (ibid., 20). He concludes by claiming that the three forces shaping public memory are the official, the vernacular, and a new force, the commercial (ibid., 251).

11. Olick and Levy, "Collective Memory and Cultural Constraint," 922.

12. Olick, "What Does it Mean to Normalize the Past?" 550. In addition, "it is not just new constellations of interests that produce new images of the past, but new images of the past that allow new power positions."

13. Rudy Koshar, *From Monuments to Traces: Artifacts of German Memory, 1870–1990* (Berkeley: University of California Press, 2000), 10.

14. Other commentators on Berlin develop similar periodizations, including Stefanie Endlich and Thomas Lutz, *Gedenken und Lernen an historischen Orten: Ein Wegweiser zu Gedenkstätten für die Opfer des Nationalsozialismus in Berlin* (Berlin: Hentrich, 1995), 152; Siobhan Kattago, *Ambiguous Memory: The Nazi Past and German National Identity* (Westport, Conn.: Praeger, 2001); Koshar, *From Monuments to Traces*; Bill Niven, *Facing the Nazi Past: United Germany and the Legacy of the Third Reich* (New York: Routledge, 2002); Peter Reichel, *Politik mit der Erinnerung: Gedächtnisorte im Streit um die nationalsozialistische Vergangenheit* (1995; Frankfurt a/M: Fischer, 1999); and Jochen Spielmann, "Gedenken und Denkmal," in *Gedenken und Denkmal*, ed. Helmut Geisert, Jochen Spielmann and Peter Ostendorff (Berlin: Berlinische Galerie, 1988), 9. Gavriel Rosenfeld's useful periodization of memorial culture in *Munich and Memory: Architecture, Monuments, and the Legacy of the Third Reich* (Berkeley: University of California Press, 2000) differs somewhat, reminding us both that there are multiple alternatives when attempting to develop a schematic overview of a period of social change, and that memorial culture was not necessarily changing uniformly, particularly in western Germany.

15. A museum was established in the building in 1967, called the "Museum of the Unconditional Capitulation" until 1994. Since 1995, the building has housed the Russian-German Museum Berlin-Karlshorst, with an exhibition created by German and Russian historians.

16. Cf. Stephen Brockmann and Frank Trommler, eds., *Revisiting Zero Hour 1945: The Emergence of Postwar German Culture*, Humanities Program Report (Washington, D.C.: American Institute of Contemporary German Studies, 1996).

17. In architecture and city planning (and of course in business, law, government, and other institutions), 1945 hardly entailed a clean break with the past as well. See, e.g., Jeffry Diefendorf, *In the Wake of War: The Reconstruction of German Cities after World War II* (Oxford: Oxford University Press, 1993); Kathleen James-Chakraborty, "Memory and the Cityscape: The German Architectural Debate about Postmodernism," *German Politics and Society* 17:3 (1999): 71–83; and Brian Ladd's treatment of these issues in *The Ghosts of Berlin* (Chicago: University of Chicago Press, 1997).

18. Diefendorf, *In the Wake of War*, 15. The skills of architects and urban planners that had been focused on reconstructing bombed-out cities in 1944 and early 1945 were also simply redirected to guide reconstruction after the fall of the Nazi regime.

19. Sabine Behrenbeck, "Between Pain and Silence: Remembering the Victims of Violence in Germany After 1949," in *Life After Death: Approaches to a Cultural and Social History of Europe During the 1940s and 1950s,* ed. Richard Bessel and Dirk Schumann (Cambridge: Cambridge University Press, 2003), 37–64; Herf, *Divided Memory,* 69–105; Ralf Kessler and Hartmut Rüdiger Peter, eds., *"An alle OdF-Betreuungsstellen Sachsen-Anhalts!" Eine dokumentarische Fallstudie zum Umgang mit Opfern des Faschismus in der SBZ/DDR, 1945–1953* (Frankfurt a/M: Peter Lang, 1996); Annette Leo and Peter Reif-Spirek, eds., *Vielstimmiges Schweigen: Neue Studien zum DDR-Antifaschismus* (Berlin: Metropol, 2001); Zeev Mankowitz, *Life Between Memory and Hope: The Survivors of the Holocaust in Occupied Germany* (Cambridge: Cambridge University Press, 2002), 192–225; Elke Reuter and Detlef Hansel, eds., *Das Kurze Leben der VVN von 1945 bis 1953* (Berlin: Ost, 1997).

20. See, e.g., "Berliners view a makeshift memorial honoring anti-fascist heroes and victims," Desig. #535.4710, W/S #11445, CD #0248; "A German woman reads a sign announcing a memorial service for 'Victims of Fascism,'" Desig. #535.4710, W/S #11449, CD #0248; and "A German pedestrian stands in front of a row of billboards on which orders from the military government of occupation are posted. Above them is a sign put up by the German Communist Party that reads, 'We commemorate our murdered anti-Fascist [comrades],'" Desig. #535.4710, W/S #11446, CD #0248; all three, Sept. 9, 1945, U.S. Holocaust Memorial Museum, Courtesy of Imperial War Museum.

21. Ulrike Puvogel, *Gedenkstätten für die Opfer des Nationalsozialismus,* vol. 2 (Bonn: Bundeszentrale für politische Bildung, 1999), 13. (Unless otherwise noted, all translations are my own.)

22. Peter Fibich, "Zur landschaftsarchitektonischen Gestaltung von Gedenkstätten und Mahnmalen für die Opfer des Nationalsozialismus in der DDR 1945–1960," in *Projekt Sozialistische Stadt: Beiträge zur Bau- und Planungsgeschichte der DDR,* ed. Holger Barth, (Berlin: Dietrich Reimer, 1998), 69–78, at 69.

23. Herf, *Divided Memory,* 74.

24. Stefanie Endlich, for example, finds that "the division of the city into four sectors, and thereby into one part administered by the Soviets and one by the Allies, at first had little effect on the development of memorial culture. In all of Berlin there were large public gatherings for all victims of persecution, even when they belonged to different political or 'weltanschauliche' groups" (Endlich, "Berlin," in Puvogel, ed., *Gedenkstätten für die Opfer des Nationalsozialismus,* vol. 2 [Bonn: Bundeszentrale für politische Bildung, 1999], 31).

25. Puvogel, "Einleitung," 13. See, e.g., "Jewish DPs from the Lechfeld displaced person camp pose with a wreath in front of the memorial to Jewish victims at the Dachau concentration camp" (1950), U.S. Holocaust Memorial Museum, courtesy of Gerzon Trzcina, Desig. #9.55, W/S #32428, CD #0267.

26. Herf, *Divided Memory,* 72.

27. J. David Case, "The Politics of Memorial Representation: The Controversy over the German Resistance Museum in 1994," *German Politics and Society* 16:1 (1998): 63.

28. Peter Reichel, *Politik mit der Erinnerung: Gedächtnisorte im Streit um die nationalsozialistische Vergangenheit* (1995; Frankfurt a/M: Fischer, 1999), 189.

29. Herf, *Divided Memory*. According to Puvogel, "Einleitung," the East German government clearly used such places and figures, including the resistance fighter and East German hero Ernst Thälmann, to "satisfy their need for legitimation" (16). For an in-depth discussion of the aesthetic styles and projects found in the East in this period, see Volker Frank, *Antifaschistische Mahnmale in der DDR: Ihre künstlerische und architektonische Gestaltung* (Leipzig: E. A. Seemann, 1970).

30. Puvogel, "Einleitung," 14; see also Herf, *Divided Memory*, 163.

31. Puvogel, "Einleitung," 14, 15.

32. Frank, *Antifaschistische Mahnmale in der DDR*, 28 (their translation). This volume also provides a good visual overview of the aesthetic techniques for representing anti-fascist resistance, relying heavily on socialist realism.

33. Stefanie Endlich, introduction to Annegret Burg, ed., *Kunst im Stadtraum: Denkmäler* (Berlin: Senatsverwaltung für Bau- und Wohnungswesen, 1994), 8.

34. Reichel, *Politik mit der Erinnerung*, 80.

35. Of course there were also monuments being built throughout East Germany for fallen Soviet soldiers, including the truly monumental Soviet memorial in the East Berlin district of Treptow. Autorenkollektiv, *Das Sowjetische Ehrenmal in Berlin-Treptow* (Berlin: Berlin-Information, 1976).

36. Herf, *Divided Memory*, 176. Herf also provides more detail about the planning for the memorials, as well as the dedication ceremonies themselves (ibid. 176–181).

37. Charles S. Maier, *The Unmasterable Past: History, Holocaust, and German National Identity* (Cambridge, Mass.: Harvard University Press, 1988), 125.

38. Puvogel, "Einleitung," 18.

39. Endlich and Lutz, *Gedenken und Lernen*, 34–35, 39–42. One of the earliest markers in the West was erected in 1953 by the Bund der Verfolgten des Naziregimes (a citizens' group), not the government: "a memorial of shell limestone from, as the inscription reads, 'the synagogue in Fasanenstraße, destroyed by the *Rassenwahn*'" (Endlich, "Berlin," 40).

40. Holger Hübner, *Das Gedächtnis der Stadt: Gedenktafeln in Berlin* (Berlin: Argon, 1997), 9.

41. Reichel, *Politik mit der Erinnerung*, 186.

42. For more on this process, see Koshar, *From Monuments to Traces*.

43. Berlin Museum, *Synagogen in Berlin: zur Geschichte einer zerstörten Architektur* (Berlin: Willmuth Arenhövel, 1983); Adolf Diamant, *Zerstörte Synagogen vom November 1938: Eine Bestandsaufnahme* (Frankfurt a/M: Adolf Diamant,

1978); Ulrich Eckhardt and Andreas Nachama, *Jüdische Orte in Berlin* (Berlin: Nicolai, 1996); Harold Hammer-Schenk, *Synagogen in Deutschland: Geschichte einer Baugattung im 19. und 20. Jahrhundert, (1780–1933)* (Hamburg: H. Christians, 1981); Carol Herselle Krinsky, *Synagogues of Europe: Architecture, History, Meaning* (Minneola, N.Y.: Dover, 1985); Sabine Offe, *Ausstellungen, Einstellungen, Entstellungen: Jüdische Museen in Deutschland und Österreich* (Berlin: Philo, 2000); Reichel, *Politik mit der Erinnerung,* 173–174.

44. In his thoughtful analysis of sites of violence and tragedy in the United States, *Shadowed Ground: America's Landscapes of Violence and Tragedy* (1997; Austin: University of Texas Press, 2003), the geographer Kenneth Foote finds four possible fates of such places in the wake of such events. They may be obliterated, rectified, designated, or sanctified.

45. See the discussion of synagogues in Chapter 5.

46. For more on this process throughout western Germany, see Diefendorf, *In the Wake of War.*

47. Offe, *Ausstellungen, Einstellungen, Entstellungen,* 70.

48. Examples are too numerous to cite here, but include a memorial (erected in response to years of citizen activism) in the form of a large sculpture by Richard Serra, accompanied by a large bronze panel set into the ground with additional information, on the site of the building that had housed the "T4" program in the western district of Tiergarten. This is where the so-called "Euthanasia Program" was directed and the deaths of up to 275,000 people, many ill or disabled, were ordered.

49. Martin Schönfeld and Annette Tietenberg, *Erhalten, Zerstören, Verändern* (Berlin: Aktives Museum / Neue Gesellschaft für Bildende Kunst, 1990), 51. It is also important to remember that these are official representations—private citizens had far more varied understandings of the past.

50. Endlich, "Berlin," 53, notes that "the remembrance of the seven anti-fascists was also misused for the legitimation of GDR politics," pointing out that the names listed represent a complex group of people, whose individual actions disappear in the monument, and who were not necessarily fighting for what the GDR had become by 1975.

51. Here again, Endlich, "Berlin," finds that the site "lists the individual victims of the 'Blutwoche' by name but misuses them at the same time for GDR politics" (65).

52. Bundesarchiv Berlin-Lichterfelde (hereafter BA), Präsidium des Ministerrats, DC 20, I/4 6003, Apr. 2, 1987, "Ordnung zur Schaffung von Denkmäler der Bildhauerkunst," 4.

53. Claus-Dieter Sprink, *Gedenkstätte Köpenicker Blutwoche Juni 1933* (Berlin: Bezirksamt Köpenick von Berlin, 1997), 62.

54. These publications include *Mahn-, Gedenk-, und Erinnerungsstätten der Arbeiterbewegung in Berlin-Köpenick* (Berlin: Bezirksleitung der SED, 1973);

Mahn-, Gedenk-, und Erinnerungsstätten der Arbeiterbewegung in Berlin-Mitte (Berlin: Bezirksleitung der SED, 1973); *Mahn-, Gedenk-, und Erinnerungsstätten der Arbeiterbewegung in Berlin-Pankow* (Berlin: Bezirksleitung der SED, 1974); *Mahn-, Gedenk-, und Erinnerungsstätten der Arbeiterbewegung in Berlin-Weißensee* (Berlin: Bezirksleitung der SED, 1978); *Mahn-, Gedenk-, und Erinnerungsstätten der Arbeiterbewegung in Berlin-Prenzlauer Berg* (Berlin: Bezirksleitung der SED, 1979); *Mahn-, Gedenk-, und Erinnerungsstätten der Arbeiterbewegung in Berlin-Treptow* (Berlin: Bezirksleitung der SED, 1979); *Mahn-, Gedenk-, und Erinnerungsstätten der Arbeiterbewegung in Berlin-Friedrichshain* (Berlin: Bezirksleitung der SED, 1981); *Mahn-, Gedenk-, und Erinnerungsstätten der Arbeiterbewegung in Berlin-Lichtenberg* (Berlin: Bezirksleitung der SED, 1982); *Mahn-, Gedenk-, und Erinnerungsstätten der Arbeiterbewegung in Berlin-Marzahn* (Berlin: Bezirksleitung der SED, 1982).

55. Anna Dora Miethe and Hugo Namslauer, *Zur Gestaltung und Pflege Politischer Gedenkstätten* (Berlin: Institut für Denkmalpflege, 1981), 2–3. Miethe and many others involved in writing the history of the Nazi era in East Germany before 1989 have continued to participate actively in this work since unification.

56. BA, Präsidium des Ministerrats, Aug. 24, 1983, DC 20 I/4 5250, pp. 162, 164. Also see Sprink, *Gedenkstätte Köpenicker Blutwoche,* 61.

57. Maier, *Unmasterable Past,* 136.

58. BA, Präsidium des Ministerrats, Apr. 2, 1987, DC 20 I/4 6003, p. 4. They were also only to be "life-size or over-life-size statues; reliefs; sculptures in connection with written forms, paintings, mosaics, tectonic elements (columns, pylons, etc.) as well as other sculpturally symbolic elements; sculptural unitary works or complexly shaped arrangements and ensembles" (ibid., 5).

59. BA, Präsidium des Ministerrats, June 10, 1987, DC 20 I/4 6045, p. 40.

60. Reichel, *Politik mit der Erinnerung,* 187.

61. Caroline Wiedmer, *The Claims of Memory: Representations of the Holocaust in Contemporary Germany and France* (Ithaca, N.Y.: Cornell University Press, 1999), 4. Also see Endlich, "Berlin," 32–33, for a discussion of the projects in East Berlin in the 1980s that focused on Jews.

62. The latter is the Koppenplatz project, which I describe elsewhere. On the Neue Synagoge, see Hermann Simon, ed., *"Tuet auf die Pforten": Die Neue Synagoge, 1866–1995* (Berlin: Stiftung Neue Synagoge Berlin—Centrum Judaicum, 1995).

63. See Brigitte Hausmann, *Duell mit der Verdrängung? Denkmäler für die Opfer des Nationalsozialismus in der Bundesrepublik Deutschland 1980 bis 1990* (Münster: Lit, 1997).

64. Endlich, "Berlin," 33–34.

65. cf. Peter Reichel, *Vergangenheitsbewältigung in Deutschland: Die Auseinandersetzung mit der NS-Diktatur von 1945 bis heute* (Munich: Beck, 2001).

66. See, e.g., Andrei Markovits and Philip Gorski, *The German Left: Red, Green, and Beyond* (Cambridge: Polity Press, 1993).

67. On the "historians' debate" see James Knowlton and Truett Cates, trans., *Forever in the Shadow of Hitler? Original Documents of the Historikerstreit, the Controversy Concerning the Singularity of the Holocaust* (Atlantic Highlands, N.J.: Humanities Press, 1993).

68. Hoffmann, "Dilemmas of Commemoration," 2.

69. Jochen Spielmann, *Denk-Mal-Prozesse* (Berlin: Senatsverwaltung für Bau- und Wohnungswesen, 1991), 5. Spielmann also points out that points 2, 3, and 5 appear in East Germany during this time as well.

70. Young, "Counter-Monument," 271; also see Noam Lupu, "Memory Vanished, Absent, and Confined," *History & Memory* 15:2 (2003): 130–164. Such monuments appeared throughout western Germany, and included projects like Horst Hoheisel's 1987 "Aschrott Fountain" in Kassel, "sunk beneath the old place in order to rescue the history of this place as a wound and as an open question, to penetrate the consciousness of the Kassel citizens so that such things never happen again" (Hoheisel, in Young, *At Memory's Edge*, 98), and Jochen Gerz and Esther Shalev-Gerz's "Harburg Monument Against War and Fascism and for Peace," dedicated in 1986—a column covered in soft metal, into which people were encouraged to inscribe their own messages, as the column disappeared into the ground in stages over seven years, a disappearing (counter)monument.

71. John Czaplicka, "History, Aesthetics, and Contemporary Commemorative Practice in Berlin," *New German Critique* 65 (1995): 155–187, at 157.

72. Endlich and Lutz, *Gedenken und Lernen*, 12–13.

73. Endlich, *Kunst im Stadtraum*, 8.

74. Offe, *Ausstellungen, Einstellungen, Entstellungen*, 81.

75. Koshar, *From Monuments to Traces*, 11. He goes on to say that "from monuments to traces, the memory landscape represented a rich field of symbols situating the national community in a historical sequence whose telling and retelling created the stretched sinews, the 'mystic chords of memory,' of that community's existence."

76. Magistratsbeschluß (East Berlin) 036/86. See also Martin Schönfeld, *Gedenktafeln in Ost-Berlin: Orte der Erinnerung an die Zeit des Nationalsozialismus* (Berlin: Contrast, 1991), 11.

77. Hübner, *Gedächtnis der Stadt*, 12.

78. M. Bienert, "Topographie des Erinnerns," *Tagesspiegel*, Sept. 18, 1997.

79. Endlich and Lutz, *Gedenken und Lernen*, 55. Many of the plaques included images of the people who had been murdered and more details of their lives and their deaths, listing occupations, political orientations, and the places where they were killed, sometimes mentioning which floor of the building the person lived on. See Schönfeld, *Gedenktafeln in Ost-Berlin*, 65–97.

80. For an in-depth discussion of the Topography of Terror, the Jewish Museum, the central Holocaust Memorial, and the Sachsenhausen concentration camp just outside of Berlin, see Karen Till's *The New Berlin: Memory, Politics, Place* (Minneapolis: University of Minnesota Press, 2005).

81. Eckhardt and Nachama, *Jüdische Orte,* 59.

82. Ulrich Paul, "Brachland ist Millionen wert," *Berliner Morgenpost,* Feb. 25, 1993.

83. Neue Gesellschaft für Bildende Kunst, *Der umschwiegene Ort* (Berlin: Neue Gesellschaft für bildende Kunst, n.d. [1988]).

84. Ladd, *Ghosts of Berlin,* 158; Ian Buruma, "Hello to Berlin," *New York Review of Books,* Nov. 19, 1998.

85. Peter Neumann, *Wo war was? 299 Infos zu Persönlichkeiten/Schauplätzen/ Ereignissen, Berlin* (Berlin: Dietz, 1990), 13.

86. Bernd Matthies, "'Grabe, wo du stehst,'" *Tagesspiegel,* July 4, 1997.

87. Rürup cited in ibid.

88. Ibid.

89. "Kein monumentales Denkmal auf Gestapo-Gelände," *DW,* June 6, 1989, 10. Also see "Verein gegen Mahnmal auf Prinz-Albrecht-Gelände," *Tagesspiegel* Apr. 29, 1989.

90. The Berlin Senate (Senat) consists of the mayor (*regierende Bürgermeister*), and eight appointed senators with various areas of responsibility (education, justice, urban planning, culture, etc., although the specific areas of responsibility and names of the different senate administrations change from time to time), overseeing the relevant state government administrations. The senators are essentially the mayor's cabinet—they are nominated by the mayor, and approved by the elected representatives in the State Assembly (Abgeordnetenhaus). See Stephanie Pruschansky, *Das Berliner Parlament* (Berlin: Präsident des Abgeordnetenhauses von Berlin, 2004).

91. Abgeordnetenhaus von Berlin (hereafter AB), Drucksache (hereafter DS) 11/549, Mitteilung—zur Kenntnisnahme, Dec. 27, 1989.

92. Matthies, "'Grabe, wo du stehst.'"

93. Advertisement paid for by *Perspektive Berlin e.V.,* in *Der Spiegel,* Apr. 3, 1989.

94. "Verein gegen Mahnmal auf Prinz-Albrecht-Gelände," *Tagesspiegel,* Apr. 29, 1989.

95. AB, DS 12/4709, no. 5523, June 2, 1994.

96. "Planung für Prinz-Albrecht-Gelände unter neuem Aspekt," *Berliner Morgenpost,* June 29, 1990.

97. Ladd, *Ghosts of Berlin,* concludes "it is probably of great importance that the consensus in favor of preservation had emerged by 1989. It had been much easier to agree that history forbade any normal use of the land when the land was

of little value anyway. The fall of the Wall delayed and complicated the planning for the site, but the basic decisions remained unchanged"(164).

98. Press release from the Berlin Senate, Oct. 23, 1990 (microfilm clippings file, Abgeordnetenhaus, Preußischer Landtag, Berlin).

99. Stefanie Endlich, "Die 'offene Wunde' in der Stadtbrache," in *Architektur in Berlin, Jahrbuch 1993/94*, ed. Martina Düttmann and Felix Zwoch (Berlin: Junius, 1994), 56.

100. Burg, ed., *Kunst im Stadtraum*, 52–57.

101. Jola Merten, "1,5 Mio. sahen Topographie des Terrors," *Berliner Morgenpost*, July 3, 1997.

102. Endlich, "Die 'offene Wunde,'" 56.

103. Marlies Emmerich, "Zumthor hat vom Senat Geld bekommen," *Berliner Zeitung*, Oct. 11, 2005.

104. Heinrich Wefing, "'Topographie des Terrors': Virus des Scheiterns," *Frankfurter Allgemeine Zeitung*, May 6, 2004; also see "Haushaltsstopp trifft weiteres jüdisches Mahnmal," *Berliner Zeitung*, Nov. 16-17, 1996; "Gedenkstätten: 'Topographie des Terrors' ohne Zumthor," *Frankfurter Allgemeine Zeitung*, May 25, 2004.

105. Endlich, "Die 'offene Wunde,'" 56.

106. The Aktives Museum conducted a project titled "Digging After History" in 1985, which led to the excavations that later became the Topography of Terror. By 1993, the museum was receiving financial support from the State Culture Administration.

107. Endlich, "Berlin," 33, 34.

108. These debates about memory and forgetting extend to the central structures for the new government as well, including the Reichstag and the new buildings of the government quarter. For a discussion of some of the dilemmas and controversies surrounding the Reichstag, including the issue of the graffiti left behind by Soviet soldiers and preserved in Foster's redesign of the building, see *Reichstag Graffiti: Essays by Norman Foster, Frederick Baker, and Deborah Lipstadt* (New York: Jovis, 2003). Also see Norman Foster and David Jenkins, *Rebuilding the Reichstag* (New York: Overlook Press, 2000). For more on the new buildings constructed for the capital (including controversies over location and symbolism), also see Helmut Engel and Wolfgang Ribbe eds., *Hauptstadt Berlin—wohin mit der Mitte? Historische, städtebauliche und architektonische Wurzeln des Stadtzentrums* (Berlin: Akad., 1993), Friedhelm Fischer and Harald Bodenschatz, *Hauptstadt Berlin: Zur Geschichte der Regierungsstandorte* (Berlin: Senatsverwaltung für Bau- und Wohnungswesen, 1992); Michael Mönninger, ed., *Das neue Berlin: Baugeschichte und Stadtplanung der deutschen Hauptstadt* (Frankfurt a/M: Insel, 1991); and Michael Wise, *Capital Dilemma: Germany's Search for a New Architecture of Democracy* (New York: Princeton Architectural Press, 1998).

109. The new memorials constructed in the 1990s are too numerous to mention here, but range from the new Jewish Museum built by Daniel Libeskind and the central Memorial to the Murdered Jews of Europe to small sites like the red porphyry statues at the site of a protest in 1943 by non-Jewish women pressing for their Jewish male relatives to be released from a detention center at Rosenstraße and the conceptual project by Renate Stih and Frieder Schnock in the western district of Schöneberg. Here the artists placed small signs on lampposts with excerpts from laws restricting the rights of Jews in the 1930s, coupled with a simple, colorful image on the reverse side—a law forbidding Jews to own house pets shows a simple image of a cat, or a law preventing "Aryan" children from playing with "non-Aryan" children is paired with an image of hopscotch. For a fine in-depth discussion of many of these sites, see Young, *At Memory's Edge*. For more on new memorial projects, see Chapter 4.

110. Hubert Staroste, "Politische Denkmäler in Ost-Berlin im Spannungsfeld von Kulturpolitik und Denkmalpflege," in *Bildersturm in Osteuropa*, ed. ICOMOS (n.p.: ICOMOS, 1994), 84.

111. Eberhard Elfert, "Die Politischen Denkmäler der DDR im ehemaligen Ost-Berlin und unser Lenin," in *Demontage . . . revolutionärer oder restaurativer Bildersturm? Bilder und Texte*, ed. Götz Aly (Berlin: Kramer, 1992), 53.

112. Dominik Wichmann, "In manchen Fragen auch verloren," *Allgemeine Jüdische Wochenzeitung*, June 17, 1993.

113. Eberhard Elfert and Martin Schönfeld, eds., *Presse-Reader: Erhalten, Zerstören, Verändern? Denkmäler der DDR in Ost-Berlin* (Berlin: Aktives Museum, 1996), n.p. The district of Mitte also established its own commission on "The Political Monuments in Mitte," whose recommendations were approved in May 1992 (BVV Mitte, DS 487/92, Beschl. no. 368/92, "Antrag an die 29. Tagung der Bezirksverordnetenversammlung Mitte von Berlin"). The first such district commission was established in November 1990, for the purpose of examining the renaming of streets and squares (BVV Mitte, DS 58/90, Beschl. no. 62/90, "Antrag: Berufung einer Kommission zur Umbenennung von Strassen und Plätzen im Stadtbezirk Berlin Mitte").

114. In part because of their efforts, a curious bureaucratic apparatus emerged at the state and district levels that was partly responsible for exercising this caution. In 1992, the Berlin senate established the Commission on the Treatment of the Postwar Political Monuments of the Former East Berlin to determine which postwar monuments in eastern Berlin should remain (including sites that dealt with the Nazi past), and which should be torn down, discussed in greater depth in Chapter 3.

115. *Vorschlag zum Umgang mit den politischen Denkmälern der Nachkriegszeit in Berlin* (Berlin: Arbeitsgruppe des Vereins Aktives Museum Faschismus und Widerstand in Berlin, 1993), 16.

116. "Denkmalsretter und -stürmer," *taz*, Mar. 3, 1992.

117. "Denkmälerkommission des Senats eingesetzt," *Tagesspiegel*, Mar. 11, 1992.

118. Staroste, "Politische Denkmäler," 84.

119. Wolfgang Kil, "Denkmäler und Geschichte," *Berliner Zeitung*, Feb. 17, 1993; *Vorschlag zum Umgang*, 14.

120. Much of this remembering does happen along political lines, which makes it difficult to speak of these sites as necessarily the product of some kind of cultural or political consensus. In general, the Greens and the Social Democrats spearhead more memorial efforts concerning the Nazi era than do the Christian Democrats or the Free Democrats, although the lines are not always that clear-cut. See, e.g., Ute Frings, "Wo die Frauen die Gestapo besiegten," *Frankfurter Rundschau*, Feb. 28, 1992, in which the author quotes the head of the Berlin Christian Democrats as saying that less is more when it comes to memorials in the cityscape.

121. In 1997, in the eastern state of Mecklenburg-Vorpommern, for example, a conference was held to discuss the role of *Gedenkstättenarbeit*, or memorial work, in attracting tourists to the region, whose economy continues to struggle. See *Gedenkstätten und Tourismus: Nicht nur ein Konferenzbericht: Güstrow, 15./16. September 1997/Projekt "Gedenkstättenarbeit in Mecklenburg-Vorpommern"* (Schwerin: Projekt "Gedenkstättenarbeit in Mecklenburg-Vorpommern," 1997). Also see Karen Till's discussion of tourism in *The New Berlin*, and Oren Stier's chapter on tourism and pilgrimage in his *Committed to Memory: Cultural Mediations of the Holocaust* (Amherst: University of Massachusetts Press, 2003), 150–190.

122. Throughout the 1990s and through today, the U.S. press has also consistently covered issues of memorialization and confrontation with the past in Berlin and in Germany more generally.

123. Young, "Berlin's Holocaust Memorial," 56.

124. Young, "Counter-Monument," 270–271.

125. Hoffmann, "The Dilemmas of Commemoration," 3. Young, "Counter-Monument," finds a situation very different from what we saw in the late 1940s, one where he can write, in response to the years of controversy surrounding the central Holocaust Memorial, that "in fact, the best German memorial to the Fascist era and its victims may not be a single memorial at all, but simply the never to be resolved debate over which kind of memory to preserve, how to do it, in whose name, and to what end. Instead of a fixed figure for memory, the debate itself— perpetually unresolved amid ever-changing conditions—might be enshrined" (270). Authenticity also continues to be a prevalent theme in memorialization, particularly in light of the planning for the central Holocaust Memorial in Berlin, which many people felt diverted both funding and attention from "authentic" sites. Christian Hunziker, "Kalter Krieg der Erinnerung," *Berliner Zeitung*, Nov. 27, 1997; Volker Müller, "Schindler Tours, nein danke," ibid., Apr. 21, 1999.

126. Jeffrey Olick and David Levy, "Collective Memory and Cultural Constraint: Holocaust Myth and Rationality in German Politics," *American Sociological*

Review 62 (December 1997): 934. While there is also much talk of a European identity, these sites emphasize one of the things that sets Germany apart from the rest of Europe, and thus these places are not directly about a European identity. At the same time, they may be a part of the entrance requirements to European, and generally international, political, economic, and military legitimacy. German collective memory of World War II, and in particular of Nazi atrocities, has tangible effects on contemporary German foreign policy according to Andrei S. Markovits and Simon Reich, *The German Predicament: Memory and Power in the New Europe* (Ithaca, N.Y.: Cornell University Press, 1997).

127. Endlich and Lutz, *Gedenken und Lernen.*

128. See Andreas Huyssen, *Present Pasts: Urban Palimpsests and the Politics of Memory* (Stanford: Stanford University Press, 2003).

CHAPTER 3: PERSISTENT MEMORY

1. This conclusion came from a report issued by leading real estate consulting agencies, including Jones Lang Wootton and Müller International. ("Die Investoren drängen nach Berlin," *FAZ*, Oct. 29, 1990). For more on the real estate market and urban development in the 1990s, see Elizabeth Strom, *Building the New Berlin: The Politics of Urban Development in Germany's Capital City* (Lanham, Md.: Lexington, 2001).

2. Liegenschaftsgesellschaft der Treuhandanstalt [TLG], *TLG MarktReport 92/93: Erfahrungen aus dem Immobilienmarkt der neuen Bundesländer* (Berlin: TLG, 1992), 22.

3. This figure is based on comparing pre-1989 and post-1989 catalogs of memorial sites (listed elsewhere, but including those of Hans Maur and Endlich et al.), and comparing these with on-site visits and newspaper coverage. The figure is necessarily approximate and will almost inevitably change as the city itself continues to change. These sites range from large-scale cemeteries and *Ehrenhaine*, or memorial fields, to small granite stones in gardens and courtyards or on traffic islands.

4. This is also an approach very consciously used by many in Berlin who have to do with memorialization, as seen in the discussion of the Memorial Plaque Commission. It is also an approach used by Kenneth Foote, *Shadowed Ground: America's Landscapes of Violence and Tragedy* (Austin: University of Texas Press, 2003).

5. "[T]he experience of the visitor at a particular site is collectively influenced by its location in the city, its accessibility, the approach to it, its topography, and the combination of elements presented at the site," John Czaplicka writes in "History, Aesthetics, and Contemporary Commemorative Practice in Berlin," *New German Critique* 65 (Spring–Summer 1995): 158.

6. Cf. Volker Hobrack, "Neue Gedenktafeln in Berlin-Mitte nach 1993" (MS,

2000); Holger Hübner, *Das Gedächtnis der Stadt: Gedenktafeln in Berlin* (Berlin: Argon, 1997); Martin Schönfeld, *Gedenktafeln in Ost-Berlin* (Berlin: Aktives Museum Faschismus und Widerstand in Berlin, 1991); id., *Gedenktafeln in West-Berlin* (Berlin: Aktives Museum Faschismus und Widerstand, 1993); Hermann Zech, *Gedenktafeln in Berlin-Mitte 1855–1996* (Berlin: Hermann Zech, 1996); Stefanie Endlich and Bernd Wurlitzer, *Skulpturen und Denkmäler in Berlin* (Berlin: Stapp, 1990); Ulrike Puvogel, ed., *Gedenkstätten für die Opfer des Nationalsozialismus, Band II* (Bonn: Bundeszentrale für politische Bildung, 1999).

7. For a more in-depth discussion of the bunker complex, see Chapter 6.

8. In addition to the most obvious and immediate levels of supply and demand, there were additional forces contributing to the explosion of real estate prices and new construction in the early 1990s. A particularly important impetus for the early boom came from the projections issued by the government and various consulting agencies. See Dietrich Flicke, ed., *Büroflächenmarkt Berlin: Tendenzen von Nachfrage und Angebot bis zum Jahr 2005*, Senatsverwaltung für Stadtentwicklung, Stadtwirtschaft 9 (Berlin: Regioverlag, 1996). Berlin was called one of the "most interesting and dynamic real estate markets in the world" (Liegenschaftsgesellschaft der Treuhandanstalt, *TLG MarktReport 92/93*, 22). The TLG predicted Berlin would need between eleven and thirteen million square meters of office space in the next fifteen to twenty years, a near doubling of the amount of office space available in 1992. The real estate analyst company Aengevelt offered a chart of the various prognoses for growth in the greater Berlin area in 1992. The population of Berlin at the time was 3.45 million, and the Statistical Office predicted three different populations based on three different scenarios, ranging from 3.71 million to an astonishing 5.19 million. Private consulting agencies were more conservative in their estimates, ranging from 3.39 million to 3.6 million. See Aengevelt Immobilien KG, *City Report Region Berlin Nr. IV 1994/95* (Berlin: Aengevelt Immobilien, 1994), 6–7. The state projections have yet to be realized—in fact the population increased by only six thousand people between 1990 and 1998, and 1999 saw the population drop to 3.39 million. But the projections did play an important role in urban change in the early 1990s, figuring not only in governmental boosterism, but in on-the-ground investment and construction as well. Population predictions thus led to similarly inflated predictions concerning the need for housing and office space. Based only on leveling living conditions between East and West (specifically, m^2 of living space per resident) and raising eastern amenities (primarily plumbing and heating) to western standards (that is, with zero population growth), the TLG estimated that 300,000 new apartments would be needed in Berlin, and 150,000 more to accommodate migrants into the city (Liegenschaftsgesellschaft der Treuhandanstalt [TLG], *TLG MarktReport 92/93*, 26). In 1992, the real estate advising company Jones Lang Wootton predicted that Berlin would need an additional 10 million m^2 of office space by 2000.

9. One category of sites that was removed were the Traditionskabinette, small rooms or museums set up in public buildings and factories to honor the history of socialism, including anti-fascist resistance during the Nazi era. In addition, a bust of Ernst Thälmann (who had become an anti-fascist martyr of sorts) and a monument called "Out of the Ashes of our Dead" (ostensibly recalling the deaths of the Nazis' victims) located in a large park (formerly called Pioneer Park Ernst Thälmann) were removed in 1995 when responsibility for the park changed hands. Indeed all "political" monuments in the park were removed at that point, including a bust of Angela Davis. The Ernst Thälmann statue in the district of Prenzlauer Berg, an immense heroic bust of the communist leader who died in a Nazi concentration camp, fell into disfavor after the Wall fell. It remains standing in part because of the immense cost of dismantling it, and increasingly because of the efforts of historical preservationists to hold on to it as a physical remnant of East German memorial culture. For more on this debate, see Brian Ladd's discussion in *Ghosts of Berlin.*

10. Jeffrey Herf, *Divided Memory: The Nazi Past in the Two Germanys* (Cambridge, Mass.: Harvard University Press, 1997).

11. See, e.g., Katherine Verdery, *The Political Lives of Dead Bodies: Reburial and Postsocialist Change* (New York: Columbia University Press, 1999).

12. Hubert Staroste, "Politische Denkmäler in Ost-Berlin im Spannungsfeld von Kulturpolitik und Denkmalpflege," in *Bildersturm in Osteuropa,* ed. ICOMOS (n.p.: ICOMOS, 1994), 84.

13. *Vorschlag zum Umgang mit den politischen Denkmälern der Nachkriegszeit in Berlin* (Berlin: Initiative Politische Denkmäler, 1993), 14. Many of the intellectuals and officials concerned with monuments and memorials made clear that they opposed the wholesale removal of official East German monuments. Volker Hobrack, Bernd Wurlitzer, Stefanie Endlich, and most of the members of the Monument Commission enforced a view that these monuments themselves had historical value. At the same time, "the extreme position expressed in public discussion, that all political monuments should remain as historical documents, was rejected as much as the suggestion to remove all political monuments from the SED era from the urban landscape" (Staroste, "Politische Denkmäler," 84).

14. Staroste, "Politische Denkmäler," 86.

15. Arguably, this phenomenon applies to more than just the memorial landscape. While the unification certainly entailed the wholesale application of western standards and practices to many aspects of society (and of the city), various observers make clear that the transfer of western practices was by no means total, and that "institutional transfer" only affected certain sectors. See Scott Gissendammer and Jan Wielgohs, "State Policy Making and Interest Groups in the Transformation of the East German Public Housing Sector," *German Politics and Society* 15:3 (1997): 73–98, and Gerhard Lehmbruch, "Institutional Change in the

East German Transformation Process," ibid. 18:3 (2000): 13–47.

16. For two of the sites that did provoke controversy, see Karin Schmidl, "Vier Ordner zum Faust," *Berliner Zeitung*, Dec. 29, 2003; Thomas Flierl, *Mythos Antifaschismus: Ein Traditionskabinett wird kommentiert* (Berlin: Christoph Links, 1992).

17. For more on these forms see Chapter 2.

18. Komitee der antifaschistischen Widerstandskämpfer, *Historischer Lehrpfad zu einigen Stätten der Verfolgung und des Widerstands gegen den faschistischen Pogrom November 1938 im Stadtbezirk Berlin-Mitte* (Berlin, 1988).

19. There is also a range of rejections of these markers that lies outside democratic debate, including the destruction of monuments and cemeteries, their defacement with graffiti, and the surreptitious removal of memorial plaques. See discussions elsewhere in this chapter.

20. This chapter only addresses selected pre-1989 sites. Other sites, ranging from museums to plaques, are described in greater detail in a range of German-language sources (cited elsewhere), although in relatively few English sources.

21. See Cindy T. Cooper and Christopher Mele, "Urban Redevelopment as Contingent Process: Implicating Everyday Practices in Berlin's Renewal," *City and Community* 1:3 (2002): 291-311.

22. For more on the Hackesche Höfe, see Dieter Hoffmann-Axthelm, "Prototyp Hackesche Höfe: Ein faszinierender Ort kommt wieder," *Architektur in Berlin 1996* (Hamburg: Junius, 1996), 40-45, and Gesellschaft Hackesche Höfe, *Die Hackeschen Höfe: Geschichte und Geschichten einer Lebenswelt in der Mitte Berlins* (Berlin: Argon, 1993).

23. See A.E., "Der 'gute Ort' der Juden—mitten in Berlin," *Tagesspiegel*, Dec. 2, 1993; DPA, "Wo Mendelssohn ruht," *Berliner Zeitung*, July 17, 1997.

24. Stefanie Endlich and Thomas Lutz, *Gedenken und Lernen an historischen Orten: Ein Wegweiser zu Gedenkstätten für die Opfer des Nationalsozialismus in Berlin* (Berlin: Hentrich, 1995), 111.

25. DPA, "Gedenken an Juden und Nazis?" *Tagesspiegel*, Oct. 6, 1997.

26. Grundbuch, Amtsgericht Mitte, April 2000.

27. Senatsverwaltung für Stadtentwicklung und Umweltschutz, ed., *Berliner Denkmalliste* (Berlin: Kulturbuch, 1995), 3248.

28. Students visiting the nearby Anne Frank Zentrum, for example, are also taken on a tour that includes the Große Hamburger Str. memorial. See "Geheimes Versteck in der Blindenwerkstatt," *Berliner Zeitung*, May 15, 2000.

29. "Gedenken an Pogromnacht vor 60 Jahren," *Berliner Zeitung*, Nov. 9, 1998.

30. OEW, "'Antisemitische Straftaten schöngeredet,'" *Tagesspiegel*, Feb. 27, 1998. Other sites were vandalized the same night, including the memorial at the Grunewald train station and the Jewish cemetery in Schönhauser Allee. Marlies Emmerich, "Nachama: Wachsamkeit gegen Mahnmal-Schändungen ist Sache aller," *Berliner Zeitung*, Jan. 2, 1998.

31. OEW, "Mahnwachen sollen den Gedenkstein schützen," *Tagesspiegel,* Mar. 4, 1998.

32. Vera Gaserow, "Mahnwache, die zum Denken anregt," *Die Zeit,* Apr. 23, 1998.

33. Such stones include the column for anti-fascist resistance fighters at the corner of Koppenstraße and Singerstraße in Friedrichshain and a stone in the corner of the Wuhlheide park in Lichtenberg for the victims of a Gestapo work camp there.

34. The *Traditionskabinette* related to Ernst Thälmann were dismantled, and a few of the dozens of memorial stones in eastern Berlin were removed by property owners, vandals, or renovation crews.

35. The stone also appears in East German guidebooks, including Hans Prang and Horst Günter Kleinschmidt, *Durch Berlin zu Fuß: Wanderungen in Geschichte und Gegenwart* (Berlin: Tourist, 1983), 77.

36. Twenty-eight other people were executed at Plötzensee, and another fifty were sentenced to heavy prison sentences, many of whom were murdered in concentration camps, according to Hans-Rainer Sandvoß, *Widerstand in Mitte und Tiergarten* (Berlin: Gedenkstätte Deutscher Widerstand, 1994), 169.

37. Helmut Caspar, "Wieder ein Ort lustvollen Verweilens," *Berlinische Monatsschrift* 7 (2001): 184–188, at 186–187.

38. Max Lautenschläger, "Viersprachiger Gedenkstein am Lustgarten," *Berliner Zeitung,* Mar. 5, 2001.

39. Uwe Aulich, "Ergänzende Worte zum Widerstand," *Berliner Zeitung,* Dec. 21, 2000.

40. Press release, www.berlin-mitte.de/index_431_de.html (accessed Oct. 24, 2005).

41. *Parkfriedhof Marzahn* (Bezirksamt Marzahn von Berlin, Naturschutz- und Grünflächenamt, Friedhofsverwaltung, n.d).

42. Another new memorial has been built in the cemetery for the "Russian Germans," German-speakers who were expelled from their homes in Russian territory by Stalin. See Birgitt Eltzel, "Russlanddeutsche bekommen Denkmal," *Berliner Zeitung,* Oct. 11, 2001.

43. Julia Haak, "Ein Spaziergang durch die Zeitgeschichte," *Berliner Morgenpost,* Nov. 17, 1997.

44. Hans Maur, *Mahn-, Gedenk-, und Erinnerungsstätten der Arbeiterbewegung in Berlin-Marzahn* (Berlin: Bezirksleitung der SED, 1982), 8.

45. Maur lists six memorial plaques for anti-fascist resistance fighters mounted on houses in Marzahn. Schönfeld provides occasional mention of the date and immediate circumstance of the mounting of a plaque (whether there was a ceremony, for instance), while Hübner also mentions little about origins.

46. For more on the origins and conditions of the camp itself, see Wolfgang Wippermann and Ute Brucker-Boroujerdi, "Nationalsozialistische Zwangslager

in Berlin, III: Das 'Zigeunerlager' Marzahn," in *Berlin-Forschungen,* ed. Wolfgang Ribbe, 2: 189–201 (Berlin: Colloquium, 1987).

47. si, "Schriftzug muß erneuert werden," *Berliner Zeitung,* July 3, 1997. The new informational plaque was designed by Götz Dorl.

48. In 1996, there was an exhibition in the district city hall on the persecution of Roma and Sinti. Mathias Raabe, "Isoliert und umgebracht," *Berliner Zeitung,* June 7, 1996.

49. "Gedenken am Sinti-Stein," *Berliner Zeitung,* June 6, 2001.

50. Parliamentary Vice President Michels, "Erinnerung an Leiden der Sinti und Roma wach halten," Gedenkveranstaltung auf dem Parkfriedhof Marzahn, May 31, 2002 (parliamentary on-line archive, www.parlament-berlin.de/archiv.nsf/o/ec5 9ef44beb353fbc1256bd700532370?OpenDocument [accessed Oct. 24, 2005]).

51. Philip Gessler, "Eine Feierstunde am Rande," *taz,* June 3, 2003; Birgitt Eltzel, "Gedenken für verschleppte Sinti," *Berliner Zeitung,* June 13, 2003.

52. Between 2000 and 2003, for example, the Berlin State Assembly extensively discussed a central memorial for Sinti and Roma murdered by the Nazis. See Abgeordnetenhaus von Berlin, 14. Wahlperiode (legislative period), cf. DS 14/471, minutes of the 11th meeting, June 8, 2000; 15. Wahlperiode, cf. minutes of the Culture Committee, Jan. 27, 2003, etc. For more on memorials related to the Roma and Sinti, see Edgar Bamberger, *Der Völkermord an den Sinti und Roma in der Gedenkstättenarbeit* (Heidelberg: Dokumentations- und Kulturzentrum Deutscher Sinti und Roma, 1993); Karin Néy, "Mosaik der Sinti-Melancholie," *Freitag* 33, Aug. 11, 2000.

53. Ingeborg Ruthe and Kirsten Reinhardt, "Dein Teil der Welt," *Berliner Zeitung,* Feb. 8, 2005. For some of the discussion of this memorial, see Abgeordnetenhaus von Berlin, 14. Wahlperiode, Inhaltsprotokoll Haupt 14/41, 4, July 2001, 32–35, and other discussions that took place in the fourteenth Wahlperiode.

54. See Volker Hobrack's description of the activities of the commission, and the list of memorial plaques it has approved since its founding in 1992, www.berlin.de/ba-mitte/index_4713_de.html (accessed September 9, 2005).

55. In their book *Jüdische Orte in Berlin* (Berlin: Nicolai, 1996), Ulrich Eckhardt and Andreas Nachama admit to the incompleteness of their account and ask their readers to send in any information they might have. Similar caveats accompany books such as Endlich and Wurlitzer's *Skulpturen und Denkmäler in Berlin* and Schönfeld's two volumes on memorial plaques in East and West Berlin.

56. See Christiane Hoss and Martin Schönfeld, *Gedenktafeln in Berlin: Orte der Erinnerung an Verfolgte des Nationalsozialismus 1991–2001* (Berlin: Aktives Museum Faschismus und Widerstand, 2002).

57. Hübner, *Gedächtnis der Stadt,* 8–10. Hübner is very clear that some plaques had disappeared by the time the book went to press, so all numbers only approxi-

mate the actual numbers of plaques in the city. The distribution of plaques in the urban topography does reveal differences based in part on neighborhood organizing, density, dominant party affiliation of neighborhood, and the visibility of the district to outsiders. As of 1997, the distribution of plaques was as follows, according to Hübner, with the first number being the total number in each district, and the second being the number of plaques relating to persecution by or resistance to the Nazi regime: Mitte 212/61, Prenzlauer Berg 52/35, Friedrichshain 58/36, Treptow 51/19, Köpenick 51/29, Lichtenberg 44/22, Weißensee 27/21, Pankow 47/31, Marzahn 15/4, Hohenschönhausen 12/5, Hellersdorf 7/6.

58. Sandvoß, *Widerstand in Mitte und Tiergarten*, 386–387. Some of the other sites he mentions are also plaques but are in some way attached to a larger complex involving noncommercial land use, e.g., the New Synagogue on Oranienburger Straße and the memorial on Große Hamburger Straße, set in a small patch of grass on the site of a since-destroyed Jewish retirement home.

59. Hermann Zech, *Gedenktafeln in Berlin-Mitte, 1855–1996* (Berlin: Hermann Zech, 1996), 6.

60. See Hoss and Schönfeld, *Gedenktafeln in Berlin*. Based on Martin Schönfeld, *Gedenktafeln in Ost-Berlin: Orte der Erinnerung an die Zeit des Nationalsozialismus* (Berlin: Aktives Museum Faschismus und Widerstand in Berlin, 1991), 91–116, there were twenty-eight memorial plaques (he includes only plaques, not monuments) in Mitte. Of the memorial plaques he lists, ten were in or on some kind of public structure, including foyers of theaters and office buildings, a bridge, a cemetery wall, museums, and other sites either owned by the state or otherwise publicly accessible. Also see "Ansprechendere Gedenktafeln," *Berliner Zeitung*, Feb. 28, 1992.

61. Schönfeld, *Gedenktafeln in Ost-Berlin*, 18–19.

62. The cost of a memorial plaque depends largely on the type of materials used. In 1991, it was at least 4,000 DM. Holger Drews, "Gedenktafeln gab's schon 1879," *Berliner Morgenpost*, Sept. 24, 1991.

63. Hübner, *Gedächtnis der Stadt*, 14–15.

64. "Wenn Gedenktafeln heimlich entfernt werden," *Tagesspiegel*, May 13, 1996.

65. Anita Kugler, "Zur Dankbarkeit erpreßt," *taz*, Sept. 28, 1994; Carmen Oesterreich, "Gedenktafel am Wohnhaus—warum Eigentümer abwinken," *Berliner Morgenpost* July 31, 1995; "Gedenktafel am Gestell," *Tagesspiegel*, Sept. 28, 1996; Michael Bienert, "Topographie des Erinnerns," ibid., Sept. 18, 1997.

66. See Jefferson Chase, "Stumbling over the Holocaust," *Boston Globe*, Apr. 11, 2004. These projects are also discussed in greater detail in Chapter 6.

67. KNA Länderdienst OST [microfilm clippings files of the Abgeordnetenhaus, Preußischer Landtag, Berlin], no. 214, Nov. 6, 1992.

68. Lothar Heinke, "Bauen Sie das Nest von oben bis unten um," *Tagesspie-*

gel, Mar. 25, 1992.

69. "Das Gedenken an Gedenktafeln," *taz,* May 10, 1991.

70. As Christine Fischer-Defoy indicates in her introduction, Schönfeld's book is less a history of fascism and resistance in Berlin than it is a history of the representation of fascism and resistance. Schönfeld, *Gedenktafeln in Ost-Berlin,* 7.

71. "Acht Gedenktafeln werden ersetzt," *Tagesspiegel,* May 4, 1993.

72. Anita Kugler, "Gedenktafel-Guerilla unterwegs," *taz,* May 8, 1993.

73. "Tafeln erinnern an Widerstand," *Volksblatt Berlin,* May 9, 1991.

74. Ralf Neukirch, "Immer mehr Gedenktafeln geklaut," *taz,* Apr. 11, 1992.

75. Herbert Mayer and Hans-Jürgen Mende, eds., *Straßennamen* (Berlin: Luisenstädtischer Bildungsverein, 1993).

76. Landesarchiv Berlin (hereafter LB), C. Rep. 100, no. 380, 5th sess., July 4, 1990, Plenarprotokolle der Stadtverordnetenversammlung, nos. 1–13 (May 28–Sept. 26 1990): 203.

77. BVV Mitte, DS 58/90, Beschluß 62/90, Nov. 5, 1990.

78. Volker Hobrack, "Neue Gedenktafeln in Berlin-Mitte nach 1993" (MS, 2000), 1.

79. Wolfgang Kil, "Denkmäler und Geschichte," *Berliner Zeitung,* Feb. 17, 1993.

80. BVV Mitte, DS 329/91, Dec. 12, 1991.

81. BVV Mitte, DS 487/92, May 14, 1992.

82. C. Liebram, "Alle 41 Gedenktafeln aus SED-Zeiten sollen bleiben," *Berliner Morgenpost,* June 10, 1992; Holger Hübner, *Das Gedächtnis der Stadt,* 11.

83. Hobrack, "Neue Gedenktafeln," 1.

84. BVV Mitte, DS 487/92, May 14, 1992.

85. BVV Mitte, DS 71/92, Beschluß no. 32/92, May 10, 1992.

86. BVV Mitte, DS 664/94, Beschluß no. 383/94, Apr. 14, 1994.

87. Christoph Schnauß, "Geschichte auf Tafeln—Erinnerungen oder . . . ?" *Scheinschlag,* June 1993; "Kompromiß im Streit um Gedenktafel-Text," *Tagesspiegel,* Nov. 22, 1996.

88. Bettina Heidkamp, "'Nichtanbringung,'" *Neues Deutschland,* Nov. 21, 1996.

89. Birgitt Eltzel, "Gedenktafel erinnert an jüdisches Leben," *Berliner Zeitung,* Aug. 29, 1994.

90. Karin Schmidl, "Die Faust wird verdeckt," *Berliner Zeitung,* May 6, 2004.

91. This site is also discussed in Chapter 5. See, e.g., Karin Schmidl, "Ein Park für alle Opfer," *Berliner Zeitung,* Jan. 10, 2003; sfk, "Blutwoche in Köpenick," *Die Welt,* June 26, 2003; Karin Schimdl, "Die Faust und kein Ende," *Berliner Zeitung,* Aug. 25, 2003; and Birgitt Eltzel, "Debatte um Betonfaust geht weiter," *Berliner Zeitung,* Sept. 27, 2003.

92. Young, *Texture of Memory,* 3.

CHAPTER 4: CHANGING PLACES

1. Neil Brenner, "Berlin's Transformations: Postmodern, Postfordist . . . or Neoliberal?" *International Journal of Urban and Regional Research* 26 (2002): 635–642; Hartmut Häußermann and Andreas Kapphan, *Berlin: Von der geteilten zur gespaltenen Stadt? Sozialräumlicher Wandel seit 1990* (Opladen: Leske + Budrich, 2000); Stefan Krätke and Renate Borst, *Berlin, Metropole zwischen Boom und Krise* (Opladen: Leske + Budrich, 2000); Eva Schweitzer, *Großbaustelle Berlin* (Berlin: Nicolai, 1997); Elizabeth Strom, *Building the New Berlin* (Lanham, Md.: Lexington, 2001).

2. For the discussion in this chapter I have chosen five of the most publicly visible sites, which received both extensive newspaper coverage and the attention of district, state, and in some cases federal officials. Approximately twenty new projects have appeared since 1989 in the eastern half of the city (some of which are discussed in Chapter 5), including a memorial in the Hausvogteiplatz, a square that once housed many fashion houses owned by Jewish businesspeople (Uwe Westphal, *Berliner Konfektion und Mode 1836–1939: Die Zerstörung Einer Tradition* [1986; Berlin: Hentrich, 1992]); "The Missing House," Große Hamburger Str. 15/16, where a vanished wing of a building is indicated only by small plaques listing the last people to live there in the 1940s (Christian Boltanski, "The Missing House," in *Die Endlichkeit der Freiheit: Berlin 1990*, ed. Wulf Herzogenrath, Joachim Sartorius, and Christoph Tannert [Berlin: Hentrich, 1990], 71–86; Michael Glasmeier, "Der gute Ort," *Bauwelt* 83:32 (1992): 1784–1791; and Dieter Hoffmann-Axthelm, "Prototyp Hackesche Höfe: Ein Faszinierender Ort kommt wieder," *Architektur in Berlin, Jahrbuch 1996* [Hamburg: Junius, 1996], 40–45); a memorial wall for the Schulze-Boysen resistance group; a series of glass plaques marking the sites of key buildings around the centers of Nazi power on Wilhelmstraße; a memorial plaque at the site of the former "Tanzhaus Clou," which was also used a deportation center. Finally, as noted throughout this book, given the dynamic qualities of the city, these lists are necessarily incomplete, and catalogs, guidebooks, and web sites are the best sources for more up to date information.

3. Likewise, of course, extensive memorial construction was continuing in the western half of the city, including many sites that are discussed in greater detail by James Young, Brian Ladd, Karen Till, and other analysts (close to three dozen sites, in addition to memorial plaques and "stumbling stones"). These include the Deportations-Mahnmal am S-Bahnhof Grunewald; the new Jewish Museum in Kreuzberg, designed by Daniel Libeskind; the "Steglitzer Spiegelwand"; the marker for the concentration camp subcamp at Sonnenallee; and the project "Mahnen und Gedenken im Bayerischen Viertel." This last memorial project began in 1991, when the Berlin Senate and the western district of Schöneberg held a competition for a project to remember the 6,000 Jews who had lived and worked

in the district. Even the initial call implied a preference for conceptual projects. "The 'markings' to be developed at this level should have the character of 'stumbling blocks'" (Camilla Blechen, "Jüdische Leidenswelten," in *Architektur in Berlin: Jahrbuch 1992*, ed. Martina Düttmann and Felix Zwoch [Hamburg: Junius, 1992], 183). In 1992, the jury selected the artist Renata Stih's and the art historian Frieder Schnock's entry, a series of pictographs mounted on lampposts representing the laws reducing the rights of Jews after 1933. The memorial project takes up no urban land but is infused into the entire neighborhood, visible above eye level at nearly every turn. Also see Cay Dobberke, "Begegnung mit der Geschichte," *Die Welt*, May 18, 1994, and Annegret Burg, ed., *Kunst im Stadtraum: Denkmäler* (Berlin: Senatsverwaltung für Bau- und Wohnungswesen, 1994). On the Jewish Museum in Berlin, see Daniel Libeskind, *Das Jüdische Museum in Berlin: Architekt Daniel Libeskind* (Berlin: Philo, 2000).

4. James E. Young, *The Texture of Memory: Holocaust Memorials and Meaning* (New Haven, Conn: Yale University Press, 1993), 2.

5. This process calls into question John Bodnar's distinctions in *Remaking America: Public Memory, Commemoration and Patriotism in the Twentieth Century* (Princeton, N.J.: Princeton, 1991) between official and vernacular memory. In a democratic setting, the two ideally exist in some kind of interactive relationship with one another.

6. Stefanie Endlich, "Berlin," in Puvogel, ed., *Gedenkstätten für die Opfer des Nationalsozialismus: eine Dokumentation* (Bonn: Bundeszentrale für politische Bildung, 1999), 105. Similar book-burnings happened in cities all across Germany.

7. LB, Magistrat von Berlin, Abt. Kultur. Rep. 121, no. 796, Denkmal zur Erinnerung an die nationalsozialistische Bücherverbrennung 1987–1990.

8. BA, Präsidium des Ministerrats, Sept. 2, 1987. Plastik zur mahnenden Erninnerung an die faschistische Bücherverbrennung am 10. Mai 1933, p. 33. DC 20 I/4 6095.

9. The plaque was removed briefly in 1989, but returned to its place, and later the date of its original mounting was added as a way of indicating to passersby that it originated in the GDR. The language of imperialism was quite specific to GDR memorial culture and political rhetoric, and often indicated Western nations in general, and the United States in particular (Endlich, "Berlin," 105). Endlich's description of the origins of the Bebelplatz memorial does not mention that the GDR had already begun the process of proposing a monument of some kind to mark the book-burning, and that the post-1989 competition and the resulting memorial site were, in part, a continuation of work begun in the East before 1989.

10. BA, Präsidium des Ministerrats, Sept. 2, 1987, p. 35, DC 20 I/4 6095; LA, Rep. 121, no. 796, Denkmal zur Erinnerung an die nationalsozialistische Bücherverbrennung 1987–1990, Magistrat von Berlin, Abt. Kultur.

11. LB, Rep. 121, no. 796, Denkmal zur Erinnerung an die nationalsozialist-ische Bücherverbrennung 1987–1990, Magistrat von Berlin, Abt. Kultur.

12. BA, Präsidium des Ministerrats, Sept. 2, 1987, p. 35, DC 20 I/4 6095.

13. LA, Kaufvertrag, Rep. 121, no. 796, Denkmal zur Erinnerung an die nation-alsozialistische Bücherverbrennung, 1987–1990, Magistrat von Berlin, Abt. Kultur.

14. Stefanie Endlich, introduction to Burg, ed., *Kunst im Stadtraum,* 9. See also Ulrich Eckhardt and Andreas Nachama, *Jüdische Orte in Berlin* (Berlin: Nicolai, 1996), 52–53.

15. AB, DS 12/3769, Jan. 21, 1994, Vorlage zur Kenntnisnahme über Denkmal "Die Bücherverbrennung vom 10. Mai 1933."

16. Ibid.

17. Senatsverwaltung für Bau- und Wohnungswesen, *Künstlerischer Wettbe-werb: Die Bücherverbrennung vom 10. Mai 1933: Ausschreibung, Berlin lebenswert bauen* (Berlin: Senatsverwaltung für Bau- und Wohnungswesen, 1993), 8.

18. Manfred Butzmann, "Denkmal für die Bücherverbrennung vom 10. Mai 1933, Bebelplatz in Berlin-Mitte," in Burg, ed., *Kunst im Stadtraum,* 50.

19. AB, DS 12/3769, Vorlage zur Kenntnisnahme über Denkmal "Die Bücherverbrennung vom 10. Mai 1933," Jan. 21, 1994.

20. BVV Mitte, DS 538/93, Beschluß no. 315/93.

21. "Mahnmal," *FAZ,* Oct. 13, 1993.

22. Endlich and Lutz, *Gedenken und Lernen,* 119–120.

23. Micha Ullmann in Burg, ed., *Kunst in Stadtraum,* 46.

24. For more on the shift from representational to conceptual memorials in Germany and elsewhere, see Chapter 2.

25. BVV Mitte, DS 1111/95, Beschluß no. 659/95, April 1995.

26. *Tagesspiegel,* Oct. 13, 1994.

27. Peter Neumann, "Unter dem Bebelplatz entsteht eine Tiefgarage," *Berliner Zeitung,* Feb. 3, 1999.

28. Rolf Lautenschläger, "Denkort Bebelplatz: Hörsturz," *taz,* May 27, 1994.

29. "FDP fordert späteren Mahnmal-Baubeginn," *Berliner Morgenpost,* May 27, 1994.

30. Uwe Aulich, "Am Bebelplatz wird gebuddelt," *Berliner Zeitung,* July 31, 2002.

31. Uwe Aulich, "Trockenen Fußes in die Oper," *Berliner Zeitung,* Dec. 12, 2004.

32. Ingeborg Ruthe, "Denkmal: Im Konflikt zwischen Mahnen und Parken," *Berliner Zeitung,* May 9, 2003.

33. Anja Seeliger, "Zu wenige lebendige Spuren der Vergangenheit," *Die Allge-meine,* Sept. 17, 1992.

34. LB, Rep. 121, no. 799, Magistrat von Berlin, Abt. Kultur, Denkmal zur Erinnerung an die Verfolgung und Deportation jüdischen Bürger, 1988–1990.

"Wettbewerb für eine Denkmalanlage zur Würdigung des Wirkens jüdischer Bürger in Berlin, zum gedenken an ihre Verfolgung und zur Würdigung ihres Widerstandes."

35. Endlich and Lutz, *Gedenken und Lernen*, 120. It should be noted that they are describing a rather small project, and at a very late date, indicating the degree to which the GDR rarely incorporated the fates of Jews into its markers related to the Nazi era.

36. LB, Rep. 121, no. 799 Denkmal zur Erinnerung an die Verfolgung und Deportation jüdischen Bürger, 1988–1990.

37. Magistratsbeschluß (East Berlin) no. 302/89, July 17, 1989.

38. Karl Biedermann, "Denkmal zur Würdigung des Wirkens jüdischer Bürger in Berlin, Koppenplatz in Berlin-Mitte," in Burg, ed., *Kunst im Stadtraum*, 30.

39. LB, Protokoll der Jury-Sitzung, 6.7.89. Magistrat von Berlin, Abt. Kultur, Denkmal zur Erinnerung an die Verfolgung und Deportation jüdischen Bürger, 1988–1990. C Rep. 121, no. 799.

40. Jürgen Stüber, "Koppenplatz: Denkmal für Holocaust-Opfer geplant," *Berliner Morgenpost*, Apr. 7, 1992.

41. BVV Mitte, DS 410/92, Mar. 12, 1992.

42. AB, DS 12/1761, no. 2224, Apr. 3, 1992.

43. Thomas Dietz, "Ein umgeworfener Stuhl," *Tagesspiegel*, Apr. 29, 1994.

44. "Ein Schriftband ziert den Koppenplatz," *Berliner Zeitung*, Sept. 27, 1996.

45. The Bayerisches Viertel is interesting for my analysis because it does not take up urban land—it is entirely on public property. Arguably it has transformed the experience, but not the use, of the land in the neighborhood. See James E. Young's discussion of this important site, *At Memory's Edge: After-Images of the Holocaust in Contemporary Art and Architecture* (New Haven, Conn: Yale University Press, 2000), 112–117.

46. Gernot Jochheim, based on eyewitness reports, in Burg, ed., *Kunst im Stadtraum*, 32. Also see Gernot Jochheim, *Frauenprotest in der Rosenstraße: "Gebt uns unsere Männer wieder"* (Berlin: Hentrich, 1993), and Nathan Stoltzfus, *Widerstand des Herzens* (Munich: dtv, 2000), both of which make mistaken claims about the protests leading to the release of the men according to Wolf Gruner, "Die Fabrik-Aktion und die Ereignisse in der Berliner Rosenstraße: Fakten und Fiktionen um den 27. Februar 1943," in *Jahrbuch für Antisemitismus-Forschung*, 11, ed. Wolfgang Benz (Berlin: Metropol, 2002), 142–143.

47. Götz Aly, "Fabrik-Aktion: Misstrauisch gegen Mythen," *Berliner Zeitung*, Feb. 28, 2003.

48. Wolfgang Benz, "Kitsch as Kitsch Can," *Süddeutsche Zeitung*, Sept. 18, 2003.

49. These findings were particularly striking in contrast to Margarethe von Trotta's film *Rosenstraße* (2003), which portrays the release of those who were

arrested as at least partially the result of the women's actions (a sequence of events that Gruner refutes in "Die Fabrik-Aktion und die Ereignisse," finding that the intention of the government had always been to release the men, regardless of the protest). For more of the discussion surrounding this article and the *Rosenstraße* film, see Benz, "Kitsch as Kitsch Can"; Aly, "Fabrik-Aktion: Misstrauisch gegen Mythen"; Philip Kennicott, "Germany's Remorse Code, Reordered by 'Rosentrasse,'" *Washington Post,* Sept. 14, 2003; Ulrich Kurzer, "Zivilcourage ohne Anlaß?" *Freitag* 10, Feb. 28, 2003.

50. Roland Korn and Klaus Weise, *Berlin: Bauten unserer Tage* (Berlin: Berlin-Information, 1985), 58.

51. Burg, ed., *Kunst im Stadtraum,* 34–35.

52. LB, Schaffung von bildkünstlerischen Denkmäler, 1987–1990, Magistrat Berlin, Abt. Kultur, Rep. 121, no. 798.

53. Alexander Eggert, Volker Herholt, Ralf Meeck, Ekkehard Münzing, Ulrich Schröder, and Sven Wierskalla, *Denkmäler zum Denken: Geschichte zum Begehen und Verstehen—antifaschistische Gedenkstätten in den östlichen Bezirken Berlins* (Berlin: DVK, 1991), 74–78.

54. Ute Frings, "Wo die Frauen die Gestapo besiegten," *Frankfurter Rundschau,* Feb. 28, 1992.

55. Eckhardt and Nachama, *Jüdische Orte,* 30.

56. Gernot Jochheim, *Frauenprotest in der Rosenstraße,* 180–181. See also Frings, "Wo die Frauen die Gestapo besiegten."

57. AB, DS 12/4406, no. 5135, Apr. 8, 1994.

58. BVV Mitte, DS 1311/95, Oct. 12, 1995.

59. Uwe Aulich, "Steine erinnern an die Fabrikaktion," *Berliner Zeitung,* Aug. 9, 1995.

60. BVV Mitte, DS 1311/95, Oct. 12, 1995.

61. Ibid..

62. BVV Mitte, DS 1062/95, Apr. 4, 1995; BVV Mitte DS 1072/95, Mar. 27, 1995.

63. BVV Mitte, DS 1062/95, Apr. 4, 1995.

64. BVV Mitte, DS 1077–A/95, Beschluß no. 648/95, Apr. 6, 1995.

65. Uwe Aulich, "Steine erinnern an die Fabrikaktion."

66. BVV Mitte, DS 1072/95, Apr. 7, 1995; BVV Mitte, DS 1077–A/95, Beschluß no. 648/95, Apr. 6, 1995.

67. Gernot Jochheim and Johannes Rösler, *Die Rosenstraße: Gestern, Heute* (Berlin: Hentrich/Alexander Plaza, 1997), 17.

68. Jochheim and Rösler, *Rosenstraße,* 20.

69. "Erinnerung in Glas," *Tagesspiegel,* Sept. 10, 1998.

70. Roger Cohen, "Wiesel urges Germany to ask Forgiveness," *New York Times,* Jan. 27, 2000.

71. See Nicolai Ouroussoff, "A Forest of Pillars, Recalling the Unimaginable," *New York Times*, May 9, 2005.

72. Christine Richter, "Das Holocaust-Mahnmal wird frühestens 2002 fertig," *Berliner Zeitung*, Jan. 27, 2000.

73. See in particular Karen Till, *The New Berlin* (Minneapolis: University of Minnesota, 2005), 161-190. Also see Michael Cullen, ed., *Das Holocaust-Mahnmal: Dokumentation einer Debatte* (Munich: Pendo, 1999); Ute Heimrod, Günter Schlusche, and Horst Seferens, eds., *Der Denkmalstreit das Denkmal? Die Debatte um das Denkmal für die ermordeten Juden Europas* (Berlin: PHILO, 1999); Michael Jeismann, ed., *Mahnmal Mitte: Eine Kontroverse* (Cologne: DuMont, 1999); Caroline Wiedmer, *The Claims of Memory: Representations of the Holocaust in Contemporary Germany and France* (Ithaca, N.Y.: Cornell University Press, 1999); Young, *At Memory's Edge*.

74. Cf. Cullen, ed., *Holocaust-Mahnmal*, 279. A competition had been held in 1983–84 for the construction of a memorial on the site of the Gestapo headquarters (now the outdoor museum Topography of Terror), a plan that was later scrapped, in part as a result of the protests of the Active Museum of Fascism and Resistance. Indeed, the winning entry envisioned covering the ground in metal plates, an approach utterly contrary to the intentions of the supporters of the Topography of Terror exhibition to expose the material remnants of the city's Nazi past in their authentic location. In 1990, the Förderkreis, the group of people (including Lea Rosh) who wanted a central memorial for Europe's murdered Jews, also rejected the site as the location for its planned memorial. See Cullen, ed., *Holocaust-Mahnmal*, 280–281, Endlich and Lutz, *Gedenken und Lernen*, 116.

75. Young, *At Memory's Edge*, 186.

76. Jane Kramer, "The Politics of Memory," in *Bauwelt Berlin Annual*, ed. Martina Düssmann and Felix Zwoch (Berlin: Birkhäuser, 1996).

77. BVV Mitte, DS 334/91, Dec. 12, 1991, nicht behandelt, Jan. 16, 1992, zur Kenntnis genommen Beschl. 282.

78. BVV Mitte, DS 334/91, Dec. 12, 1991.

79. Elke Kleinwächter-Jarnot and Annalie Schön, *Bürgerbeteiligung im Parlaments- und Regierungsviertel: Stadtteilvertretungen stellen sich vor* (Berlin: Senatsverwaltung für Bau- und Wohnungswesen, Hauptstadtreferat, 1994), 20.

80. Young, *At Memory's Edge*, 87.

81. Ulrich Eckhardt, ed., *Berlin: Open City—The City on Exhibition* (Berlin: Nicolai, 1999), 118.

82. Christian Hunziker, "Kalter Krieg der Erinnerung," *Berliner Zeitung*, Nov. 27, 1997; Volker Müller, "Schindler Tours, nein danke," *Berliner Zeitung*, Apr. 21, 1999.

83. Cullen, ed., *Holocaust-Mahnmal*, 279, 281.

84. Ibid., 291–292; Richard Bernstein, "Berlin Holocaust Shrine Stays with Company Tied to Nazi Gas," *New York Times*, Nov. 14, 2003.

85. James E. Young, "Die Bezwingung der Mahnmals-Dämonen," *Berliner Zeitung*, Jan. 27, 2000.

86. BVV Mitte, DS 661/94, Beschluß no. 381/94, Apr. 14, 1994. Antrag zur Bereithaltung von Flächen für das Holocaust-Denkmal.

87. James E. Young, "The Counter-Monument: Memory Against Itself in Germany Today," *Critical Inquiry* 18 (Winter 1992): 270; id., *At Memory's Edge*, 193.

88. LB, C Rep. 131/1 Zg. 380/8, Ehem. Rat des Stadtbezirkes, Bezirksbürgermeister: Berichte vom Bezirksamt Mitte, Bereich Großveranstaltungen, Berlin, den 22.10.90.

89. Andreas Huyssen, "The Voids of Berlin," *Critical Inquiry* 24:1 (1997): 65.

90. English translation of Mayor Eberhard Diepgen's speech at the dedication ceremony for the new Sony buildings (Oct. 11, 1996); available from www.sony.co.jp.

91. Grundbuch, Amtsgericht, Mitte, April 2000.

92. Eckhardt and Nachama, *Jüdische Orte*, 9.

93. They wrote that "the building substance of the side wing [is] completely worn out. Due to economic grounds, a renovation is not approved." LB, Rosenthaler Straße 39, C Rep 110 Mü, no. 4159.

94. See www.haus-schwarzenberg.org (accessed September 10, 2005).

95. Nancy Krahlisch, "Aller guten Dinge sind drei: Haus Schwarzenberg am Hackeschen Markt konnte bei einer Zwangsversteigerung gerettet werden," *Berliner Zeitung*, July 30, 2004.

96. There are exceptions, and some property owners have chosen to mark the difficult past of their buildings or streets, in which case, memorial use and other uses coexist on the same site.

CHAPTER 5: FORGETTING PLACES

1. There are other potential categories of largely unmarked sites, including places where so-called *stille Helden,* or silent heroes, helped Jews who had gone into hiding or otherwise provided assistance to people fleeing persecution by the Nazis. See Inge Deutschkron, *Sie blieben im Schatten: Ein Denkmal für Stille Helden* (Berlin: Hentrich, 1997).

2. Jochen Spielmann, *Denk-Mal-Prozesse* (Berlin: Senatsverwaltung für Bau- und Wohnungswesen, 1991), 16.

3. On resistance, for example, see the series issued by the Gedenkstätte Deutscher Widerstand, written by Hans-Rainer Sandvoß, including *Widerstand in Friedrichshain und Lichtenberg* (Berlin: Gedenkstätte Deutscher Widerstand, 1998), *Widerstand in Mitte und Tiergarten* (Berlin: Gedenkstätte Deutscher Widerstand, 1998), *Stätten des Widerstandes in Berlin, 1933–1945* (Berlin: Gedenkstätte Deutscher Widerstand, n.d. [198?]).

4. Every act of remembrance that Marita Sturken studied in the United States—the Vietnam War Memorial, the nurses' memorial, the three soldiers statue, and the AIDS quilt—originated from a group of advocates, a model that fits what I have found in Berlin. See Sturken, *Tangled Memories: The Vietnam War, the AIDS Epidemic, and the Politics of Remembering* (Berkeley: University of California Press, 1997).

5. Throughout the 1990s, a series of books recounting the history of Jews in Berlin's different districts was released, including the following: Monika Becker, *Juden in Treptow: Sie haben geheissen wir ihr heisst* (Berlin: Hentrich, 1993); Annegret Ehmann, *Juden in Berlin, 1671–1945: Ein Lesebuch* (Berlin: Nicolai, 1988); Regina Girod, Reiner Lidschun, and Otto Pfeiffer, *Nachbarn: Juden in Friedrichshain* (Berlin: Kulturring in Berlin, 2000); Carola Jüllig, *Juden in Kreuzberg* (Berlin: Hentrich, 2001); Alois Kaulen, *Juden in Spandau: Vom Mittelalter bis 1945* (Berlin: Hentrich, 1988); Thea Koberstein and Norbert Stein, *Juden in Lichtenberg: Mit den früheren Ortsteilen in Friedrichshain, Hellersdorf und Marzahn* (Berlin: Hentrich, 1995).

6. Kurt Schilde, *Erinnern—und nicht vergessen: Dokumentation zum Gedenkbuch für die Opfer des Nationalsozialismus aus dem Bezirk Tempelhof* (Berlin: Bezirksamt Tempelhof, 1988).

7. In a 1994 press release, for example, the Christian Democratic state parliament member Klaus Landowsky criticized "the current inundation of the capital's urban landscape with memorial plaques and memorial sites, which, in his view, do not serve the task of confronting history [*Geschichtsbewältigung*]," Ute Frings noted in "Bescheiden im Erinnern, gewaltig im Sprücheklopfen," *Frankfurter Rundschau*, Apr. 30, 1994.

8. M. Günther-Kaminski, *"—als wäre es nie gewesen.": Juden am Ku'damm* (Berlin: Berliner Geschichtswerkstatt, 1989).

9. *Berlin, kurz gefaßt* (Berlin: Presse- und Informationsamt Berlin, 1995), 7.

10. Ulrich Eckhardt and Andreas Nachama, *Jüdische Orte in Berlin* (Berlin: Nicolai, 1996), 6.

11. Clearly, there is much more detail here than I can convey in this chapter, and the examples presented are drawn from an analysis of far more sites than I can describe in detail.

12. Veronika Bendt and Rolf Bothe, "Vorwort," in Berlin Museum, *Synagogen in Berlin: Zur Geschichte einer zerstörten Architektur* (Berlin: Willmuth Arenhövel, 1983), 1: 5.

13. Adolf Diamant, *Zerstörte Synagogen vom November 1938: Eine Bestandsaufnahme* (Frankfurt a/M: Adolf Diamant, 1978), 6–13.

14. Reichel, *Politik mit der Erinnerung*, 172.

15. Bendt and Bothe, "Vorwort," 1: 5.

16. Inge Lammel, *Jüdisches Leben in Pankow: Eine zeitgeschichtliche Dokumentation* (Berlin: Hentrich, 1993), 88.

17. Indeed, "because a synagogue's sanctity comes from the activity pursued within it, the congregation may sell the building and move elsewhere. . . . A synagogue may be anything from a small room to a grand church-like edifice." Carol Krinsky, *Synagogues of Europe: Architecture, History, Meaning* (Minneola, N.Y.: Dover, 1985), 8.

18. For more on synagogues, see Berlin Museum, *Synagogen in Berlin*; Eckhardt and Nachama, *Jüdische Orte*; Petra Kruse, *Synagogen in Deutschland: Eine virtuelle Rekonstruktion: Kunst- und Ausstellungshalle der Bundesrepublik Deutschland, 17. Mai bis 16. Juli 2000 in Bonn* (Bonn: Kunst- und Ausstellungshalle der Bundesrepublik Deutschland, 2000); Harold Hammer-Schenk, *Synagogen in Deutschland: Geschichte einer Baugattung im 19. und 20. Jahrhundert, (1780–1933)* (Hamburg: H. Christians, 1981).

19. Marlies Emmerich and Michael Helberg, "'Wir hatten noch geglaubt, so schlimm würde es nicht werden,'" *Berliner Zeitung*, Nov. 9, 1998.

20. Throughout Europe, synagogues were destroyed and misused. Krinsky, *Synagogues of Europe*, 97, notes: "During the Second World War, a synagogue in a conquered country might become a stable, warehouse, laundry, hospital, garbage dump, brothel, or prison for deportees. Churches were not used for such things, lest the Christian majority be additionally aroused against their conquerors. Synagogues also suffered from arsonists, vandals, and thieves who stole building materials. Bombs dropped by both sides ruined many synagogues as well as churches, including the eighteenth-century synagogues in London, Livorno, and Rotterdam."

21. Hammer-Schenk, *Synagogen in Deutschland*, 512–513, writes of the chronic lack of adequate synagogue space for Berlin's Jewish residents in the first third of the twentieth century, and the particular difficulty of finding room for everyone on high holidays. For a discussion of the symbolism behind the larger synagogues constructed across Europe in the nineteenth and early twentieth centuries, see L. Scott Lerner, "The Narrating Architecture of Emancipation," *Jewish Social Studies* 6:3 (2000): 1–30. Before 1938, these were places of life, hope, community, normalcy, politics, daily life, and all of the regular practices that take place in synagogues around the world. Because the life that filled these structures and spaces was by and large destroyed, synagogue sites thus serve in part as reminders both of prewar Jewish life and of its destruction.

22. For more on this process throughout western Germany, see Jeffry Diefendorf, *In the Wake of War: The Reconstruction of German Cities after World War II* (Oxford: Oxford University Press, 1993).

23. This discussion is based in part on the accounts in the following sources: Klaus Arlt et al., *Zeugnisse jüdischer Kultur: Erinnerungsstätten in Mecklenburg-Vorpommern, Brandenburg, Berlin, Sachsen-Anhalt, Sachsen und Thüringen* (Berlin: Tourist, 1992); Becker, *Juden in Treptow*; Diamant, *Zerstörte Synagogen vom November 1938*; Eckhardt and Nachama, *Jüdische Orte*; Hammer-Schenk, *Syna-*

gogen in Deutschland; Jüllig, *Juden in Kreuzberg*; Koberstein and Stein, *Juden in Lichtenberg*; Krinsky, *Synagogues of Europe*; Lammel, *Jüdisches Leben in Pankow*; Berlin Museum, *Synagogen in Berlin*; Mario Offenberg, *Adass Jisroel: Die jüdische Gemeinde in Berlin (1869–1942): vernichtet und vergessen* (Berlin: Museumspädagogischen Dienst Berlin, 1986).

24. Some of the sites of such demolitions include Freiheit 8, Artillerie Str. 31 (Tucholsky Str.), Heidereutergasse 4, Johannisstr. 16, Oranienburger Str. 30 (the main synagogue building), Lindenstr. 48–50, Lützowstr. 16, Fasanenstr. 79–80, Levetzowstr. 7–8, Prinzregentenstr. 69–70, Passauer Str. 2 (which is now occupied by the parking lot of the large department store in western Berlin, KDW), Münchener Str., Markgraf-Albrecht-Str. 11–12, Franzensbader Str. 7–8, Siegmundshof 11 (of these, Freiheit 8, Heidereutergasse, Oranienburger Str., and Artillerie Str. were in the East).

25. Eckhardt and Nachama, *Jüdische Orte*, 103.

26. Krinsky, *Synagogues of Europe*, 10, writes that "a Synagogue in ruins may be used only for certain secular purposes, because some sanctity remains associated with it. Ideally, the ruin would be left untouched, with wild grass and weeds growing to arouse compassion in the viewer."

27. Diane Barthel, *Historic Preservation: Collective Memory and Historical Identity* (New Brunswick, N.J.: Rutgers University Press, 1996); Rudy Koshar, *Germany's Transient Pasts: Preservation and National Memory in the Twentieth Century* (Chapel Hill: University of North Carolina Press, 1998).

28. Bendt and Bothe, "Vorwort," 1: 5. In 1998, the Active Museum—a group engaged in many different projects related to the marking of Berlin's Nazi past in the landscape—hung posters near many of the memorial plaques connected with the events of the pogrom on November 9, 1938, when the Nazis burned synagogues, vandalized shops and other buildings owned by Jews, and arrested many of Berlin's Jewish residents. At that point, fifty years after the fact, twenty-seven plaques mentioned the events of November 9, 1938. It is also important to remember that the dozens of synagogues in use before the pogroms constituted a very heterogeneous group of original structures, reflecting the heterogeneity of Berlin's prewar Jewish population.

29. These include Heidereutergasse 4, Friedenstr. 3, Konrad-Wolf Str. 91, Freiheit 8, Tucholsky Str. 40, Behaimstr. 11, Lindenstr. 48–50, Levetzowstr. 7–8, Isarstr. 8, Münchener Str. 37, Passauer Str. 2, Lindenufer 12, Wrangelstr. 6–7, Mussehlstr. 22, Lützowstr. 16, Lessingstr. 6, Prinzenallee 87, Franzensbader Str. 7–8, Prinzregentenstr. 69–70, Markgraf-Albrecht Str. 11–12, Schönhauser Allee 162, Mühlenstr. 77, and Siegmunds Hof 11.

30. Hermann Simon, ed., *"Tuet auf die Pforten": Die Neue Synagoge, 1866–1995* (Berlin: Stiftung Neue Synagoge Berlin—Centrum Judaicum, 1995), 33.

31. Ibid. Here ownership is also crucial. For more on issues of ownership and

restitution with respect to synagogues and other Jewish community property, see Ayaka Takei, "The 'Gemeinde Problem': The Jewish Restitution Successor Organization and the Postwar Jewish Communities in Germany, 1947–1954," *Holocaust and Genocide Studies* 16:2 (2002): 266–288.

32. Simon, *"Tuet auf die Pforten,"* 36.

33. BA, Beschluß zur Bildung eines internationalen Kuratoriums und einer Stiftung zum Wiederaufbau der Neuen Synagoge in der Oranienburger Straße, June 24, 1988. Beschlüsse des Sekretariats des ZK der SED, Microfilm.

34. LB, Oranienburger Straße 30, C Rep 110 Mü, no. 4169.

35. The lot had been purchased by the Jüdische Gemeinde in 1856. Grundbuchamt, Amtsgericht Mitte, April 2000.

36. Endlich, "Berlin," in Puvogel, ed., *Gedenkstätten in Berlin,* 77.

37. The structure has gained increasing interest lately, and has recently been the site of public exhibits and of presentations in Berlin's "Long Night of the Synagogues," when many of the city's synagogue buildings were opened for tours, lectures, exhibits, and other public events. For more on the Synagoge Beth Zion, see Uwe Aulich, "Kerzen und Wein zur langen Nacht," *Berliner Zeitung,* Nov. 24, 2003; Marlies Emmerich, "Alte Synagoge wird religiöses Zentrum," *Berliner Zeitung,* Nov. 3, 2001; Stefan Melle, "Eingemauerte Säulen, Gutachten: Eine ehemalige Privatsynagoge könnte historisch getreu wieder hergerichtet werden," *Berliner Zeitung,* Sept. 20, 2001. A local women's group, Frauentreff Brunnhilde, has been particularly active in bringing the structure's history to light.

38. Eckhardt and Nachama, *Jüdische Orte,* 107.

39. Ibid., 109.

40. Horst Seferens, *Ein Deutscher Denkmalstreit: Die Kontroverse um die Spiegelwand in Berlin-Steglitz* (Berlin: Hentrich, 1995).

41. Endlich, "Gedenkstätten in Berlin," 78.

42. Eckhardt and Nachama, *Jüdische Orte,* 31.

43. Marlies Emmerich, "'Ein Unort wird zu einem jüdischen Ort': Grundmauern und Tafel erinnern an erste Synagoge," *Berliner Zeitung,* Sept. 15, 2000.

44. Michael Engel, "Die Vereinssynagogen—Einleitung," in Berlin Museum, *Synagogen in Berlin,* 2: 11.

45. Walking down Almstadtstraße in this neighborhood for example, the pedestrian would pass by numbers 16, 18, 26, and 28, all of which once housed small prayer spaces. (Eckhardt and Nachama, *Jüdische Orte,* 23–24).

46. Engel, "Vereinssynagogen—Einleitung," 10.

47. Girod, Lidschun, and Pfeiffer, *Nachbarn,* 255.

48. See, e.g., the many publications in the 1990s treating the neighborhood of Spandauer Vorstadt in the heart of Berlin, including Gesellschaft Hackesche Höfe, *Die Spandauer Vorstadt: Utopien und Realitäten zwischen Scheunenviertel und Friedrichstraße* (Berlin: Argon, 1995); Verein Stiftung Scheunenviertel, ed., *Das*

Scheunenviertel: Spuren eines verlorenen Berlins (Berlin: Haude & Spener, 1994); Frank Schumann, *Die Szene: Neue Geschichten aus dem Scheunenviertel* (Berlin: Neues Leben, 1993); Adolf Sommerfeld, *Das Ghetto von Berlin: Aus dem Scheunenviertel* (Berlin: Neues Leben, 1992); Ulrike Steglich and Peter Kratz, *Das Falsche Scheunenviertel: Ein Vorstadtverführer* (Berlin: Altberliner Bücherstube, 1997).

49. Clearly, the basement of a local bar cannot really be called a camp (*Lager*), so the distinction between "wild" concentration camps and *Folterkeller* is an important one. "In addition to the concentration camps erected by the state after the Reichstag fire, there were also so-called 'wild camps.' They were set up above all in the *Sturmlokalen* of the SA, as well as in former prisons. In Berlin alone, there are over one hundred known terror sites [*Terrororte*]" (Kurt Schilde, *Vom Columbia-Haus zum Schulenburgring: Dokumentation mit Lebensgeschichten von Opfern des Widerstands und der Verfolgung von 1933 bis 1945 aus dem Bezirk Tempelhof* [Berlin: Hentrich, 1987], 41).

50. Helmut Bräutigam and Oliver C. Gliech, "Nationalsozialistische Zwangslager in Berlin, I: Die 'wilden' Konzentrationslager und Folterkeller 1933/34," in *Berlin-Forschungen,* ed. Wolfgang Ribbe, 2: 139–140 (Berlin: Colloquium, 1987). They also point out that "the concept 'wild' concentration camp does not appear in the eyewitness reports that we are aware of. Its use in the course of the Nuremberg trials, however, leads to the suspicion that this term was already common in the Nazi era."

51. Claus-Dieter Sprink, *Gedenkstätte Köpenicker Blutwoche Juni 1933* (Berlin: Bezirksamt Köpenick von Berlin, 1997), 10. In "Nationalsozialistische Zwangslager in Berlin, I," Bräutigam and Gliech cite tallies ranging from fifty to two hundred sites that qualify either as "wild" concentration camps or torture sites (148).

52. Bräutigam and Gliech, "Nationalsozialistische Zwangslager in Berlin, I," 152.

53. Ibid., 139.

54. See, e.g., the use of terms like "historical toxic waste" in Michael Mönninger, "Der Giftmüll der NS-Geschichte," *Berliner Zeitung,* Oct. 28, 1999.

55. See Kenneth Foote's discussion of the sites of mass murders and other kinds of violence in the U.S. context, *Shadowed Ground: America's Landscapes of Violence and Tragedy* (Austin: University of Texas Press, 2003).

56. Bräutigam and Gliech, "Nationalsozialistische Zwangslager in Berlin, I," 151.

57. It is also entirely possible that many people, victims and perpetrators alike (albeit for profoundly different reasons), want this past to fade away.

58. These sites are the barracks at General-Pape-Straße, the Columbiahaus, the third floor of Hedemannstraße 31, the so-called Gutschow-Keller at Friedrichstraße 234, and the SA residence Drechsel in Spandau (Bräutigam and Gliech, "Nationalsozialistische Zwangslager in Berlin, I," 147). Of these, only General-

Pape-Straße and the Columbiahaus are marked.

59. Bräutigam and Gliech, "Nationalsozialistische Zwangslager in Berlin, I," 140.

60. The Nazis were at this point predominantly "arresting" low- and middle-ranking members of the Communist Party, the Democratic Socialist Party, and unions, as well as people singled out for personal or extortionate reasons. "Jews were also already hauled off as well. These were in no way only Jews who were members of the SPD or KPD," Bräutigam and Gliech note. They cite a few sources adding up to 16 Jews murdered in 1933. Ibid., 148–150.

61. Ibid., 155–167, 167–172.

62. Ibid., 151.

63. Schönfeld, *Gedenktafeln in Ost-Berlin,* 152; Endlich, "Berlin," 164–165.

64. Three of these are in the western half of the city (Rathaus Spandau, General-Pape-Str., and the Columbia-Haus), the other seven in the eastern half (Petersburger Str., the Wasserturm, and the Köpenick sites). This count is drawn in part on the following sources: a list provided by Bräutigam and Gliech, "Nationalsozialistische Zwangslager in Berlin, I," 155–172; the volumes by Hans-Rainer Sandvoß on resistance in the different districts of Berlin, including *Widerstand in Mitte und Tiergarten* (Berlin: Gedenkstätte Deutscher Widerstand, 1998); Endlich, "Berlin"; Martin Schönfeld, *Gedenktafeln in Ost-Berlin: Orte der Erinnerung an die Zeit des Nationalsozialismus* (Berlin: Aktives Museum Faschismus und Widerstand in Berlin, 1991), and id., *Gedenktafeln in West-Berlin* (Berlin: Aktives Museum Faschismus und Widerstand, 1993).

65. Amtsgericht Köpenick Gefängnis, Demuth, Seidler, Wendenschloß, and Gladenbecksche Villa. See Sandvoß, *Widerstand in Köpenick und Treptow,* 269; Schönfeld, *Gedenktafeln in Ost-Berlin,* 60, 66.

66. This was the "Zum Keglerheim" site, where the plaque was remounted in May 1995, with a small ceremony. See "Gedenktafel wurde wieder angebracht," *Berliner Zeitung,* May 3, 1995; Sandvoß, *Widerstand in Friedrichshain und Lichtenberg,* 330; Schönfeld, *Gedenktafeln in Ost-Berlin,* 42.

67. Claus-Dieter Sprink, *Gedenkstätte Köpenicker Blutwoche Juni 1933* (Berlin: Bezirksamt Köpenick von Berlin, 1997).

68. Relatively little has been published on this site, but Irene Mayer has written a master's thesis about it, "Das frühe Konzentrationslager am Wasserturm in Berlin-Prenzlauer Berg in seiner Zeit und in der Erinnerungsgeschichte" (Zentrum für Antisemitismusforschung, Technische Universität zu Berlin, 2003). Also see her chapter, "Das Konzentrationslager am Wasserturm Prenzlauer Berg in Berlin," in Wolfgang Benz and Barbara Distel, eds., *Instrumentarium der Macht: Geschichte der Konzentrationslager, 1933–1945* (Berlin: Metropol, 2003), 71–88.

69. Mayer, "Das Konzentrationslager am Wasserturm Prenzlauer Berg in Berlin," 80.

70. Ibid., 84–85.

71. Ibid., 85.

72. Johannes Tuchel and Kurt Schilde, *Columbia-Haus: Berliner Konzentrations-lager, 1933–1936* (Berlin: Hentrich / Bezirksamt Tempelhof von Berlin, 1990), 13.

73. Endlich, "Berlin," 175.

74. Tuchel and Schilde, *Columbia-Haus*, 10.

75. Endlich, "Berlin," 175.

76. Tuchel and Schilde, *Columbia-Haus*, 203.

77. Kurt Schilde, Rolf Scholz, and Sylvia Walleczek, *SA-Gefängnis Papestrasse: Spuren und Zeugnisse* (Berlin: Overall, 1996), 10.

78. Press release from the Robert Koch-Institut, June 16, 1999.

79. Endlich, "Berlin," 176.

80. Marion Jentsch, "Ehemalige Häftlinge meldeten sich," *Berliner Zeitung,* June 8, 1995.

81. Schilde et al., *SA-Gefängnis Papestrasse*, 19. The plaque was put up in 1980, according to Wolfgang Wippermann, "Nationalsozialistische Zwangslager in Berlin, II: Das 'Arbeitserziehungslager' Wuhlheide," in *Berlin-Forschungen,* ed. Wolfgang Ribbe, 2: 27 (Berlin: Colloquium, 1987).

82. Endlich, "Berlin," 176; Schönfeld, *Gedenktafeln in West-Berlin,* 180.

83. Schilde et al., *SA-Gefängnis Papestrasse*, 10.

84. Marion Jentsch, "Hakenkreuze noch nicht verblichen," *Berliner Zeitung,* Mar. 2, 1995.

85. Marion Jentsch, "Ehemalige Häftlinge meldeten sich," *Berliner Zeitung,* June 8, 1995.

86. Schilde et al., *SA-Gefängnis Papestrasse*, 9.

87. Quoting Sylvia Walleczek, one of the authors, in Thomas Helmut Schwarz, "Dokumentation über 'willige Vollstrecker,'" *Berliner Zeitung,* Sept. 7, 1996.

88. Elmar Schütze, "Ein Zeitzeuge berichtet über den Nazi-Terror," *Berliner Zeitung,* Oct. 10, 1997.

89. Hans-Rainer Sandvoß, *Widerstand in Kreuzberg* (Berlin: Gedenkstätte Deutscher Widerstand, 1997), 30–31.

90. Other such locations include the SA *Sturmlokal* on Pfarrstraße in the eastern district of Friedrichshain (Endlich, "Berlin," 93) and the "Glaskasten" on Prinzenallee 33, which was "transformed into an SA *Sturmlokal.* The bowling lanes served as a torture cellar" (Uwe Aulich, "Jazz im Glaskasten," *Berliner Zeitung,* Feb. 15, 2002).

91. Sandvoß, *Widerstand in Mitte und Tiergarten,* 93.

92. In "Topographie und Nutzungsgeschichte der 700 Zwangsarbeiterlager in und um Berlin 1939 bis 1945," in *Zwangsarbeit während der NS-Zeit in Berlin und Brandenburg: Formen, Funktion und Rezeption,* ed. W. Meyer and K. Neitmann (Potsdam: Verlag für Berlin und Brandenburg, 2001), 91, Rainer Kubatzki speaks

of 700 forced labor camps, but with the caveat that this number "is not precise, but rather an approximation of reality." In *Zwangsarbeiter- und Kriegsgefangenenlager: Standorte und Topographie in Berlin und im brandenburgischen Umland 1939 bis 1945: Eine Dokumentation* (Berlin: A. Spitz, 2001), 10–11, Kubatzki writes, "at any rate, for Berlin and its outskirts [stretching to the Autobahn ring around the city] one can reach the figure of 1,000." The historian Laurenz Demps has counted 1,000 forced labor camps and factories in Berlin, and 100 Gestapo sites. They cannot all be marked, he says, but they are there (from a conversation in his doctoral seminar, Humboldt University, Berlin, May 1999). See also Laurenz Demps and Reinhard Hölzer, *Zwangsarbeiter und Zwangsarbeiterlager in der faschistischen Reichshauptstadt Berlin, 1939–1945* (Berlin: Gesellschaft für Heimatgeschichte und Denkmalpflege Berlin im Kulturbund der DDR, 1986).

93. These processes are also taking place throughout Germany, not only in Berlin. In April 2003, for example, a plaque was placed at the front of the train station in Rahnsdorf (Wilhelmshagen), which served as a transit camp (*Durchgangslager*) for thousands of forced laborers (Karin Schmidl, "Gedenktafel für NS-Zwangsarbeiter," *Berliner Zeitung*, Apr. 10, 2003).

94. Helmut Bräutigam, "Nationalsozialistische Zwangslager in Berlin, IV: Fremdarbeiterlager 1939 bis 1945," in *Berlin-Forschungen*, ed. Wolfgang Ribbe, 4: 245 (Berlin: Colloquium, 1989).

95. Rainer Kubatzki, "Irgendein Lager gleich um die Ecke," *Berlinische Monatsschrift* 9 (2000): 71. Also see Bräutigam, "Nationalsozialistische Zwangslager in Berlin, IV," 242. Kubatzki also insists that these camps must not only be understood in terms of economics in general and arms production in particular but were also "closely linked to the political, racist, and *völkisch* goals of the National Socialists" (*Zwangsarbeiter- und Kriegsgefangenenlanger*, 22). My premise is not to assert that all such sites should necessarily be marked in similar ways, but rather to begin to understand in greater depth how some places emerge into the memorial landscape, while other, similar places do not.

96. It is also important to note the separate category of "KZ-Außenlager," work camps in the city but operating as satellites of the concentration camps. These included sites at the Grunewald train station (where there is no marker regarding forced labor), on Sonnenallee, on Wismarer Str., and in the area of Lichtenrade. Also see Wolf Gruner's discussion of Jewish forced labor in particular, *Der geschlossene Arbeitseinsatz deutscher Juden: Zur Zwangsarbeit als Element der Verfolgung, 1938–1943* (Berlin: Metropol, 1997), as well as Meyer and Neitmann, *Zwangsarbeit während der NS-Zeit*.

97. These changes are easy to see in the records of the Berlin state assembly. In the thirteenth session, the only mention of forced laborers is in the context of discussions over the payment of damages to forced laborers who worked for Siemens: see, e.g., "Annahme einer Entschliessung über Entschädigungszahlungen für ehe-

malige Zwangsarbeiterinnen und Zwangsarbeiter bei Siemens," AB, 13. Wahlperiode, DS 1371 (Feb. 13, 1997). In the fourteenth session, the number of discussions of paying damages to forced laborers increases and mention is made of setting up a research center: see, e.g., "Beteiligung des Landes Berlin am Entschädigungsfonds für ehemalige NS-Zwangsarbeiter/-innen," DS 127 (Jan. 18, 2000).

98. During its stay in the district of Pankow, the exhibition showed "to the precise address, where forced laborers were housed" (Philip Gessler, "Als der Feind die Zeit raubte," *taz*, Oct. 10, 2003).

99. See Arbeitskreis Berliner Regionalmuseen, *Zwangsarbeit in Berlin, 1938–1945* (Berlin: Metropol, 2003), the book that went with the "Forced Labor In Berlin, 1938–1945" exhibition in 2002 and 2003.

100. Cf. Stichting Holländerei, *Niederländer und Flamen in Berlin, 1940–1945: KZ-Häftlinge, Inhaftierte, Kriegsgefangene und Zwangsarbeiter* (Berlin: Hentrich, 1996); Leonore Scholze-Irrlitz and Karoline Noack, eds., *Arbeit für den Feind: Zwangsarbeiter-Alltag in Berlin und Brandenburg (1939–1945)* (Berlin: be.bra, 1998); Christine Steer, *Versklavt und fast Vergessen: Zwangsarbeit im Berliner Bezirk Lichtenberg 1939–1945* (Berlin: Trafo, 2001).

101. Much of the academic work at the time relating to forced labor had to do with the damages paid to workers in the 1990s, as well as thorough inquiries into the conditions of forced labor not only in Berlin, but throughout Germany. Some examples include Klaus Barwig, Günter Saathoff, and Nicole Weyde, eds., *Entschädigung für NS-Zwangsarbeit: Rechtliche, historische und politische Aspekte* (Baden Baden: Nomos Verlagsgesellschaft, 1998); Berliner Geschichtswerkstatt, ed., *Zwangsarbeit in Berlin, 1940–1945: Erinnerungsberichte aus Polen, der Ukraine und Weißrußland* (Erfurt: Sutton, 2000); Gruner, *Geschlossene Arbeitseinsatz deutscher Juden*; Ulrike Winkler, ed. *Stiften gehen: NS-Zwangsarbeit und Entschädigungsdebatte.* (Cologne: PapyRossa, 2000).

102. Bräutigam, "Nationalsozialistische Zwangslager in Berlin, IV," 235.

103. Ibid., 237. Laurenz Demps and Reinhard Hölzer, *Zwangsarbeiter und Zwangsarbeiterlager in der faschistischen Reichshauptstadt Berlin, 1939–1945* (Berlin: Gesellschaft für Heimatgeschichte und Denkmalpflege Berlin im Kulturbund der DDR, 1986).

104. Wolfgang Ribbe, 'Vorwort,' in Kubatzki, *Zwangsarbeiter- und Kriegsgefangenenlanger*, 8. In 2001, Ribbe could write that "the analysis of the sources is in full swing," indicated in part by a conference on "Forced Labor During the Nazi period in Berlin and Brandenburg: Forms, Function, and Reception," supported by the Gedenkstätte Sachsenhausen, the Historische Kommission zu Berlin, and the Brandenburgische Landeshauptarchiv.

105. Kubatzki, *Zwangsarbeiter- und Kriegsgefangenenlanger*, 10.

106. Ribbe, "Vorwort," in Kubatzki, ibid., 7-8. In Kubatzki's registry of forced labor camps (ibid.), the descriptions are curt, conveying nothing of the experience of

the workers, e.g., "Mentioned as a foreigner camp with French female forced laborers"; "Mentioned as foreigner camp for the Julius Pintsch Company . . . destroyed by an air raid on November 23, 1943." Kubatzki's aim in *Zwangsarbeiter- und Kriegsgefangenenlanger* is not to flesh out the stories of the individual camps (this is done by other historians), but rather to provide as exhaustive an account as possible of the precise locations and numbers of forced labor camps, thus offering a context for the other research being done on living conditions, resistance, deaths, etc.

107. Bräutigam, "Nationalsozialistische Zwangslager in Berlin, IV," 239. The term *Zwangsarbeiterlager* (forced labor camp) has come to replace *Fremdarbeiterlager* (foreign worker camp), the term used at the time (Kubatzki, *Zwangsarbeiter- und Kriegsgefangenenlanger*, 11). It is also important to remember that not all forced laborers were foreigners. German political prisoners and German Jews were also forced laborers, and often under worse conditions than, for example, French and Italian forced laborers.

108. Kubatzki, *Zwangsarbeiter- und Kriegsgefangenenlager*, 10–11.

109. Bräutigam, "Nationalsozialistische Zwangslager in Berlin, IV," 251.

110. Ibid., 236.

111. Kubatzki, *Zwangsarbeiter- und Kriegsgefangenenlanger*, 21.

112. Kubatzki, "Irgendein Lager gleich um die Ecke," 71.

113. The Berlin History Workshop has a web site dedicated to forced labor sites. Other markers are located in the district of Spandau and in Friedrichshain, on the edge of the Volkspark, at Sophienstr. 18, Wendenschloß Str. 154–158, the Sophie-Scholl Schule, and the interior courtyard of the Siemens building. Unmarked sites include Schönhauser Allee 22, a building that had many different uses in the 1930s and 1940s, including as a Jewish rest home, then a deportation center, and as housing for Ukrainian forced laborers who worked in the nearby brewery complex (Endlich, "Berlin," 139). One of the consistent dangers to forced laborers was the unavailability of air raid shelters. At Joachimsthaler Str. 11 in Charlottenburg, in November 1943, eighteen young Czech workers were killed in a bombing, and a plaque now marks the site: "Eighteen Czech young people died here on November 23, 1943, in an air raid. They were employed by the Technical Emergency Service, to remove bombing damage." The Berliner Geschichtswerkstatt initiated the plaque, sponsored by Allianz insurance, which was dedicated on July 10, 2000, in the presence of the Czech ambassador and the district mayor. www.luise-berlin.de/Gedenktafeln/Index1024.htm (accessed Oct. 31, 2005, search by "Tschechische Zwangsarbeiter").

114. Endlich, "Berlin," 62. Another mass forced laborer grave can be found in the Lankwitz cemetery on Lange Str. (ibid., 171).

115. Ibid., 95; "Wirbel um geräumtes Mahnmal," *Berliner Zeitung,* May 26, 1997.

116. Birgitt Eltzel, "Stele erinnert an Zwangsarbeiter," *Berliner Zeitung,* Sept. 17, 2002.

117. schoe, "Gedenken an Opfer der NS-Herrschaft," *Berliner Morgenpost,* Jan. 28, 2004.

118. Endlich, "Berlin," 201.

119. Wippermann, "Nationalsozialistische Zwangslager in Berlin, II: Das 'Arbeitserziehungslager' Wuhlheide," 181.

120. Ibid., 185–188.

121. Endlich, "Berlin," 89.

122. Philip Gessler, "Als der Feind die Zeit raubte," *taz,* Oct. 10, 2003.

123. Endlich, "Berlin," 192.

124. AB, Antrag der Fraktion der CDU über Sicherung des NS-Zwangsarbei-terlagers Niederschöneweide als Denkmal und Begegnungsstätte, 15. Wahlperiode, DS 15/791.

125. AB, DS 15/1392.

126. AB, DS 15/1901, June 24, 2003.

127. AB, Green Party Representative Michael Cramer, 15. Wahlperiode, Inhalts-protokoll Kult 15/9, Aug. 26, 2002, pp. 15–16.

128. Endlich, "Berlin," 158.

129. See the report written by the teacher at the Sophie-Scholl-Oberschule, Elßholzstr. 34–37, who has been most closely involved in these efforts, Bodo Förster, titled "Zwangsarbeiter in Deutschland: 'Du erwartest in Deutschland eine anständige Behandlung,'" http://learning.dada.at/res/pdf/DC001PRO.PDF (accessed September 10, 2005).

130. Endlich, "Berlin," 165.

131. Marcel Gäding, "Der beste Platz für das Denkmal," *Berliner Zeitung,* Aug. 19, 2003.

132. Marcel Gäding, "Einigung um Standort für Denkmal," *Berliner Zeitung,* Sept. 8, 2003.

133. Endlich, "Berlin," 30.

134. Marlies Emmerich, "Tausend Lager in der ganzen Stadt," *Berliner Zeitung,* Jan. 28, 2000.

135. Wolfgang Benz, ed., *Überleben im Dritten Reich: Juden im Untergrund und ihre Helfer* (Munich: C. H. Beck, 2003).

136. For more on the issue of Jewish forced labor, see Gruner, *Geschlossene Arbeitseinsatz deutscher Juden.*

CHAPTER 6: BERLIN AND BEYOND

1. Wilbur Zelinsky, *Nation into State: The Shifting Symbolic Foundations of American Nationalism* (Chapel Hill: University of North Carolina Press, 1988), 175.

2. For more on this process in the United States, see Kenneth Foote, *Shadowed*

Ground: America's Landscapes of Violence and Tragedy (Austin: University of Texas Press, 2003).

3. Michael Schudson, "Culture and the Integration of National Societies," in *The Sociology of Culture*, ed. Diane Crane (Cambridge, Mass.: Blackwell, 1994), 26.

4. Walter Firey, "Sentiment and Symbolism as Ecological Variables," *American Sociological Review* 10:2 (1944): 140.

5. "Not only is there the usual sanctity which attaches to all cemeteries, but in those of Boston there is an added sacredness growing out of the age of the grounds and the fact that the forebears of many of New England's most distinguished families as well as a number of colonial and Revolutionary leaders lie buried in these cemeteries. There is thus a manifold symbolism to these old burying-grounds, pertaining to family lineage, early nationhood, civic origins, and the like, all of which have strong sentimental associations" (ibid., 145). "Thank Heaven, the tide of money making must break and go around" Boston Common, one citizen proclaimed, while another said: "Here, in short, are all our accumulated memories, intimate, public, private" (ibid., 144). Of course, these places may also function as tourist attractions, a phenomenon arguably more pronounced today than at the time when Firey was writing, and noticeably absent from his analysis.

6. Ibid., 144. Gerald Suttles found unpersuasive Firey's "procedure . . . essentially to identify what he took as departures from a rational, economic model of land use." "The Cumulative Texture of Local Urban Culture," *American Journal of Sociology* 90:2 (1984): 285. Suttles felt that Firey was mistaken in identifying intense pockets of meaning in the landscape as residual and also in seeing them as simply fitting into a functionalist arrangement of urban space (where the collective "need" for meaning has to be balanced with the need for commerce, for example).

7. In explaining the uneven landscape of Boston, Firey depicted a clear-cut battle between real estate and meaning (an opposition echoed in later analyses of the city as well), pitching commerce and memory against each other in what seems to be a winner-take-all battle of money against community. Somewhat similar oppositions employed by Michel De Certeau, David Harvey, Henri Lefebvre, and Harvey Molotch (in his earlier work) have been augmented by more layered analyses of the interaction of symbols and commerce in the cityscape. See Michel de Certeau, *The Practice of Everyday Life* (Berkeley: University of California Press, 1984); David Harvey, *The Condition of Postmodernity: An Enquiry into the Origins of Cultural Change* (Cambridge, Mass.: Blackwell, 1990); Henri Lefebvre, *The Production of Space* (Oxford: Blackwell, 1974); and Harvey Molotch, "The City as a Growth Machine: Toward a Political Economy of Place," *American Journal of Sociology* 82:2 (1976): 309–332. Other analysts have inquired into the ways in which sentiment and symbolism interact with real estate markets, boosterism, shopping districts, and other forms of commerce, often finding that spaces of collective memory are intertwined with (and not always in opposition to) the

economic pressures of urban change. See Manuel Castells, *The City and the Grass-roots: A Cross-Cultural Theory of Urban Social Movements* (Berkeley: University of California Press, 1983); Tom Gieryn, "A Space for Place in Sociology," *Annual Review of Sociology* 26 (2000): 463–496; Jan Lin, "Ethnic Places, Postmodernism, and Urban Change in Houston," *Sociological Quarterly* 36:4 (1995): 629–647; Christopher Mele, *Selling the Lower East Side: Culture, Real Estate, and Resistance in New York City* (Minneapolis: University of Minnesota Press, 2000); Harvey Molotch, William Freudenberg, and Krista E. Paulsen, "History Repeats Itself, but How? City Character, Urban Tradition, and the Accomplishment of Place," *American Sociological Review* 65:6 (2000): 791–823; Suttles, "Cumulative Texture of Local Urban Culture"; Sharon Zukin, *The Cultures of Cities* (Cambridge, Mass.: Blackwell, 1995); and Sharon Zukin, Robert Baskerville, and Courtney Guthreau, "From Coney Island to Las Vegas in the Urban Imaginary: Discursive Practices of Growth and Decline," *Urban Affairs Review* 33:5 (1998): 627–654.

8. Many of these studies place much of the weight of their analysis on the symbols and sentiments themselves, and at times, they leave unanswered questions of more precise empirical links between the symbolic and the economic arenas. Molotch et al., however, embark on a more integrative approach, attempting to understand the political, symbolic, and economic components of "the complex configurations that distinguish 'place'" in Santa Barbara and Ventura, California (Molotch et al., "History Repeats Itself," 792). They also invoke Firey, for whom "'sentiment and symbolism' were 'ecological variables' of equal standing to quantitative economic elements." In their efforts to understand the ways in which place construction happens differentially in the seemingly similar communities of Santa Barbara and Ventura, they find path dependence, and they reject the search for a single independent variable. Following the results of their inquiry, cities and other places must be explained in terms of a combination of happenstance and intention, as well as different kinds of social and material preconditions. They posit a "rolling inertia" that "allows for continuous flux within a stable mode of operation," and this way of understanding place is also useful here, even though my object of analysis differs from theirs (ibid., 819).

9. Conflict figures prominently in the process of memorialization in Berlin, but is largely absent from Durkheim's and Halbwachs's formulations of collective memory. "Durkheim's own focus on already-functioning religions has tended to draw attention to the functional aspects of religion—the way in which it promotes social solidarity through moral obligation—rather than to the sacred as a potential arena for conflict, change, and violence," Lynn Hunt observes in "The Sacred and the French Revolution," in *Durkheimian Sociology: Cultural Studies*, ed. Jeffrey Alexander (Cambridge: Cambridge University Press, 1988), 39.

10. Émile Durkheim, *The Elementary Forms of the Religious Life* (1915; New York: Free Press, 1965), 52.

11. Like many sociologists before him, Halbwachs distinguished between the countryside, where land housed both law and memory, and the city, where land itself is comparatively unimportant, because "this is the world of money transaction, where specific objects, bought and sold, are unimportant and what matters is the capacity to acquire or dispose of anything." Yet he points out that spatial and legal memory are still important in the city but do not encompass very much or reach very far back. See Maurice Halbwachs, *The Collective Memory* (1950; New York: Harper Colophon Books, 1980), 138.

12. Like James Young, and like Jeffrey Olick and Joyce Robbins, David Chidester and Edward T. Linenthal emphasize the centrality of conflict in the generation of collective memory, in contrast to the consensus-based formulations of Durkheim, Halbwachs, and Eliade. Chidester and Linenthal react in particular to Eliade's emphasis on consensus, which they see as an inaccurate theoretical formulation of the sacred. See Chidester and Linenthal, eds., *American Sacred Space* (Bloomington: Indiana University Press, 1995), 16. But Durkheim's understanding of "the social fact" may be useful in thinking about how symbolic places are created and sustained in the urban landscape. He writes that "the social fact is sometimes so far materialized as to become an element of the external world. For instance, a definite type of architecture is a social phenomenon; but it is partially embodied in houses and buildings of all sorts which, once constructed, become autonomous realities, independent of individuals" (Émile Durkheim, *Suicide* [Glencoe, Ill.: Free Press, 1951], 313–315). Frequently, memorial projects also become "autonomous realities, independent of individuals."

13. Mary Douglas, "Symbolic Pollution," in *Culture and Society: Contemporary Debates*, ed. Jeffrey Alexander and Steven Seidman (Cambridge: Cambridge University Press, 1990), 159.

14. Keith Basso, "'Stalking with Stories': Names, Places, and Moral Narratives Among the Western Apache," in *Text, Play, and Story: The Construction and Reconstruction of Self and Society*, ed. E. M. Bruner (n.p.: American Ethnological Society, 1984), 19–55; quotation at 23.

15. Ibid., 44–45.

16. We "are responsible for 'past' Berlin and the many layers, proper names, works, this memory entails. We are responsible to all of them—all of those ghosts—neither living nor simply dead," Jacques Derrida observes, for example, in "The Berlin City Forum: Jacques Derrida, Kurt Forster, and Wim Wenders," *Architectural Design* 26:11–12 (1992): 46–47.

17. Stefanie Endlich and Thomas Lutz, *Gedenken und Lernen an historischen Orten: Ein Wegweiser zu Gedenkstätten für die Opfer des Nationalsozialismus in Berlin* (Berlin: Hentrich, 1995), 45–47.

18. The Haus der Wannsee-Konferenz also serves pedagogical purposes, hosting school groups and seminars "for political education." See *Erinnern für die*

Zukunft (Berlin: Gedenkstätte Haus der Wannsee-Konferenz, 1992).

19. Stefanie Endlich and Thomas Lutz, *Gedenken und Lernen an historischen Orten*, 46.

20. *Erinnern für die Zukunft* (Berlin: Gedenkstätte Haus der Wannsee-Konferenz, 1992), 3.

21. Brian Ladd, *The Ghosts of Berlin* (Chicago: University of Chicago Press, 1997), 154.

22. Ibid., 131; Alfred Kernd'l, "Archäologie der Neuzeit: Denkmalschutz und Zeitgeist in der Hauptstadt," in *Geschichtswerkstatt Spree-Insel: Historische Topographie—Stadtarchäologie—Stadtentwicklung*, ed. Helmut Engel, Jörg Haspel, and Wolfgang Ribbe (Potsdam: Verlag für Berlin-Brandenburg: 1998), 151.

23. "Im alten Bunker der Reichskanzlei wachsen Tropfsteine von der Decke," *Tagesspiegel*, Aug. 10, 1990.

24. "Ein Freskenraum der Leibstandarte," *Tagesspiegel*, Jan. 8, 1991. For more on Kernd'l, see Ladd, *Ghosts of Berlin*, as well as Kernd'l's own extensive publications.

25. "Ein Freskenraum der Leibstandarte," *Tagesspiegel*, Jan. 8, 1991.

26. Kernd'l, "Archäologie der Neuzeit," 149, 151.

27. "Reichskanzleigelände wird dokumentiert," *Tagesspiegel*, Mar. 10, 1992. The federal government intended to build the new foreign ministry here, while the landscape designer Ingo Kowarik called for the area to become a public green space (*Grünzone*). Minister for Urban Development Volker Hassemer argued, however, in favor of locating the offices of the German states on the site, which he saw as a more appropriate use for it than the foreign ministry. Given its Nazi past, he said, "passing over [*Übergehen*] the historical traces" was impossible (Rolf Lautenschläger, "Offene Räume—geschlossenes Denken," *taz*, June 22, 1992). The state assembly commissioned a report on the bunkers in March 1992. The archaeological investigation of the bunkers was carried out from May 11 to 14, 1992. At the same time, regardless of the results of the study, the assembly planned to begin the process of placing the best-preserved bunkers under historical preservation. See AB, DS 12/1769, Mitteilung zur Kenntnisnahme über Dokumentation der historischen Topographie des Geländes der ehemaligen Reichskanzlei, July 13, 1992. Also see Alfred Kernd'l, *Zeugnisse der historischen Topographie auf dem Gelände der Ehemaligen Reichskanzlei Berlin-Mitte* (Berlin: Archäologisches Landesamt Berlin, 1993).

28. Steffen Winter, "UNESCO-Schutz für Hitlers Bunker?" *Der Spiegel*, Nov. 15, 1999, 80-82. See also Michael Mönninger, "Der Giftmüll der NS-Geschichte," *Berliner Zeitung*, Oct. 28, 1999; Dietmar Arnold, "Stolpersteine der Vergangenheit," *Berliner Zeitung*, Nov. 13, 1999.

29. "Hitler-Bunker unter Denkmalschutz," *taz*, July 2, 1992.

30. Marlies Emmerich, "Hitler-Bunker bald unter Denkmalschutz," *Berliner Zeitung*, July 2, 1992.

31. Ottomar Harbauer, "Hitler-Bunker: Mahn-oder Kultstätte?" *Berliner Zeitung,* July 3, 1992.

32. "Keine Wallfahrt zum Bunker," *Tagesspiegel,* July 4, 1992.

33. Anita Kugler, "Gegen die Mythenbildung," *taz,* Oct. 23, 1992.

34. These included Christoph Stölzl and Reinhard Rürup. Earlier, Christine Fischer-Defoy had suggested that the only way to make this bunker publicly accessible would be in conjunction with the nearby Topography of Terror exhibit, a position that she abandoned at this discussion. Under this initial suggestion, people could be allowed into the bunkers, but only in tours led by guides trained in anti-fascist education. In January 1993, the participants at another hearing organized by the Active Museum concluded that the site was not worth preservation and advocated focusing on the Wannsee Villa, the Gedenkstätte Plötzensee, the Museum of German Resistance, and the future Holocaust Memorial as more legitimate sites of memory (*Stätten der Erinnerung*), given their greater significance to the Holocaust than the bunkers of Hitler's drivers. See Marlies Emmerich, "Diskussion über Nazi-Kunst," *Berliner Zeitung,* July 14, 1992; "Disput um Hitler-Bunker," *taz,* Jan. 27, 1993.

35. Michael Mönninger, "Der Giftmüll der NS-Geschichte," *Berliner Zeitung,* Oct. 28, 1999.

36. Nikolaus Bernau, "Stein des Anstoßes," *Tagesspiegel,* Aug. 29, 1992.

37. Daniela Pogade, "Gefrorene Apokalypse," *Berliner Zeitung,* Aug. 29–30, 1992.

38. "Ödland mit Kaninchen," *Der Spiegel,* Apr. 18, 1995.

39. Johannes Leithäuser, "Streit um die Denkmalwürdigkeit eines ehemaligen SS-Bunkers," *FAZ,* Feb. 1, 1997.

40. An odd slippage occurred in most of these discussions, conflating the site for the Holocaust Memorial with the site of Hitler's bunkers. Hitler's bunker itself sits beneath existing construction. Most of this discussion, including the question of historical preservation, centered, not on Hitler's bunker, the "Führerbunker," but rather on his drivers' bunker, the "Fahrerbunker" (interview with Alfred Kernd'l by Marlies Emmerich, "Gemeinsam gegen das Vergessen: Archäologe Alfred Kernd'l will NS-Bunker auf dem Potsdamer Platz erhalten," *Berliner Zeitung,* July 27, 1992). See also Anita Kugler, "Gegen die Mythenbildung: Diskussion über die Zukunft der unterirdischen Reste am Potsdamer Platz," *taz,* Oct. 23, 1992; "Ödland mit Kaninchen," *Der Spiegel,* Apr. 18, 1995.

41. BIS, "Kampf um die Rest von Hitlers Bunker," *Berliner Zeitung,* May 25, 1997.

42. It should be noted that most of the bunkers are in poor condition; the drivers' bunker seems to be the most intact.

43. Kernd'l, "Archäologie der Neuzeit," 149.

44. Winter, "UNESCO-Schutz für Hitlers Bunker?" It is also important to

note the controversy around another "contaminated" site, Hitler's mountain retreat, Berchtesgaden, where the luxury InterContinental Resort Berchtesgaden opened in March, 2005. Many questioned the appropriateness of creating a resort on this "stained" site, as well as the demolitions of some remaining "authentic structures" by the Bavarian government. There have definitely been instances of neo-Nazi pilgrimage (well before the opening of the hotel). But there is also a documentation center chronicling the Nazi era not far from the hotel, attracting tens of thousands of visitors since the center opened in 1999. See Richard Bernstein, "Hotel Hopes to Thrive on Beauty that Predates Nazi Era," *New York Times*, Mar. 6, 2005, and "Where Hitler Played, Should the Rich do Likewise?" *New York Times*, Oct. 21, 2004. Also see Frank Junghänel, "Über die Ruinen wächst kein Gras," *Berliner Zeitung*, Nov. 7, 1997.

45. Senatsverwaltung für Bau- und Wohnungswesen, *Parlament- und Regierungsviertel Berlin: Ergebnisse der Vorbereitenden Untersuchungen* (Berlin: Senatsverwaltung für Bau- und Wohnungswesen, 1993), 50.

46. Laurenz Demps, *Berlin-Wilhelmstraße: Eine Topographie preußisch-deutscher Macht* (Berlin: Ch. Links, 1994), 279–280.

47. Wolfgang Schäche, "Geschichte und stadträumliche Bedeutung der 'Ministergärten,'" in *Architektur in Berlin: Jahrbuch 1992*, ed. N. Baumeister (Hamburg: Junius, 1992), 66.

48. Demps, *Berlin-Wilhelmstraße*, 289. "Apparently little more than its floor still remains, forty feet below an expanse of playground, parking lot, and lawn adjoining the new apartment buildings. Typical German treatment of a historically burdened site, Kernd'l observed sardonically, is either to plant it with greenery or to use it for parking, and here we have both" (Ladd, *Ghosts of Berlin*, 133).

49. AB, DS 12/1361, March 1992.

50. "Bürgerinitiative schlägt Kompromiß für Ex-SS-Häuser vor," *Berliner Morgenpost*, Oct. 12, 1997.

51. One particularly well known example of this process is the shift from the Vietnam Veterans Memorial as a subject of great controversy to the widely accepted memorial that it is today. See Marita Sturken, *Tangled Memories: The Vietnam War, the AIDS Epidemic, and the Politics of Remembering* (Berkeley: University of California Press, 1997).

52. Cf. Stefanie Lehnart, "Niederschöneweide: Gedenken an Zwangsarbeiter, Ausstellungen im alten Lager," *Berliner Zeitung*, June 22, 2002; www.zwangsarbeit-in-berlin.de (accessed September 10, 2005).

53. Jefferson Chase, "Stumbling over the Holocaust," *Boston Globe*, Apr. 11, 2004.

54. Claudia Fuchs, "Stolpersteine," *Berliner Zeitung*, Apr. 11, 2003; Andreas Rosenfelder, "Messingplatten als Kölner Steine des Anstoßes," *FAZ*, Nov. 13, 2003.

55. Kirsten Grieshaber, "Plaques for the Nazi Victims Offer a Personal Impact,"

New York Times, Nov. 29, 2003. The Munich city government justified its refusal to grant permission for *Stolpersteine* by claiming that it did not want to support the placement of such markers in the sidewalk, where they would be walked on and otherwise sullied, and that these markers also only identified a small percentage of victims rather than being more inclusive. See www.muenchen.de/Rathaus/dir/presse/archiv/2004/pressemitteilungen/97751/stolpersteine.html (accessed September 10, 2005).

56. Karin Schmidl, "15 neue 'Stolpersteine,'" *Berliner Zeitung,* May 4, 2004.

57. This argument is expressed by many of the classical sociological theorists, as well as E. Relph, *Place and Placelessness* (London: Pion, 1976); Marc Augé, *Non-Places: An Anthropology of Super-Modernity* (London: Verso, 1995); and Tony Hiss, *The Experience of Place* (New York: Knopf, 1990).

58. For more on questions of place and globalization, see Jennifer Jordan, "Collective Memory and Locality in Global Cities," in *Global Cities: Cinema, Architecture, and Urbanism in a Digital Age,* ed. Linda Krause and Patrice Petro (New Brunswick, N.J.: Rutgers University Press, 2003), 31–48.

59. This attention to authenticity and the development of memorials in eastern Berlin, more generally, demonstrate an elaborate specificity of place precisely at a moment of globalization and the consolidation of Europe. For more on questions of place and modernity, see Rick Biernacki and Jennifer Jordan, "The Place of Space in the Study of the Social," in *The Social in Question: New Bearings in History and the Social Sciences,* ed. Patrick Joyce (London: Routledge, 2002), 133–150.

60. One article that sets out in this direction is L. Meskell, "Negative Heritage and Past Mastering in Archaeology," *Anthropological Quarterly* 75:3 (2002): 557–574.

61. For analyses of the United States, see John Bodnar, *Remaking America: Public Memory, Commemoration and Patriotism in the Twentieth Century* (Princeton, N.J.: Princeton, 1991); M. Kammen, *Mystic Chords of Memory: The Transformation of Tradition in American Culture* (New York: Knopf, 1991); George Lipsitz, *Time Passages: Collective Memory and American Popular Culture* (Minneapolis: University of Minnesota Press, 1990); Barry Schwartz, *George Washington: The Making of an American Symbol* (New York: Free Press, 1987); Lynn Spillman, *Nation and Commemoration: Creating National Identities in the United States and Australia* (Cambridge: Cambridge University Press, 1997); Sturken, *Tangled Memories;* Wilbur Zelinsky, *Nation into State: The Shifting Symbolic Foundations of American Nationalism* (Chapel Hill: University of North Carolina, 1988).

62. Cf. Stefanie Endlich and Thomas Lutz, *Gedenken und Lernen an historischen Orten: Ein Wegweiser zu Gedenkstätten für die Opfer des Nationalsozialismus in Berlin* (Berlin: Hentrich, 1995).

63. Keith Basso paints an intriguing picture in "'Stalking with Stories'" of one possible constellation of memory, morality, and landscape. He finds that place-

specific "historical tales are 'about' what it means to *be* a Western Apache, or, to make the point less dramatically, what it is that being an Apache should normally and properly entail" (36). The landscape instructs, warns, and reminds, but through social activity.

64. This is a point emphasized by many analysts of memory. See, e.g., Andreas Huyssen, *Present Pasts: Urban Palimpsests and the Politics of Memory* (Stanford: Stanford University Press, 2003), and Edward Linenthal, *The Unfinished Bombing: Oklahoma City in American Memory* (New York: Oxford University Press, 2001).

65. Some of the same issues raised by the Topography of Terror in the former Gestapo headquarters in Berlin also appear in the Tuol Sleng Museum of Genocidal Crimes in Cambodia, in the Apartheid Museum in South Africa, and in the Vietnam Veterans Memorial in Washington, D.C.

Appendix: Maps

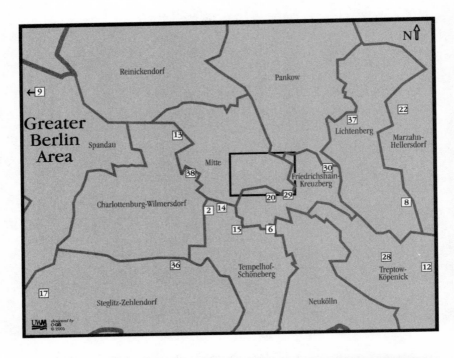

Greater
Berlin
Area

Reinickendorf

Pankow

←9

Spandau

13

Mitte

Charlottenburg-Wilmersdorf

38

2 14

15 6

37

Lichtenberg

22

Marzahn-
Hellersdorf

30

Friedrichshain-
Kreuzberg

20 29

8

36

Tempelhof-
Schöneberg

28

Treptow-
Köpenick

12

17

Steglitz-Zehlendorf

Neukölln

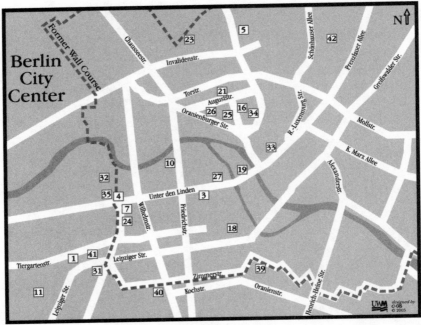

Berlin
City
Center

Former Wall Course

Chausseestr.

Invalidenstr.

23

5

Schönhauser Allee

42

Prenzlauer Allee

Greifswalder Str.

Torstr.

Auguststr.

21

26 25

16 34

Oranienburger Str.

R. Luxemburg Str.

Mollstr.

33

K. Marx Allee

10

32

35 4

Unter den Linden

27

19

Alexanderstr.

Wilhelmstr.

7

24

3

Friedrichstr.

18

Tiergartenstr.

1 41

Leipziger Str.

31

Leipziger Str.

Zimmerstr.

39

11

40

Kochstr.

Oranienstr.

Heinrich-Heine Str.

LEGEND

1. Aktion T4 site
2. Bayerisches Viertel
3. Bebelplatz
4. Brandenburger Tor
5. Brunnenstraße 33
6. Columbia-Haus
7. Denkmal für die ermordeten Juden Europas / Memorial for the Murdered Jews of Europe
8. Deutsch-Russisches Museum Berlin-Karlshorst
9. Evangelisches Waldkrankenhaus Spandau
10. Friedrichstraße plaque
11. Gedenkstätte Deutscher Widerstand
12. Gedenkstätte Köpenicker Blutwoche
13. Gedenkstätte Plötzensee
14. Gedenktafel für die homosexuellen Opfer des Nationalsozialismus / Plaque for the Homosexual Victims of Nazism
15. General-Pape-Straße
16. Große Hamburger Straße
17. Haus der Wannseekonferenz
18. Hausvogteiplatz
19. Herbert Baum Gedenkstein
20. Jüdisches Museum
21. Koppenplatz
22. Marzahner Parkfriedhof
23. Mauer Gedenkstätte / Berlin Wall Memorial
24. Ministergärten
25. Missing House
26. Neue Synagoge
27. Neue Wache
28. Niederschöneweide/Treptow forced labor camp
29. Oranienstraße (Stolpersteine)
30. Petersburger Straße 94
31. Potsdamer Platz
32. Reichstag
33. Rosenstraße
34. Rosenthaler Straße 39/Blind Trust
35. Sinti and Roma Memorial (planned)
36. Steglitzer Spiegelwand
37. Synagoge Konrad-Wolf-Straße
38. Synagoge Levetzowstraße
39. Synagoge Lindenstraße
40. Topographie des Terrors
41. Volksgerichtshof site
42. Wasserturm

Please note that locations are approximate. The district names shown here reflect the district consolidation that occurred in 2001. In cases where the original district name was omitted from the new name, the pre-2001 district names used in this book are shown in parentheses: Charlottenburg-Wilmersdorf, Friedrichshain-Kreuzberg, Lichtenberg (Hohenschönhausen, Lichtenberg), Marzahn-Hellersdorf, Mitte (Mitte, Tiergarten, Wedding), Pankow (Pankow, Prenzlauer Berg, Weißensee), Neukölln, Reinickendorf, Spandau, Steglitz-Zehlendorf, Tempelhof-Schöneberg, Treptow-Köpenick. Maps created by Donna Genzmer and the Cartography and Geographic Information Science Center at the University of Wisconsin-Milwaukee.

Select Bibliography

Adamczyck, Amy. "On Thanksgiving and Collective Memory: Constructing the American Tradition." *Journal of Historical Sociology* 15:3 (2002): 343–365.

Aengevelt Immobilien KG. *City Report Region Berlin Nr. IV 1994/95*. Berlin: Aengevelt Immobilien, 1994.

Arbeitskreis Berliner Regionalmuseen. *Zwangsarbeit in Berlin, 1938–1945*. Berlin: Metropol, 2003.

Arlt, Klaus, et al. *Zeugnisse jüdischer Kultur: Erinnerungsstätten in Mecklenburg-Vorpommern, Brandenburg, Berlin, Sachsen-Anhalt, Sachsen und Thüringen*. Berlin: Tourist, 1992.

Autorenkollektiv. *Das Sowjetische Ehrenmal in Berlin-Treptow*. Berlin: Berlin-Information, 1976.

Bahrmann, Hannes and Christoph Links. *Chronik der Wende: Die Ereignisse in der DDR zwischen 7. Oktober 1989 und 18. März 1990*. Rheda-Wiedenbrück: RM-Buch-und-Media-Vertrieb, 1999.

Bamberger, Edgar. *Der Völkermord an den Sinti und Roma in der Gedenkstättenarbeit*. Heidelberg: Dokumentations- und Kulturzentrum Deutscher Sinti und Roma, 1993.

Barnack, Wolfgang, et al. *Denkmale und Plastiken im Stadtbezirk Berlin-Prenzlauer Berg*. Berlin: Rat des Stadtbezirks Berlin-Prenzlauer Berg, Abteilung Kultur, 1980.

Barthel, Diane. *Historic Preservation: Collective Memory and Historical Identity*. New Brunswick, N.J.: Rutgers University Press, 1996.

Barwig, Klaus, Günter Saathoff, and Nicole Weyde, eds. *Entschädigung für NS-Zwangsarbeit: rechtliche, historische und politische Aspekte*. Baden Baden: Nomos Verlagsgesellschaft, 1998.

Basso, Keith. "'Stalking with Stories': Names, Places, and Moral Narratives among the Western Apache." In *Text, Play, and Story: The Construction and Reconstruction of Self and Society*, ed. E. M. Bruner, 19–55. N.p.: American Ethnological Society, 1984.

Becker, Howard. *Outsiders: Studies in the Sociology of Deviance.* New York: Free Press, 1963.

Becker, Monika. *Juden in Treptow: Sie haben geheissen wir ihr heisst.* Berlin: Hentrich, 1993.

Behrenbeck, Sabine. "Between Pain and Silence: Remembering the Victims of Violence in Germany After 1949." In *Life After Death: Approaches to a Cultural and Social History of Europe During the 1940s and 1950s,* ed. Richard Bessel and Dirk Schumann, 37–64. Cambridge: Cambridge University Press, 2003.

Bell, Michael M. "The Ghosts of Place." *Theory and Society* 26 (1997): 813–836.

Bendt, Veronika, and Rolf Bothe. "Vorwort." In *Synagogen in Berlin: Zur Geschichte einer zerstörten Architektur,* ed. Berlin Museum. Berlin: Willmuth Arenhövel, 1983.

Benz, Wolfgang, ed. *Überleben im Dritten Reich: Juden im Untergrund und ihre Helfer.* Munich: C. H. Beck, 2003.

Berlin Museum. *Synagogen in Berlin: Zur Geschichte einer zerstörten Architektur.* 2 vols. Berlin: Willmuth Arenhövel, 1983.

Berlin, kurz gefaßt. Berlin: Presse- und Informationsamt Berlin, 1995.

Berliner Geschichtswerkstatt, ed. *Zwangsarbeit in Berlin, 1940–1945: Erinnerungsberichte aus Polen, der Ukraine und Weissrussland.* Erfurt: Sutton, 2000.

Berlin-Information. *Bauten unter Denkmalschutz: Berlin, Hauptstadt d. DDR.* Berlin: Berlin-Information, 1980.

Biernacki, Richard. *The Fabrication of Labor: Germany and Britain, 1640–1914.* Berkeley: University of California Press, 1995.

Biernacki, Richard, and Jennifer A. Jordan. "The Place of Space in the Study of the Social." In *The Social in Question,* ed. Patrick Joyce, 133–150. London: Routledge, 2002.

"Blindes Vertrauen." *nebenanders: Journal des Anne Frank Zentrums* 1 (1999): 23.

Bodnar, John. *Remaking America: Public Memory, Commemoration and Patriotism in the Twentieth Century.* Princeton, N.J.: Princeton University Press, 1991.

Boltanski, Christian. "The Missing House." In *Die Endlichkeit der Freiheit: Berlin 1990,* ed. Wulf Herzogenrath, Joachim Sartorius, and Christoph Tannert, 71–86. Berlin: Hentrich, 1990.

Boonstra, Janrense, and Marie-José Rijnders. *Anne Frank House: A Museum with a Story.* The Hague: Sdu Uitgeverij Koninginnegracht, 1992.

Boyer, M. Christine. *The City of Collective Memory: Its Historical Imagery and Architectural Entertainments.* Cambridge, Mass.: MIT Press, 1994.

Bräutigam, Helmut. "Nationalsozialistische Zwangslager in Berlin, IV: Fremdarbeiterlager 1939 bis 1945." In *Berlin-Forschungen,* ed. Wolfgang Ribbe, 4: 235–280. Einzelveröffentlichungen der Historischen Kommission zu Berlin. Berlin:

Colloquium, 1989.

Bräutigam, Helmut, and Oliver C. Gliech. "Nationalsozialistische Zwangslager in Berlin, I: Die 'wilden' Konzentrationslager und Folterkeller 1933/34." In *Berlin-Forschungen*, ed. Wolfgang Ribbe, 2: 139–178. Einzelveröffentlichungen der Historischen Kommission zu Berlin. Berlin: Colloquium, 1987.

Brenner, Neil. "Berlin's Transformations: Postmodern, Postfordist . . . or Neoliberal?" *International Journal of Urban and Regional Research* 26 (2002): 635–642.

Brockmann, Stephen, and Frank Trommler, eds. *Revisiting Zero Hour 1945: The Emergence of Postwar German Culture.* Humanities Program Report. Washington, D.C.: American Institute of Contemporary German Studies, 1996.

Burg, Annegret, ed. *Kunst im Stadtraum: Denkmäler.* Städtebau und Architektur, 29. Berlin: Senatsverwaltung für Bau- und Wohnungswesen, 1994.

Buruma, Ian. *The Wages of Guilt.* New York: Farrar Straus & Giroux, 1994.

Case, J. David. "The Politics of Memorial Representation: The Controversy over the German Resistance Museum in 1994." *German Politics and Society* 16:1 (1998): 58–81.

Casey, Edward S. *The Fate of Place: A Philosophical History.* Berkeley: University of California Press, 1997.

Caspar, Helmut. "Wieder ein Ort lustvollen Verweilens." *Berlinische Monatsschrift* 7 (2001): 184–188.

Castells, Manuel. *The City and the Grassroots: A Cross-Cultural Theory of Urban Social Movements.* Berkeley: University of California Press, 1983.

Chidester, David, and Edward T. Linenthal, eds. *American Sacred Space.* Bloomington: Indiana University Press, 1995.

Confino, Alon, and Peter Fritzsche, eds. *The Work of Memory: New Directions in the Study of German Society and Culture.* Urbana: University of Illinois Press, 2002.

Cullen, Michael, ed. *Das Holocaust-Mahnmal: Dokumentation einer Debatte.* Munich: Pendo, 1999.

Czaplicka, John. "History, Aesthetics, and Contemporary Commemorative Practice in Berlin." *New German Critique* 65 (Spring–Summer 1995): 155–187.

Davis, Fred. *Yearning for Yesterday: A Sociology of Nostalgia.* New York: Free Press, 1979.

De Certeau, Michel. *The Practice of Everyday Life.* Berkeley: University of California Press, 1984.

Demps, Laurenz. *Berlin-Wilhelmstraße: Eine Topographie preußisch-deutscher Macht.* Berlin: Ch. Links, 1994.

Demps, Laurenz, and Reinhard Hölzer. *Zwangsarbeiter und Zwangsarbeiterlager in der faschistischen Reichshauptstadt Berlin, 1939–1945.* Miniaturen zur Geschichte,

Kultur und Denkmalpflege Berlins, 20–21. Berlin: Gesellschaft für Heimatgeschichte und Denkmalpflege Berlin im Kulturbund der DDR, 1986.

Derrida, Jacques, Kurt Forster, and Wim Wenders. "The Berlin City Forum: Jacques Derrida, Kurt Forster, and Wim Wenders." *Architectural Design* 26, no. 11–12 (1992): 46–47.

Deutschkron, Inge. *Ich trug den gelben Stern.* Munich: dtv, 1978.

———. *Sie blieben im Schatten: Ein Denkmal für Stille Helden.* Berlin: Hentrich, 1997.

Diamant, Adolf. *Zerstörte Synagogen vom November 1938: Eine Bestandsaufnahme.* Frankfurt a/M: Adolf Diamant, 1978.

Diefendorf, Jeffry. *In the Wake of War: The Reconstruction of German Cities after World War II.* Oxford: Oxford University Press, 1993.

DiMaggio, Paul. "Cultural Entrepreneurship in Nineteenth-Century Boston, Part I: The Creation of an Organizational Base for High Culture in America." *Media, Culture and Society* 4:1 (Winter 1982), 33–50.

———. "Cultural Entrepreneurship in Nineteenth-Century Boston, Part II: The Classification and Framing of American Art." *Media, Culture and Society* 4:4 (Autumn 1982), 303–321.

Dolff-Bonekämper, Gabi. "Sites of Hurtful Memory." *Getty Conservation Institute Newsletter,* 2002, 11–16.

Douglas, Mary. "Symbolic Pollution." In *Culture and Society: Contemporary Debates,* ed. Jeffrey Alexander and Steven Seidman. Cambridge: Cambridge University Press, 1990: 155–159.

Durkheim, Émile. *The Elementary Forms of Religious Life.* 1915. New York: Free Press, 1965.

Düssmann, Martina, and Felix Zwoch, eds. *Bauwelt Berlin Annual: Chronology of Building Events 1996 to 2001: 1996.* Berlin: Birkhäuser, 1996.

Eckhardt, Ulrich, ed. *Berlin: Open City—The City on Exhibition.* Berlin: Nicolai, 1999.

Eckhardt, Ulrich, and Andreas Nachama. *Jüdische Orte in Berlin.* Berlin: Nicolai, 1996.

Eggert, Alexander, et al. *Denkmäler zum Denken: Geschichte zum Begehen und Verstehen—antifaschistische Gedenkstätten in den östlichen Bezirken Berlins.* Berlin, DVK, 1991.

Ehmann, Annegret. *Juden in Berlin, 1671–1945: Ein Lesebuch.* Berlin: Nicolai, 1988.

Elfert, Eberhard. "Die Politischen Denkmäler der DDR im ehemaligen Ost-Berlin und unser Lenin." In *Demontage . . . revolutionärer oder restaurativer Bildersturm? Bilder und Texte,* ed. Götz Aly. Berlin: Kramer, 1992: 53–58.

Elfert, Eberhard, and Martin Schönfeld, eds. *Presse-Reader: Erhalten, Zerstören, Verändern? Denkmäler der DDR in Ost-Berlin.* Berlin: Aktives Museum, 1996.

Eliade, Mircea. *The Sacred and the Profane: The Nature of Religion.* 1959. San Diego: Harcourt Brace, 1987.

Endlich, Stefanie. *Gestapo-Gelände: Entwicklungen, Diskussionen, Meinungen, Fordergungen, Perspektiven: Eine Untersuchung mit Interviews.* Berlin: Akademie der Künste, 1988.

Endlich, Stefanie, and Bernd Wurlitzer. *Skulpturen und Denkmäler in Berlin.* Berlin: Stapp, 1990.

Endlich, Stefanie, and Thomas Lutz. *Gedenken und Lernen an historischen Orten: Ein Wegweiser zu Gedenkstätten für die Opfer des Nationalsozialismus in Berlin.* Berlin: Hentrich, 1995.

Endlich, Stefanie. "Berlin." In *Gedenkstätten für die Opfer des Nationalsozialismus,* 2, ed. Ulrike Puvogel, 27–227. Bonn: Bundeszentrale für politische Bildung, 1999.

Engel, Helmut, and Wolfgang Ribbe, eds. *Hauptstadt Berlin—wohin mit der Mitte? Historische, städtebauliche und architektonische Wurzeln des Stadtzentrums.* Berlin: Akad, 1993.

Fibich, Peter. "Zur landschaftsarchitektonischen Gestaltung von Gedenkstätten und Mahnmalen für die Opfer des Nationalsozialismus in der DDR 1945–1960." In *Projekt Sozialistische Stadt: Beiträge zur Bau- und Planungsgeschichte der DDR,* ed. Holger Barth, 69–78. Berlin: Dietrich Reimer, 1998.

Firey, Walter. "Sentiment and Symbolism as Ecological Variables," *American Sociological Review* 10:2 (1944): 140–148.

Fischer, Friedhelm, and Harald Bodenschatz. *Hauptstadt Berlin: Zur Geschichte der Regierungsstandorte.* Berlin: Senatsverwaltung für Bau- und Wohnungswesen, 1992.

Flicke, Dietrich, ed. *Büroflächenmarkt Berlin: Tendenzen von Nachfrage und Angebot bis zum Jahr 2005.* Senatsverwaltung für Stadtentwicklung, Stadtwirtschaft, 9. Berlin: Regioverlag, 1996.

Flierl, Thomas. *Mythos Antifaschismus: Ein Traditionskabinett wird kommentiert.* Berlin: Christoph Links, 1992.

Foote, Kenneth E. *Shadowed Ground: America's Landscapes of Violence and Tragedy.* Austin: University of Texas Press, 1997.

Foster, Norman, and David Jenkins. *Rebuilding the Reichstag.* New York: Overlook Press, 2000.

Foster, Norman, Frederick Baker, and Deborah Lipstadt. *Reichstag Graffiti: Essays by Norman Foster, Frederick Baker, and Deborah Lipstadt.* New York: Jovis, 2003.

Frank, Volker. *Antifaschistische Mahnmale in der DDR: Ihre künstlerische und architektonische Gestaltung.* Leipzig: E. A. Seemann, 1970.

Gedenkstätten und Tourismus: Nicht nur ein Konferenzbericht: Güstrow, 15./16. September 1997/Projekt "Gedenkstättenarbeit in Mecklenburg-Vorpommern." Schwerin: "Gedenkstättenarbeit in Mecklenburg-Vorpommern," 1997.

Gesellschaft Hackesche Höfe. *Die Hackeschen Höfe: Geschichte und Geschichten einer Lebenswelt in der Mitte Berlins.* Berlin: Argon, 1993.

————. *Die Spandauer Vorstadt: Utopien und Realitäten zwischen Scheunenviertel und Friedrichstraße.* Berlin: Argon, 1995.

Gieryn, Tom. "A Space for Place in Sociology." *Annual Review of Sociology* 26 (2000): 463–496.

Girod, Regina, Reiner Lidschun, and Otto Pfeiffer. *Nachbarn: Juden in Friedrichshain.* Berlin: Kulturring in Berlin, 2000.

Gissendammer, Scott, and Jan Wielgohs. "State Policy Making and Interest Groups in the Transformation of the East German Public Housing Sector." *German Politics and Society* 15:3 (1997): 73–98.

Griswold, Wendy. *Cultures and Societies in a Changing World.* Thousand Oaks, Calif.: Pine Forge Press, 1994.

Gruner, Wolf. *Der geschlossene Arbeitseinsatz deutscher Juden: Zur Zwangsarbeit als Element der Verfolgung, 1938–1943.* Berlin: Metropol, 1997.

————. "Die Fabrik-Aktion und die Ereignisse in der Berliner Rosenstrasse: Fakten und Fiktionen um den 27. Februar 1943." In *Jahrbuch für Antisemitismusforschung,* 11, ed. Wolfgang Benz, 137–177. Berlin: Metropol, 2002.

Gruzdz, Kai. "Blindes Vertrauen." *nebenanders: Journal des Anne Frank Zentrums,* 1(1999): 23.

Günther-Kaminski, M. *"—als wäre es nie gewesen.": Juden am Ku'damm.* Berlin: Berliner Geschichtswerkstatt, 1989.

Halbwachs, Maurice. *The Collective Memory.* 1950. New York: Harper Colophon Books, 1980.

Hammer-Schenk, Harold. *Synagogen in Deutschland: Geschichte einer Baugattung im 19. und 20. Jahrhundert (1780–1933).* Hamburg: H. Christians, 1981.

Harvey, David. *The Condition of Postmodernity: An Enquiry into the Origins of Cultural Change.* Cambridge, Mass.: Blackwell, 1990.

Haus der Wannsee-Konferenz, ed. *Erinnern für die Zukunft: Haus der Wannsee-Konferenz 20. Januar 1942. Ansprachen und Vorträge zur Eröffnung der Gedenkstätte.* Berlin: Haus der Wannsee-Konferenz, 1992.

Hausmann, Brigitte. *Duell mit der Verdrängung? Denkmäler für die Opfer des Nationalsozialismus in der Bundesrepublik Deutschland 1980 bis 1990.* Münster: Lit, 1997.

Häußermann, Hartmut, and Andreas Kapphan. *Berlin: Von der geteilten zur gespaltenen Stadt?* Berlin: Leske + Budrich, 2000.

Heesch, Johannes, and Ulrike Braun. *Orte Erinnern: Spuren des NS-Terrors in Berlin: Ein Wegweiser.* Berlin: Nicolai, 2003.

Heimrod, Ute, Günter Schlusche, and Horst Seferens, eds. *Der Denkmalstreit das Denkmal? Die Debatte um das Denkmal für die ermordeten Juden Europas.* Berlin: PHILO, 1999.

Herf, Jeffrey. *Divided Memory: The Nazi Past in the Two Germanys.* Cambridge, Mass.: Harvard University Press, 1997.

Hobrack, Volker. "Neue Gedenktafeln in Berlin-Mitte nach 1993." MS. 2000.

Hoffmann, Christhard. "Dilemmas of Commemoration: Introduction." *German Politics and Society* 17:3 (1999): 1–8.

Hoffmann-Axthelm, Dieter. "Prototyp Hackesche Höfe: Ein faszinierender Ort kommt wieder." In *Architektur in Berlin, 1996,* 40–45. Hamburg: Junius, 1996.

Hoss, Christiane, and Martin Schönfeld. *Gedenktafeln in Berlin: Orte der Erinnerung an Verfolgte des Nationalsozialismus 1991–2001.* Berlin: Aktives Museum Faschismus und Widerstand, 2002.

Hübner, Holger. *Das Gedächtnis der Stadt: Gedenktafeln in Berlin.* Berlin: Argon, 1997.

Hunt, Lynn. "The Sacred and the French Revolution." In *Durkheimian Sociology: Cultural Studies,* ed. Jeffrey Alexander, 25–43. Cambridge: Cambridge University Press, 1988.

Huyssen, Andreas. *Present Pasts: Urban Palimpsests and the Politics of Memory.* Stanford: Stanford University Press, 2003.

———. *Twilight Memories: Marking Time in a Culture of Amnesia.* New York: Routledge, 1995.

James-Chakraborty, Kathleen. "Memory and the Cityscape: The German Architectural Debate About Postmodernism." *German Politics and Society,* 17:3 (1999): 71–83.

Jeismann, Michael, ed. *Mahnmal Mitte: Eine Kontroverse.* Cologne: DuMont, 1999.

Jochheim, Gernot. *Frauenprotest in der Rosenstraße: "Gebt uns unsere Männer wieder."* Deutsche Vergangenheit, Stätten der Geschichte Berlins, 85. Berlin: Hentrich, 1993.

Jochheim, Gernot, and Johannes Rösler. *Die Rosenstraße: Gestern, Heute.* Berlin: Hentrich / Alexander Plaza, 1997.

Johnson, Nuala. "Cast in Stone: Monuments, Geography, and Nationalism." *Environment and Planning D: Society and Space* 13:1 (1995): 51–65.

Jordan, David. *Transforming Paris: The Life and Labors of Baron Haussmann.* Chicago: University of Chicago Press, 1995.

Jordan, Jennifer. "Collective Memory and Locality in Global Cities." In *Global Cities: Cinema, Architecture, and Urbanism in a Digital Age*, ed. Patrice Petro and Linda Krause, 31–48. New Brunswick, N.J.: Rutgers University Press, 2003.

Jüllig, Carola. *Juden in Kreuzberg*. Berlin: Hentrich, 1991.

Kaminsky, Annette, ed. *Orte des Erinnerns. Gedenkzeichen, Gedenkstätten und Museen zur Diktatur in SBZ und DDR*. Leipzig: Forum, 2004.

Kammen, Michael. *Mystic Chords of Memory: The Transformation of Tradition in American Culture*. New York: Knopf, 1991.

Kattago, Siobhan. *Ambiguous Memory: The Nazi Past and German National Identity*. Westport, Conn.: Praeger, 2001.

Kaulen, Alois. *Juden in Spandau: Vom Mittelalter bis 1945*. Berlin: Hentrich, 1988.

Kernd'l, Alfred. "Archäologie der Neuzeit: Denkmalschutz und Zeitgeist in der Hauptstadt." In *Geschichtswerkstatt Spree-Insel: Historische Topographie—Stadtarchäologie—Stadtentwicklung*, ed. Helmut Engel, Jörg Haspel, and Wolfgang Ribbe. Potsdam: Verlag für Berlin-Brandenburg, 1998.

———. *Zeugnisse der historischen Topographie auf dem Gelände der Ehemaligen Reichskanzlei Berlin-Mitte*. Berlin: Archäologisches Landesamt Berlin, 1993.

Kessler, Ralf, and Hartmut Rüdiger Peter, eds. *"An alle OdF-Betreuungsstellen Sachsen-Anhalts!" Eine dokumentarische Fallstudie zum Umgang mit Opfern des Faschismus in der SBZ/DDR, 1945–1953*. Frankfurt a/M: Peter Lang, 1996.

Kleinwächter-Jarnot, Elke, and Annalie Schoen. *Bürgerbeteiligung im Parlaments- und Regierungsviertel: Stadtteilvertretungen stellen sich vor*. Berlin: Senatsverwaltung für Bau- und Wohnungswesen, Hauptstadtreferat, 1994.

Knowlton, James and Truett Cates, trans. *Forever in the Shadow of Hitler? Original Documents of the* Historikerstreit, *the Controversy Concerning the Singularity of the Holocaust*. Atlantic Highlands, N.J.: Humanities Press, 1993.

Koberstein, Thea, and Norbert Stein. *Juden in Lichtenberg: Mit den früheren Ortsteilen in Friedrichshain, Hellersdorf und Marzahn*. Berlin: Hentrich, 1995.

Komitee der antifaschistischen Widerstandskämpfer. *Historischer Lehrpfad zu einigen Stätten der Verfolgung und des Widerstands gegen den faschistischen Pogrom November 1938 im Stadtbezirk Berlin-Mitte* Berlin, 1988.

Korn, Roland, and Klaus Weise. *Berlin: Bauten unserer Tage*. Berlin: Berlin-Information, 1985.

Koshar, Rudy. *From Monuments to Traces: Artifacts of German Memory, 1870–1990*. Berkeley: University of California Press, 2000.

———. *Germany's Transient Pasts: Preservation and National Memory in the Twentieth Century*. Chapel Hill: University of North Carolina Press, 1998.

Krätke, Stefan. "Berlin: Towards a Global City?" *Urban Studies* 38:10 (2001): 1777–1799.

Krinsky, Carol Herselle. *Synagogues of Europe: Architecture, History, Meaning.* Minneola, N.Y.: Dover, 1985.

Kubatzki, Rainer. "Irgendein Lager gleich um die Ecke." *Berlinische Monatsschrift* 9 (2000): 70–77.

———. "Topographie und Nutzungsgeschichte der 700 Zwangsarbeiterlager in und um Berlin 1939 bis 1945." In *Zwangsarbeit während der NS-Zeit in Berlin und Brandenburg: Formen, Funktion und Rezeption,* ed. W. Meyer and K. Neitmann, 89–109. Potsdam: Verlag für Berlin und Brandenburg, 2001.

———. *Zwangsarbeiter- und Kriegsgefangenenlanger: Standorte und Topographie in Berlin und im brandenburgischen Umland 1939 bis 1945: Eine Dokumentation.* Berlin-Forschungen der Historischen Kommission zu Berlin, 1. Berlin: A. Spitz, 2001.

LaCapra, Dominick. *Representing the Holocaust: History, Theory, Trauma.* Ithaca, N.Y.: Cornell University Press, 1996.

Ladd, Brian. *The Ghosts of Berlin: Confronting German History in the Urban Landscape.* Chicago: University of Chicago Press, 1997.

Lammel, Inge. *Jüdisches Leben in Pankow: eine zeitgeschichtliche Dokumentation.* Berlin: Hentrich, 1993.

Landsberg, Alison. *Prosthetic Memory: The Transformation of American Remembrance in the Age of Mass Culture.* New York: Columbia University Press, 2004.

Ledgerwood, Judy. "The Cambodian Tuol Sleng Museum of Genocidal Crimes: National Narrative." *Museum Anthropology* 21:1 (1997): 82–98.

Lefebvre, Henri. *The Production of Space.* Oxford: Blackwell, 1974.

Lehmbruch, Gerhard. "Institutional Change in the East German Transformation Process." *German Politics and Society* 18:3 (2000): 13–47.

Leo, Annette, and Peter Reif-Spirek, eds. *Vielstimmiges Schweigen: Neue Studien zum DDR-Antifaschismus.* Berlin: Metropol, 2001.

Lerner, L. Scott. "The Narrating Architecture of Emancipation," *Jewish Social Studies* 6:3 (2000): 1–30.

Levinson, Sanford. *Written in Stone.* Durham, N.C.: Duke University Press, 1998.

Libeskind, Daniel. *Das Jüdische Museum in Berlin: Architekt Daniel Libeskind.* Berlin: Philo, 2000.

Liegenschaftsgesellschaft der Treuhandanstalt [TLG]. *TLG MarktReport 92/93: Erfahrungen aus dem Immobilienmarkt der neuen Bundesländer.* Berlin: Liegenschaftsgesellschaft der Treuhandanstalt, 1992.

Lin, Jan. "Ethnic Places, Postmodernism, and Urban Change in Houston." *Sociological Quarterly* 36:4 (1995): 629–647.

Linenthal, Edward. *Preserving Memory: The Struggle to Create America's Holocaust Museum.* New York: Viking Press, 1995.

————. *The Unfinished Bombing: Oklahoma City in American Memory*. Oxford: Oxford University Press, 2001.

Lipsitz, George. *Time Passages: Collective Memory and American Popular Culture*. Minneapolis: University of Minnesota Press, 1990.

Lowenthal, David. *The Past Is a Foreign Country*. Cambridge: Cambridge University Press, 1985.

Lupu, Noam. "Memory Vanished, Absent, and Confined." *History & Memory* 15:2 (2003): 130–164.

Madison, James H. *A Lynching in the Heartland: Race and Memory in America*. New York: Palgrave, 2001.

Maier, Charles S. *The Unmasterable Past: History, Holocaust, and German National Identity*. Cambridge, Mass.: Harvard University Press, 1988.

Mankowitz, Zeev. *Life Between Memory and Hope: The Survivors of the Holocaust in Occupied Germany*. Cambridge: Cambridge University Press, 2002.

Marcuse, Harold. *Legacies of Dachau: The Uses and Abuses of a Concentration Camp, 1933–2001*. Cambridge: Cambridge University Press, 2001.

Markovits, Andrei, and Philip Gorski. *The German Left: Red, Green, and Beyond*. Cambridge: Polity Press, 1993.

Markovits, Andrei S., and Simon Reich. *The German Predicament: Memory and Power in the New Europe*. Ithaca, N.Y.: Cornell University Press, 1997.

Maur, Hans. *Mahn-, Gedenk-, und Erinnerungsstätten der Arbeiterbewegung in Berlin-Friedrichshain*. Berlin: Bezirksleitung der SED, 1981.

————. *Mahn-, Gedenk-, und Erinnerungsstätten der Arbeiterbewegung in Berlin-Köpenick*. Berlin: Bezirksleitung der SED, 1973.

————. *Mahn-, Gedenk-, und Erinnerungsstätten der Arbeiterbewegung in Berlin-Lichtenberg*. Berlin: Bezirksleitung der SED, 1982.

————. *Mahn-, Gedenk-, und Erinnerungsstätten der Arbeiterbewegung in Berlin-Marzahn*. Berlin: Bezirksleitung der SED, 1982.

————.*Mahn-, Gedenk-, und Erinnerungsstätten der Arbeiterbewegung in Berlin-Mitte*. Berlin: Bezirksleitung der SED, 1973.

————. *Mahn-, Gedenk-, und Erinnerungsstätten der Arbeiterbewegung in Berlin-Pankow*. Berlin: Bezirksleitung der SED, 1974.

————. *Mahn-, Gedenk-, und Erinnerungsstätten der Arbeiterbewegung in Berlin-Prenzlauer Berg*. Berlin: Bezirksleitung der SED, 1979.

————. *Mahn-, Gedenk-, und Erinnerungsstätten der Arbeiterbewegung in Berlin-Treptow*. Berlin: Bezirksleitung der SED, 1979.

————. *Mahn-, Gedenk-, und Erinnerungsstätten der Arbeiterbewegung in Berlin-Weißensee*. Berlin: Bezirksleitung der SED, 1978.

Mayer, Herbert and Hans-Jürgen Mende, eds. *Straßennamen*. Berlin: Luisenstädtischer Bildungsverein, 1993.

Mayer, Irene. "Das frühe Konzentrationslager am Wasserturm in Berlin-Prenzlauer Berg in seiner Zeit und in der Erinnerungsgeschichte." Master's thesis, Zentrum für Antisemitismusforschung, Technische Universität zu Berlin, 2003.

———. "Das Konzentrationslager am Wasserturm Prenzlauer Berg in Berlin." In *Instrumentarium der Macht: Geschichte der Konzentrationslager 1933–1945*, ed. Wolfgang Benz and Barbara Distel, 71–88. Berlin: Metropol, 2003.

Mele, Christopher. *Selling the Lower East Side: Culture, Real Estate, and Resistance in New York City.* Minneapolis, University of Minnesota Press, 2000.

Meskell, L. "Negative Heritage and Past Mastering in Archaeology." *Anthropological Quarterly* 75:3 (2002): 557–574.

Miethe, Anna Dora, and Hugo Namslauer. *Zur Gestaltung und Pflege Politischer Gedenkstätten.* Berlin: Institut für Denkmalpflege, 1981.

Molotch, Harvey. "The City as a Growth Machine: Toward a Political Economy of Place." *American Journal of Sociology* 82:2 (1976): 309–332.

Molotch, Harvey, William Freudenberg, and Krista Paulsen. "History Repeats Itself, but How? City Character, Urban Tradition, and the Accomplishment of Place." *American Sociological Review* 65:6 (2000): 791–823.

Mönninger, Michael, ed. *Das neue Berlin: Baugeschichte und Stadtplanung der deutschen Hauptstadt.* Frankfurt a/M: Insel, 1991.

Mukerji, Chandra. *Territorial Ambitions and the Gardens of Versailles.* Cambridge: Cambridge University Press, 1997.

Musil, Robert. *Posthumous Papers of a Living Author.* Hygiene, Colo.: Eridanos Press, 1987.

Neue Gesellschaft für Bildende Kunst. *Der umschwiegene Ort.* Berlin: Neue Gesellschaft für bildende Kunst, n.d. [1988].

Neumann, Klaus. *Shifting Memories: The Nazi Past in the New Germany.* Ann Arbor, Mich.: University of Michigan Press, 2000.

Neumann, Peter. *Wo war was? 299 Infos zu Persönlichkeiten/Schauplätzen/Ereignissen, Berlin.* Berlin: Dietz, 1990.

Niven, Bill. *Facing the Nazi Past: United Germany and the Legacy of the Third Reich.* New York: Routledge, 2002.

Nora, Pierre, ed. *Realms of Memory: Rethinking the French Past.* Translated by Arthur Goldhammer. 3 vols. New York: Columbia University Press, 1996. Originally published as *Les Lieux de mémoire* (Paris: Gallimard, 1984).

Offe, Sabine. *Ausstellungen, Einstellungen, Entstellungen: Jüdische Museen in Deutschland und Österreich.* Berlin: Philo, 2000.

Offenberg, Mario. *Adass Jisroel: Die jüdische Gemeinde in Berlin (1869–1942): vernichtet und vergessen.* Berlin: Museumspädagogischen Dienst Berlin, 1986.

Ohliger, Rainer and Ulrich Raiser. *Integration und Migration in Berlin: Zahlen-Daten-Fakten.* Berlin: Der Beauftragte des Senats von Berlin für Integration und Migration, 2005.

Olick, Jeffrey. "What Does It Mean to Normalize the Past?" *Social Science History* 22:4 (1998): 547–570.

Olick, Jeffrey, and David Levy. "Collective Memory and Cultural Constraint: Holocaust Myth and Rationality in German Politics." *American Sociological Review* 62 (December 1997): 921–936.

Olick, Jeffrey, and Joyce Robbins. "Social Memory Studies: From 'Collective Memory' to the Historical Sociology of Mnemonic Practices." *Annual Review of Sociology* 24:1 (1998): 105–141.

Prang, Hans, and Horst Günter Kleinschmidt. *Durch Berlin zu Fuß: Wanderungen in Geschichte und Gegenwart.* Berlin: Tourist, 1983.

Puvogel, Ulrike, ed. *Gedenkstätten für die Opfer des Nationalsozialismus.* Bonn: Bundeszentrale für politische Bildung, 1999.

Reichel, Peter. *Politik mit der Erinnerung: Gedächtnisorte im Streit um die nationalsozialistische Vergangenheit.* 1995. Frankfurt a/M: Fischer, 1999.

————. *Vergangenheitsbewältigung in Deutschland: Die Auseinandersetzung mit der NS-Diktatur von 1945 bis heute.* Munich: Beck, 2001.

Reimann, Bettina. *Städtische Wohnquartiere: Der Einfluss der Eigentümerstruktur: Eine Fallstudie aus Berlin-Prenzlauer Berg.* Opladen: Leske + Budrich, 2000.

Renan, Ernest. "What Is a Nation?" 1882. In *Nation and Narration,* ed. Homi K. Bhabha, 8–22. New York: Routledge, 1990.

Reuter, Elke, and Detlef Hansel, eds. *Das Kurze Leben der VVN von 1945 bis 1953.* Berlin: Ost, 1997.

Rosenfeld, Gavriel. *Munich and Memory: Architecture, Monuments, and the Legacy of the Third Reich.* Berkeley: University of California Press, 2000.

Rotenberg, Robert. *Landscape and Power in Vienna.* Baltimore: Johns Hopkins University Press, 1995.

Sandvoß, Hans-Rainer. *Stätten des Widerstandes in Berlin, 1933–1945.* Berlin: Gedenkstätte Deutscher Widerstand, n.d. [198+?].

————. *Widerstand in Friedrichshain und Lichtenberg.* Schriftenreihe über den Widerstand in Berlin von 1933 bis 1945, 10. Berlin: Gedenkstätte Deutscher Widerstand, 1998.

————. *Widerstand in Kreuzberg.* Schriftenreihe über den Widerstand in Berlin von 1933 bis 1945, 11. Berlin: Gedenkstätte Deutscher Widerstand, 1997.

————. *Widerstand in Mitte und Tiergarten.* Schriftenreihe über den Widerstand in Berlin von 1933 bis 1945, 8. Berlin: Gedenkstätte Deutscher Widerstand, 1994.

Savage, Kirk. *Standing Soldiers, Kneeling Slaves: Race, War, and Monument in Nine-teenth-Century America.* Princeton, N.J.: Princeton University Press, 1999.

Schäche, Wolfgang. "Geschichte und stadträumliche Bedeutung der 'Minis-tergärten.'" In *Architektur in Berlin: Jahrbuch 1992*, ed. N. Baumeister, 58–67. Hamburg: Junius, 1992.

Schilde, Kurt. *Erinnern—und nicht vergessen: Dokumentation zum Gedenkbuch für die Opfer des Nationalsozialismus aus dem Bezirk Tempelhof.* Berlin: Bezirksamt Tempelhof, 1988.

————. *Vom Columbia-Haus zum Schulenburgring: Dokumentation mit Lebensge-schichten von Opfern des Widerstands und der Verfolgung von 1933 bis 1945 aus dem Bezirk Tempelhof.* Berlin: Hentrich, 1987.

Schilde, Kurt, Rolf Scholz, and Sylvia Walleczek. *SA-Gefängnis Papestrasse: Spuren und Zeugnisse.* Berlin: Overall, 1996.

Scholze-Irrlitz, Leonore, and Karoline Noack, eds. *Arbeit für den Feind: Zwangsar-beiter-Alltag in Berlin und Brandenburg (1939–1945).* Berlin: be.bra, 1998.

Schönfeld, Martin. *Gedenktafeln in Ost-Berlin: Orte der Erinnerung an die Zeit des Nationalsozialismus.* Schriftenreihe des Aktiven Museums, 4. Berlin: Aktives Museum Faschismus und Widerstand in Berlin, 1991.

————. *Gedenktafeln in West-Berlin.* Schriftenreihe des Aktiven Museums, 6. Ber-lin: Aktives Museum Faschismus und Widerstand in Berlin, 1993.

Schönfeld, Martin, and Annette Tietenberg. *Erhalten, Zerstören, Verändern.* Ber-lin: Aktives Museum / Neue Gesellschaft für Bildende Kunst, 1990.

Schudson, Michael. "Culture and the Integration of National Societies." In *The So-ciology of Culture*, ed. Diane Crane, 21–45. Cambridge, Mass.: Blackwell, 1994.

Schumann, Frank. *Die Szene: Neue Geschichten aus dem Scheunenviertel.* Berlin: Neues Leben, 1993.

Schwartz, Barry. *Abraham Lincoln and the Forge of National Memory.* Chicago: University of Chicago Press, 2000.

————. *George Washington: The Making of an American Symbol.* New York: Free Press, 1987.

Schweitzer, Eva. *Großbaustelle Berlin: Wie die Hauptstadt verplant wird.* Berlin: Nicolai, 1996.

Seferens, Horst. *Ein Deutscher Denkmalstreit: Die Kontroverse um die Spiegelwand in Berlin-Steglitz.* Berlin: Hentrich, 1995.

Senatsverwaltung für Bau- und Wohnungswesen. *Parlament- und Regierungsviertel Berlin: Ergebnisse der Vorbereitenden Untersuchungen.* Berlin: Senatsverwaltung für Bau- und Wohnungswesen, 1993.

Senatsverwaltung für Stadtentwicklung und Umweltschutz, ed. *Berliner Denkmal-liste.* Beiträge zur Denkmalpflege in Berlin, vol. 5. Berlin: Kulturbuch, 1995.

Simon, Hermann, ed. *"Tuet auf die Pforten": Die Neue Synagoge, 1866–1995.* Berlin: Stiftung Neue Synagoge Berlin—Centrum Judaicum, 1995.

Sommerfeld, Adolf. *Das Ghetto von Berlin: Aus dem Scheunenviertel.* Berlin: Neues Leben, 1992.

Sorkin, Michael, and Sharon Zukin, eds. *After the World Trade Center: Rethinking New York City.* New York: Routledge, 2002.

Soysal, Yasemin. *Limits of Citizenship: Migrants and Postnational Membership in Europe.* University of Chicago Press, 1994.

Spielmann, Jochen. *Denk-Mal-Prozesse.* Berlin: Senatsverwaltung für Bau- und Wohnungswesen, 1991.

————. "Gedenken und Denkmal." In *Gedenken und Denkmal,* ed. Helmut Geisert, Jochen Spielmann, and Peter Ostendorff. Berlin: Berlinische Galerie, 1988, 7–46.

Spillman, Lynn. *Nation and Commemoration: Creating National Identities in the United States and Australia.* Cambridge: Cambridge University Press, 1997.

Sprink, Claus-Dieter. *Gedenkstätte Köpenicker Blutwoche Juni 1933.* Berlin: Bezirksamt Köpenick von Berlin, 1997.

Staroste, Hubert. "Politische Denkmäler in Ost-Berlin im Spannungsfeld von Kulturpolitik und Denkmalpflege." In *Bildersturm in Osteuropa,* ed. ICOMOS. N.p.: ICOMOS, 1994.

Steer, Christine. *Versklavt und fast Vergessen: Zwangsarbeit im Berliner Bezirk Lichtenberg, 1939–1945.* Berlin: Trafo, 2001.

Steglich, Ulrike, and Peter Kratz. *Das Falsche Scheunenviertel: Ein Vorstadtverführer.* Berlin: Altberliner Bücherstube, 1997.

Stichting Holländerei. *Niederländer und Flamen in Berlin, 1940–1945: KZ-Häftlinge, Inhaftierte, Kriegsgefangene und Zwangsarbeiter.* Berlin: Hentrich, 1996.

Stier, Oren. *Committed to Memory: Cultural Mediations of the Holocaust.* Amherst: University of Massachussetts Press, 2003.

Stoltzfus, Nathan. *Widerstand des Herzens.* Munich: dtv, 2000.

Strom, Elizabeth. *Building the New Berlin.* Lanham, Md.: Lexington Books, 2001.

Sturken, Marita. *Tangled Memories: The Vietnam War, the AIDS Epidemic, and the Politics of Remembering.* Berkeley: University of California Press, 1997.

Suttles, Gerald. "The Cumulative Texture of Local Urban Culture." *American Journal of Sociology* 90:2 (1984): 283–304.

Till, Karen. *The New Berlin: Memory, Politics, Place.* Minneapolis: University of Minnesota Press, 2005.

Tuchel, Johannes, and Kurt Schilde. *Columbia-Haus: Berliner Konzentrationslager, 1933–1936.* Berlin: Hentrich / Bezirksamt Tempelhof von Berlin, 1990.

Verdery, Katherine. *The Political Lives of Dead Bodies: Reburial and Postsocialist*

Change. New York: Columbia University Press, 1999.

Verein Stiftung Scheunenviertel, ed. *Das Scheunenviertel: Spuren eines verlorenen Berlins*. Berlin: Haude & Spener, 1994.

Vinitzky-Seroussi, Vered. "Commemorating a Difficult Past: Yitzhak Rabin's Memorials." *American Sociological Review* 67:1 (2002): 30–51.

Vorschlag zum Umgang mit den politischen Denkmälern der Nachkriegszeit in Berlin. Berlin: Initiative Politische Denkmäler, 1993.

Wagner-Pacifici, Robin, and Barry Schwartz. "The Vietnam Veterans Memorial: Commemorating a Difficult Past." *American Journal of Sociology* 97:2 (1991): 376–420.

Westphal, Uwe. *Berliner Konfektion und Mode, 1836–1939: Die Zerstörung Einer Tradition*. 1986. Berlin: Hentrich, 1992.

Wexler, Laura. *Fire in a Canebreak: The Last Mass Lynching in America*. New York: Scribner, 2003.

Wiedmer, Caroline. *The Claims of Memory: Representations of the Holocaust in Contemporary Germany and France*. Ithaca, N.Y.: Cornell University Press, 1999.

Winkler, Ulrike, ed. *Stiften gehen: NS-Zwangsarbeit und Entschädigungsdebatte*. Cologne: PapyRossa, 2000.

Wippermann, Wolfgang. "Nationalsozialistische Zwangslager in Berlin, II: Das 'Arbeitserziehungslager' Wuhlheide." In *Berlin-Forschungen,* ed. Wolfgang Ribbe, 2: 179–188. Einzelveröffentlichungen der Historischen Kommission zu Berlin. Berlin: Colloquium, 1987.

Wippermann, Wolfgang, and Ute Brucker-Boroujerdi. "Nationalsozialistische Zwangslager in Berlin, III: Das 'Zigeunerlager' Marzahn." In *Berlin-Forschungen,* ed. Wolfgang Ribbe, 2: 189–201. Einzelveröffentlichungen der Historischen Kommission zu Berlin. Berlin: Colloquium, 1987.

Wise, Michael. *Capital Dilemma: Germany's Search for a New Architecture of Democracy*. New York: Princeton Architectural Press, 1998.

Young, James E. *At Memory's Edge: After-Images of the Holocaust in Contemporary Art and Architecture*. New Haven, Conn.: Yale University Press, 2000.

———. "Berlin's Holocaust Memorial: A Report to the Bundestag Committee on Media and Culture, 3 March 1999." *German Politics and Society* 17:3 (1999): 54–70.

———. "The Counter-Monument: Memory Against Itself in Germany Today." *Critical Inquiry* 18 (Winter 1992), 269.

———. *Mahnmale des Holocaust: Motive, Rituale und Stätten des Gedenkens*. Munich: Prestel-Verlag, 1993.

———. *The Texture of Memory: Holocaust Memorials and Meaning*. New Haven, Conn.: Yale University Press, 1993.

Zech, Hermann. *Gedenktafeln in Berlin-Mitte 1855–1996.* Berlin: Hermann Zech, 1996.

Zelinsky, Wilbur. *Nation into State: The Shifting Symbolic Foundations of American Nationalism.* Chapel Hill: University of North Carolina Press, 1988.

Zolberg, Vera. "Museums as Contested Sites of Remembrance: The Enola Gay Affair." In *Theorizing Museums: Representing Identity and Diversity in a Changing World,* ed. Gordon Fyfe and Sharon Macdonald, 69–83. Oxford: Blackwell, 1996.

Zukin, Sharon. *The Cultures of Cities.* Cambridge, Mass.: Blackwell, 1995.

Zukin, Sharon, Robert Baskerville, and Courtney Guthreau. "From Coney Island to Las Vegas in the Urban Imaginary: Discursive Practices of Growth and Decline." *Urban Affairs Review* 33:5 (1998): 627–654.

Index

Page numbers in italic type refer to figures.

Cultural Memory | in the Present

Jacques Derrida and Elisabeth Roudinesco, *For What Tomorrow . . . : A Dialogue*

Elisabeth Weber, *Questioning Judaism: Interviews by Elisabeth Weber*

Jacques Derrida and Catherine Malabou, *Counterpath: Traveling with Jacques Derrida*

Martin Seel, *Aesthetics of Appearing*

Nanette Salomon, *Shifting Priorities: Gender and Genre in Seventeenth-Century Dutch Painting*

Jacob Taubes, *The Political Theology of Paul*

Jean-Luc Marion, *The Crossing of the Visible*

Eric Michaud, *The Cult of Art in Nazi Germany*

Anne Freadman, *The Machinery of Talk: Charles Peirce and the Sign Hypothesis*

Stanley Cavell, *Emerson's Transcendental Etudes*

Stuart McLean, *The Event and its Terrors: Ireland, Famine, Modernity*

Beate Rössler, ed., *Privacies: Philosophical Evaluations*

Bernard Faure, *Double Exposure: Cutting Across Buddhist and Western Discourses*

Alessia Ricciardi, *The Ends Of Mourning: Psychoanalysis, Literature, Film*

Alain Badiou, *Saint Paul: The Foundation of Universalism*

Gil Anidjar, *The Jew, the Arab: A History of the Enemy*

Jonathan Culler and Kevin Lamb, eds., *Just Being Difficult? Academic Writing in the Public Arena*

Jean-Luc Nancy, *A Finite Thinking*, edited by Simon Sparks

Theodor W. Adorno, *Can One Live after Auschwitz? A Philosophical Reader*, edited by Rolf Tiedemann

Patricia Pisters, *The Matrix of Visual Culture: Working with Deleuze in Film Theory*

Andreas Huyssen, *Present Pasts: Urban Palimpsests and the Politics of Memory*

Talal Asad, *Formations of the Secular: Christianity, Islam, Modernity*

Dorothea von Mücke, *The Rise of the Fantastic Tale*

Marc Redfield, *The Politics of Aesthetics: Nationalism, Gender, Romanticism*

Emmanuel Levinas, *On Escape*

Dan Zahavi, *Husserl's Phenomenology*

Rodolphe Gasché, *The Idea of Form: Rethinking Kant's Aesthetics*

Michael Naas, *Taking on the Tradition: Jacques Derrida and the Legacies of Deconstruction*

Herlinde Pauer-Studer, ed., *Constructions of Practical Reason: Interviews on Moral and Political Philosophy*

Jean-Luc Marion, *Being Given That: Toward a Phenomenology of Givenness*

Theodor W. Adorno and Max Horkheimer, *Dialectic of Enlightenment*

Ian Balfour, *The Rhetoric of Romantic Prophecy*

Martin Stokhof, *World and Life as One: Ethics and Ontology in Wittgenstein's Early Thought*

Gianni Vattimo, *Nietzsche: An Introduction*

Jacques Derrida, *Negotiations: Interventions and Interviews, 1971–1998*, ed. Elizabeth Rottenberg

Brett Levinson, *The Ends of Literature: The Latin American 'Boom" in the Neoliberal Marketplace*

Timothy J. Reiss, *Against Autonomy: Cultural Instruments, Mutualities, and the Fictive Imagination*

Hent de Vries and Samuel Weber, eds., *Religion and Media*

Niklas Luhmann, *Theories of Distinction: Re-Describing the Descriptions of Modernity*, ed. and introd. William Rasch

Johannes Fabian, *Anthropology with an Attitude: Critical Essays*

Michel Henry, *I am the Truth: Toward a Philosophy of Christianity*

Gil Anidjar, *"Our Place in Al-Andalus": Kabbalah, Philosophy, Literature in Arab-Jewish Letters*

Hélène Cixous and Jacques Derrida, *Veils*

F. R. Ankersmit, *Historical Representation*

F. R. Ankersmit, *Political Representation*

Elissa Marder, *Dead Time: Temporal Disorders in the Wake of Modernity (Baudelaire and Flaubert)*

Reinhart Koselleck, *The Practice of Conceptual History: Timing History, Spacing Concepts*

Niklas Luhmann, *The Reality of the Mass Media*

Hubert Damisch, *A Childhood Memory by Piero della Francesca*

Hubert Damisch, *A Theory of /Cloud/: Toward a History of Painting*

Jean-Luc Nancy, *The Speculative Remark: (One of Hegel's bon mots)*

Jean-François Lyotard, *Soundproof Room: Malraux's Anti-Aesthetics*

Jan Patočka, *Plato and Europe*

Hubert Damisch, *Skyline: The Narcissistic City*

Isabel Hoving, *In Praise of New Travelers: Reading Caribbean Migrant Women Writers*

Richard Rand, ed., *Futures: Of Jacques Derrida*

William Rasch, *Niklas Luhmann's Modernity: The Paradoxes of Differentiation*

Jacques Derrida and Anne Dufourmantelle, *Of Hospitality*

Jean-François Lyotard, *The Confession of Augustine*

Kaja Silverman, *World Spectators*

Samuel Weber, *Institution and Interpretation: Expanded Edition*

Jeffrey S. Librett, *The Rhetoric of Cultural Dialogue: Jews and Germans in the Epoch of Emancipation*

Ulrich Baer, *Remnants of Song: Trauma and the Experience of Modernity in Charles Baudelaire and Paul Celan*

Samuel C. Wheeler III, *Deconstruction as Analytic Philosophy*

David S. Ferris, *Silent Urns: Romanticism, Hellenism, Modernity*

Rodolphe Gasché, *Of Minimal Things: Studies on the Notion of Relation*

Sarah Winter, *Freud and the Institution of Psychoanalytic Knowledge*

Samuel Weber, *The Legend of Freud: Expanded Edition*

Aris Fioretos, ed., *The Solid Letter: Readings of Friedrich Hölderlin*

J. Hillis Miller / Manuel Asensi, *Black Holes / J. Hillis Miller; or, Boustrophedonic Reading*

Miryam Sas, *Fault Lines: Cultural Memory and Japanese Surrealism*

Peter Schwenger, *Fantasm and Fiction: On Textual Envisioning*

Didier Maleuvre, *Museum Memories: History, Technology, Art*

Jacques Derrida, *Monolingualism of the Other; or, The Prosthesis of Origin*

Andrew Baruch Wachtel, *Making a Nation, Breaking a Nation: Literature and Cultural Politics in Yugoslavia*

Niklas Luhmann, *Love as Passion: The Codification of Intimacy*

Mieke Bal, ed., *The Practice of Cultural Analysis: Exposing Interdisciplinary Interpretation*

Jacques Derrida and Gianni Vattimo, eds., *Religion*